CAST A COLD EYE

CAST A COLD EYE

Edited by

JAMES RIDGEWAY AND JEAN CASELLA

WITH RESEARCH BY LOREN BERGER

Foreword by

JOHN B. OAKES

FOUR WALLS EIGHT WINDOWS
NEW YORK

A Four Walls Eight Windows First Edition.

First printing November 1991.

Library of Congress Cataloging-in-Publication Data

Cast a cold eye : american opinion writing 1990–1991 / James Ridgeway and Jean Casella, editors; foreword by John B. Oakes

p. cm.

ISBN 0-941423-54-9 : $12.95 / ISBN 0-941423-55-7 : $25.00

1. Reportage literature, American. 2. American newspapers–Sections, columns, etc. 3. Public Opinion—United States. 4. United States—Social conditions—1980– I. Ridgeway, James, 1936– . II. Casella, Jean, 1961– .
PN4853.C37 1991
081—dc20 91-10124
CIP

Four Walls Eight Windows
PO Box 548
Village Station
New York, N.Y. 10014

Designed by Martin Moskof.

Printed in the United States of America.

Contents

Foreword

THE FIRST AMENDMENT TO THE CONSTITUTION, IN THE words of former Supreme Court Justice William J. Brennan Jr., implies "a profound national commitment to the principle that debate on public issues should be uninhibited, robust and wide open." *(New York Times v. Sullivan).*

This is the spirit that infuses Ridgeway and Casella's provocative selection of independent columns and commentary in the American press on some of the most controversial public issues of the last two years.

Uninhibited public debate by individual and independent commentators has scarcely been a major objective of the mainstream American press, usually more mindful of its First Amendment privileges than of its First Amendment responsibilities.

Yet in the increasingly restrictive atmosphere of the past decade, we need more—not less—of free-wheeling, independent, robust and reasoned commentary if we are to prevent our democracy, already endangered by public indifference, from ossifying altogether.

With the steadily lowering intellectual level of public debate and its correspondingly rising decibel level, too frequently promoted by the press itself, new thoughts, new information, new perspectives, even new insights are often lost or totally ignored. The confrontational tone of much of the debate today places a steadily increasing obligation on the part of the American press to give the broadest possible access to individual, reasoned expressions of fact and opinion from laymen and scholars alike, right across the political spectrum.

This was essentially the thinking behind establishment of the Op Ed page of *The New York Times* more than 20 years ago. The basic purpose was to open up the "public debate" to qualified individuals who had something interesting or important to say, irrespective of their political, social, professional, or personal orientation. The success of the Op Ed page demonstrates that the newspaper can only benefit by making its columns more accessible to outsiders—and the texture of democracy can only be strengthened.

The writers and commentators whose observations Ridgeway and Casella have culled in this spirit from a wide variety of publications range from well-known public figures to obscure private citizens. Their one point in common is that in the editors' judgment they contribute—from varying points of view—to the ongoing debate over the events of transcendant importance that we have been living through during the past 18 months.

The face of the country and the world has profoundly changed in these opening years of the final decade of the 20th century. In the United States, we have been experiencing a widening gap between rich and poor, a rise in crime and decline in social services, a burgeoning environmental crisis, intensification of social strife and weakening of the educational system, political and economic scandals of grotesque proportions, a confusion between standards of personal morality and impersonal public policy. Abroad, in that same short time, we have gone through a victorious military war without a peace and a victorious ideological peace without a war, topped by the demise of the worldwide Communist Party and the convulsive yet (so far) peaceful collapse of the Soviet Union itself.

Each of these developments has been reported by the American press. Each one of them raises issues that need thorough debate. They have not always had it, or at least not enough of it.

The cumulative effect of the commentary Ridgeway and Casella have selected, covering a wide range of viewpoints and at times raising neglected and disturbing questions, offers a new and stimulating perspective on current history.

—John B. Oakes
New York
September 1991

Editors' Note

THIS BOOK IS INTENDED TO PROVIDE A LOOK BACK AT some of the events, issues, and opinions of the last year and a half, with an emphasis on domestic American issues. Most of the work included comes from the pages—particularly, the op-ed pages and regular columns—of daily and weekly newspapers, though we have selected some pieces from magazines as well. In arranging the order of the articles, we followed the chronology of events rather than the dates of publication, giving thematic considerations precedence over strict chronology in order to provide some continuity and counterpoint on important issues (particularly in 1991, where we devote one chapter exclusively to the war). The first book in a bi-annual series which will henceforth run from mid-year to mid-year, this 1990/91 edition includes articles written throughout 1990 and most of 1991, allowing the book to appear within the 1991 calendar year. For historians, who tend to mark off time according to wars, this span may appear particularly suitable: The period covered began with the end of the Cold War, and ended in the aftermath of the Persian Gulf war and the collapse of Soviet Communism.

The selection, arrangement, and introduction of these articles is, like the articles themselves, opinionated. While we attempt to provide a diversity of perspectives on the most resonant American political and social issues of the recent past, we cannot claim to have been either comprehensive or objective in our choice of under a hundred pieces out of the thousands at hand in the U.S. press. Nor can we claim to have altogether resisted the temptation to pinpoint trends or glean broader significance from the issues and events addressed by the columnists. Our introductions are intended to provide context and analysis—in our opinion.

We are indebted to all of the writers whose work makes up the heart of this book, and to the publications which generously granted us permission to include that work. We also owe a special debt of thanks to Loren Berger, who did the formidable first round of research, combing through newspapers and magazines for likely candidates; and to John B. Oakes—who, as editorial page editor of *The New York Times,* conceived of the first op-ed page—for contributing the foreword.

Our thanks to the writers whose work provided valuable resources for our introductions: Richard Bolton on the NEA controversy; William Arkin, Damian Durrant, and Marianne Cherni of Greenpeace on the effects of the Persian Gulf war; Theresa Funicello on poverty in America; Dan Bischoff on Earth Day; and all the others duly credited in the footnotes. Thanks also to the *Village Voice,* where portions of the introductory material originally appeared in somewhat different form.

We are grateful to the following individuals and organizations, who generously provided assistance and advice, or sent us articles to consider for the book (even if some of them ended up on the cutting room floor): Steve Rendall of Fairness and Accuracy in Reporting, John Richard of Essential Information, Pat Gish of the *Mountain Eagle,* Jay Walljasper of the *Utne Reader,* John Cavanagh of the Institute for Policy Studies, Herb Berkowitz of the Heritage Foundation, Julie Stewart of the CATO Institute, Sarah Kerr of the *New York Review of Books,* Sandy Close of the Pacific News Service, Peter Dykstra and Andre Carothers of Greenpeace, the Worldwatch Institute, the Data-Center, the Southwest Voter Registration Education Project, the Southern Finance Project, Solidarity, Inc., and Jim Ledbetter, Dan Buck, Mark Ritchie, Brian Ahlberg, Richard Goldstein, Judy Coburn, Jason Simon, Susannah Abbey, Anne Schreiber, Meryl Schwartz, Anne Galperin, and Peter Newman.

We would like to thank the people at Four Walls Eight Windows: John G.H. Oakes; Chris O'Brien; Abigail Scherer for her patient work in securing permissions; Ted Quester for last-minute research; Eliza Galaher and Adam Black for copyediting and proofreading; and Dan Simon for his essential help in planning, shaping, and editing the book.

Finally, special thanks to Morris Simon, for first suggesting the idea for this book; and to Dolores and Stephen Casella, Pat and David Ridgeway, Amy Willis, and Felix Caro, for all their support.

—James Ridgeway.
—Jean Casella
New York
July 1991

CAST A COLD EYE

PART ONE

AFTER THE COLD WAR

JANUARY–MARCH 1990

TO MANY IT MUST HAVE SEEMED AS IF THE WHOLE world had lost its moorings. The ideological struggle between East and West, Communism and capitalism, which had dictated the way millions of people on both sides of the Iron Curtain lived their lives since the end of the Second World War, had disappeared overnight. The Soviet Union, the Evil Empire of Ronald Reagan's dreams, stood revealed—in the eyes of the U.S., at any rate—as just another large, poor, "Third World" nation, on the verge of being torn to pieces by internal turmoil, and ready to be revived by the bracing breezes of free enterprise.

The United States became the world's only true super power, awash in triumphant rhetoric, but also exposed to a new role as the world's sole policeman. The nations of Eastern Europe, for forty years colonies of the Soviet Union, stood for a moment between East and West, envisioning an independent Central Europe with an identity and future of its own.

The moment would not last long: Eastern Europe would quickly be immersed in the internal political chaos that accompanied a rekindled nationalism. Violent resurgent racism would become an unexpected factor in shaping Europe's political future. The economic future of the Eastern bloc appeared increasingly confused and bleak, and, as the Iron Curtain dropped, the world for the first time got a close look at the environmental pollution and mismanagement that threatened many more Chernobyls.

The changes in Eastern Europe reverberated within the Soviet Union itself, in the Baltic republics whose attachment to the U.S.S.R. had been relatively recent, and in the Central Asian republics. Gorbachev traveled to Lithuania in an effort to dampen secessionist moves there, and then ordered troops to quell violent uprisings in Azerbaijan, which had become the Soviet Union's Muslim Ulster.

In March East Germany, for the first time in its history, held a free election. With the autumn euphoria now over, the Lutheran leaders who had played such an instrumental role in organizing and protecting the peaceful revolution receded to an obscure spot on a larger political canvas. The nascent homegrown political groupings in East Germany were overshadowed by appendages of the West German Social Democrats and Christian Democrats. And the East Germans, who had thrown off the phony Communist election machinery for their first chance in forty years to cast a real vote, instead found themselves bit players in a complicated political game that came to a head not in their own elections, but in those of West Germany. West German chancellor Helmut Kohl, a Christian Democrat, aimed for speedy reunification, while the Social Democrats argued for a slower course. The real issue at stake was the rate of exchange for the deutsche mark, the value by which life in the east would be judged. Meanwhile, the influx of East Germans across the border continued. In Berlin the exchange was already well underway: East Berliners were working as maids and street vendors in the west, and West Berlin's artists and students headed east to take advantage of cheap apartments. The disparities in living styles, social security, welfare, and job security would become the root problems of reunification. Both in East Germany and later that month in Hungary, Christian Democratic candidates and coalitions prevailed. The new Central Europe headed rightward.

While the changes in Eastern Europe and the Soviet Union continued, the United States remained a prisoner of past policies and Cold War thinking. This was nowhere more evident than in Panama—which, as the year began, was still feeling the aftershocks of the Christmas-week invasion by U.S. forces. To the resurgent Right of the 1980s, the Panama Canal had been the symbol of American hegemony in the Western Hemisphere. Its scheduled return to Panamanian sovereignty in 1992 would, they believed, be an important cessation of U.S. power in the region, and clear the way for Kremlin surrogates to burrow their way into the United States from Nicaragua, El Salvador, and other points south. For the Right, regaining tacit control of the Panama Canal was the paramount goal in the politics of the hemisphere.

Though estimates of civilian casualties in the invasion ran as high as 3,000, most carnage was kept from the public eye by an unprecedented level of military censorship, and the action won high approval ratings from the American people. The invasion was a triumph for the Bush administration: It not only recovered American influence over the strategic canal, but also showed that an evil drug lord could prove a useful replacement for the now-defunct Evil Empire.

Panama was not the only seeming triumph for the Reagan Doctrine in Latin America. In Nicaragua, the February elections resulted in an astonishing victory for the proponents of roll back. Throughout the 1980s, the Reagan government had sought to topple the Sandinistas by waging a covert war, channelling substantial funds and support to the anti-government contras. It was in pursuit of that goal that the Iran-contra scandal unfolded, exposing the tactics used by the New Right revolutionaries to circumvent Congress, the State Department, and the Pentagon. Once exposed, Reagan—and later Bush—shifted strategies. While scaling back their support for guerrilla warfare, both administrations argued for the export of American democratic institutions in the form of elections, and then took steps to ensure that these elections would have the desired effect of defeating the Sandinistas. According to one report, U.S. tax dollars channelled into the election via the National Endowment for Democracy totalled ten dollars per Nicaraguan voter.[1] This effort was accompanied by a full trade embargo and other forms of devastating economic pressure, destined to continue as long as the Sandinistas were in power. In February these tactics prevailed in the presidential election, which toppled the eleven-year-old Sandinista government and installed the pro-American government of Violeta Chamorro. After these two Central American victories, any government in the hemisphere would think twice about challenging the United States.

On the other side of the globe, Nelson Mandela, the African National Congress leader who had become a symbol of conscience and principle, was freed by his South African captors after twenty-seven years in prison, and quickly took his place as a practical politician in the peace negotiations initiated by President F.W. DeKlerk.

For DeKlerk, a leader whose party had pursued repressive apartheid politics for thirty years, the release of Mandela and the opening of negotiations amounted to an abrupt about-face in national policy. Patrick Lekota, the publicity secretary of the United Democratic Front, the largest anti-apartheid group inside the country, attributed the shift largely to the "sheer tenacity" of those South Africans pressing for change. "The way we responded to the worst excesses they could bring on us," he told Anthony Lewis, "the resilience we had when they cut off our leaders, our creativity in always finding a new way, showed that we were simply irrepressible." Lekota cited other factors, including the changing attitudes of a new generation of Afrikaners, the need for South Africa to overcome its isolation in the global community, and the example set by the tide of change in Eastern Europe.[2]

In fact, what De Klerk set out to do was in many ways more radical and more difficult than what Gorbachev was doing in Eastern Europe, because of the racial prejudices at the core of the problem in South Africa. As *The Economist* observed, "Yesterday's Leninist rulers of Eastern Europe are being replaced by people who think differently but look the same. Perhaps, in liberal principle, handing over to people of a different color should be just as easy. In truth, it is much harder."[3] The transition would certainly not be easy: Within a month of Mandela's release, South Africa was experiencing a powerful backlash from racialist, right-wing factions, as well as an increase in African-against-African violence, often spurred on by elements within the police forces.

Race was the cause of increasing turmoil within the United States as well. As the defining role of the Cold War diminished, a new kind of politics, steeped in racial division, gained ground.

Race resonated through furor that surrounded the murder of a young, pregnant white woman in Boston. Her husband identified the assailant as an African-American man, and after the police combed the black sections of the city he even pointed out a suspect in a line-up. Then Charles Stuart committed suicide, and it became clear that he, not any black man, had killed his wife and their unborn child. Commenting, along with many others, on how easily a race-based hysteria had been aroused in Boston, Jesse Jackson wrote that "Charles Stuart . . . knew how racism worked in America . . . [he] knew that pulling the race-cord would ring the bells of fear."[4]

Underlying such incidents were the harsh facts of life for minority citizens in the United States—the economic disparaties that were exacerbated by entrenched discrimination, and now by a drug war that increasingly targeted African-American men. In 1990, blacks were more than twice as likely as whites to be unemployed. Nearly one third of all blacks, as opposed to 10 percent of whites, lived below the poverty line. Individuals living in poverty included 45 percent of all black children, as opposed to 15 percent of white children. A newborn black baby was twice as likely to die before its first birthday as a white infant. The thirty-one million African Americans made up 12 percent of the general population, but nearly half the prison population, and in Washington, D.C., one out of every four African-

American men went to jail at some time in his life. A black man was six times as likely as a white man to be murdered, and homicide was the leading cause of death among young black men.[5] Later in the year, a report by the National Center for Health Statistics would reveal that the life expectancy for black men had dropped to 69.2 years, while white men's life expectancy rose to 75.6.[6]

As the 1990s began, the changing social structure of the United States was increasingly characterized by extremes of wealth and poverty and a shrinking middle class. During the 1980s the rich had gotten richer and the poor had gotten poorer. By 1990 the richest 10 percent of families controlled 70 percent of the nation's net wealth. Thirty-three million Americans lived below the poverty line; 60 percent of these were families in which one or more members were employed, proof of the growing numbers of working poor.

Also growing was the number of poor women and children in the United States. By the late 1980s, 42.3 percent of the families living below 75 percent of the poverty line were one-parent families headed by women. And the nation's more than 10 million impoverished children—who were poor because their mothers were poor—faced an increasingly bleak future, where even their survival was in question: According to one Maine survey, they were twelve times more likely than nonpoor children to die in fires and eight times more likely to die of disease and, if born with low birth weight, they were thirty times more likely to die in their first year of life. Theresa Funicello wrote in *Ms.* magazine that "what has happened over the last quarter century has been an income redistribution scheme, the most disturbing one this country has ever seen: a redistribution from poor women and children to middle-class professionals—with men at the top calling the shots."[7]

Such statistics took their place in the ongoing debate over the nature and costs of social services in the U.S. The country has historically spent very little on direct payments to the poor: In 1987, federal payments to Aid to Families with Dependent Children (AFDC) totalled $8.8 billion—less than one percent of the federal budget, and likewise one percent of the projected cost of bailing out the savings and loan industry. Instead, the bulk of funds earmarked for the poor has gone to large social service institutions, to maintain the so-called poverty industry that had grown exponentially since its origins in the New Deal.

Criticism of the "poverty industry" came from many sides in the debate over social programs in the 1990s. Some radical voices, including many within the social service sector, were calling for approaches aimed at changing the structure of society—such as massive jobs programs and income redistribution—and for the maximum feasible participation by the poor themselves. Conservatives wanted to slash publicly funded social programs altogether, and leave the poor to be uplifted by the trickling down benefits of supply-side economics and by the elusive thousand points of light.

The Bush administration's response to such issues, as reflected in the president's February 1990 State of the Union address, offered little new insight. His sketchy agenda included a plan to cut the federal deficit by $36.5 billion. Half of this would come from cuts in domestic spending, and only one-sixth from the Pentagon—even though the Soviets had just agreed to reduce their European troop strength by 65 percent. Bush's speech, like much of the rhetoric of early 1990, had a self-congratulatory edge: American ideals of democracy and free enterprise, he said, were being "validated" by "remarkable events" all over the world.

MURRAY KEMPTON
Keeping Up with the News

Events on the eve of the new decade seemed to promise a dramatically new and different future for Eastern Europe and the world community. But Murray Kempton observed that "fewer great historical events are brought about by the power of the new than by the enduring strength of the old," and turned to literature for insight into current events.

Communism has been driven to yield over its Eastern European garrisons to an unknowable future, not by force of arms but by the collapse of its will for further struggle under the weight of all the history that had piled up before it seized what it had felt assured would be its time. If there is such a thing as an inevitability in history, it is that those who think that they can ordain what will henceforth be always end up finding themselves overcome by what has ever been.

Fewer great historical events are brought about by the power of the new than by the enduring strength of the old. It is altogether more serviceable for us to search for the destiny of nations in the permanence of their culture than in the transience of their political systems. That is why the novelist can always teach us more than the political scientist, because the realm called fiction is ruled by what is real, and the territory called fact has to make do with the dubieties of the fancied.

I remember talking once to a Soviet official who was overimpressed enough with my imprecise and useless familiarity with Stalin's quarrels with Trotsky to ask, "How do you know so much? Are you a Sovietologist?"

I replied that three weeks in Russia had persuaded me that the only sound Sovietologist was Anton Chekhov and, to my surprise, there passed over that hitherto immobile face the smile of recognition that makes it plain that you have said what your auditor had come to think well before you had.

Chekhov had been dead for eighty-five years when first I took notice of his credentials as an analyst of Soviet society. I had glimpsed his authority earliest when I read "My Life," the long story whose protagonist learns that he had been abandoned by his wife in a letter in which she tells him that she has prepared herself to begin again by buying a ring like the one that King David had engraved "All things pass."

"If I wanted a ring myself," Chekhov's hero reflects, "the inscription I should choose would be 'Nothing passes away.'"

That thought had struck me then as the epitome of the Russia that had resisted every Soviet effort to transform it and survived so immutably that Chekhov was as up-to-date a guide now as he had been in 1892 and that "Ward 6" does not merely anticipate the Gulag but is its very model.

And the most enlightening guide I have found to Central America is not the product of a social scientist's research but *Nostromo,* the novel Joseph Conrad published in 1904 when his direct experience with the neighborhood was nearly thirty years past and had never extended beyond a tarrying or so in ports when he had sailed as a schooner deck officer in the Gulf of Mexico. Yet, here as nowhere in the reports of embassies and the monographs of researchers, is the El Salvador of a few weeks ago where, in Conrad's words, "the cruelty of things stood unveiled in the levity and sufferings of that incorrigible people."There are the poor of the barrios walking stoically about their errands with grenades crumping and machine guns chattering to the near distance, awesomely brave and pitifully passive and unchanged from the citizens of Conrad's Sulaco who were "surprised but not indignant" when the cavalry of the revolution suddenly lowered lances and cleared them from the streets, because "no Costaguanero had ever learned to question the eccentricities of a military force."

There is the president of Salvador who has just the look of the "more pathetic than promising" of Conrad's freshly installed soon-to-be-unseated chief of state. There is the western diplomat who observes that, "There is no center in El Salvador" and who but echoes the judgment of Conrad's Englishman that "The fault of this country is the want of measure in political life." Conrad's disenchanted liberal remembers Bolivar's bitter summation that "[South and Central] America is ungovernable. Those who worked for her independence have ploughed the sea."

Conrad's Spanish elite hate their Catholic vicar-general who, they not unreasonably suspect, has roused the Indian peasantry for land reform, and sympathize with the bandits who control the countryside. "If it had not been for the lawless tyranny of your government," the wife of the administrator of Sulaco's silver mine says to its superintendent, "many an outlaw would be living peaceable and happy by the honest work of his hands."

"No wonder there are bandits in the campo," he answers, "when there are none but thieves and swindlers and sanguinary [posturers] to rule us."

The cruelty and indifference of misgovernment explain the bandits of Conrad's Costaguana, and perhaps the same things explain the FMLN in El Salvador's hills today. We must look to the novelist if we hope to understand. His is the matter of fact. Social science and intelligence reports are the mere poor stuff of an unadorned imagination.

New York Newsday *December 10, 1989*

VACLAV HAVEL
The Great Moral Stake of the Moment

Vaclav Havel's searching New Year's Day address to Czechoslovakia, widely excerpted in the American press, set a high moral tone for debate over the future of the new Eastern Europe. The new president urged his citizens to take responsibility both for the past, when they kept "the totalitarian machine running," and for the future, in which they would become the guardians of their own freedom.

For the past 40 years on this day you have heard my predecessors utter variations on the same theme, about how our country is prospering, how many more billion tons of steel we have produced, how happy we all are, how much we trust our government and what beautiful prospects lie ahead. I do not think you put me into this office so that I, too, should lie to you.

Our country is not prospering. The great creative and spiritual potential of our nation is not being used to its fullest. Whole sectors of industry are producing things in which no one is interested, while things we need are in short supply.

The state, which calls itself a state of the working people, is humiliating and exploiting the workers. Our outdated economy is squandering energy. . . . A country which could once be proud of the standard of education of its people spends so little on education that today it ranks 72nd in the world. We have laid waste to our soil and the rivers and the forests our forefathers bequeathed us, and we have the worst environment in all of Europe today. . . .

The worst thing is that we are living in a decayed moral environment. We have become morally ill, because we have become accustomed to saying one thing and thinking another. We have learned not to believe in anything, not to care about one another and only to look after ourselves. Notions such as love, friendship, compassion, humility and forgiveness have lost their depth and dimension, and for many of us they represent merely some kind of psychological idiosyncrasy, or appear as some kind of stray relic from times past, something rather comical in the era of computers and space rockets. . . .

The previous regime, armed with its arrogant and intolerant ideology, denigrated man into a production force and nature into a production tool. In this way it attacked their very essence and the relationship between them. It made talented people who were capable of managing their own affairs . . . into cogs in some kind of monstrous, ramshackle, smelly machine whose purpose no one can understand. It can do nothing more than slowly but surely wear itself down, along with all the cogs in it.

When I talk about a decayed moral environment... I mean all of us, because all of us have become accustomed to the totalitarian system, accepted it as an inalterable fact and thereby kept it running. In other words, all of us are responsible, each to a different degree, for keeping the totalitarian machine running. None of us is merely a victim of it, because all of us helped to create it together.

Why do I mention this? It would be very unwise to see the sad legacy of the past 40 years as something alien, handed down to us by some distant relatives. On the contrary, we must accept this legacy as something which we have brought upon ourselves. If we can accept this, then we will understand that it is up to all of us to do something about it. We cannot lay all the blame on those who ruled us before, not only because this would not be true but also because it could detract from the responsibility each of us now faces—the responsibility to act on our own initiative, freely, sensibly and quickly. . . .

Throughout the world, people are surprised that the acquiescent, humiliated, skeptical Czechoslovak people who apparently no longer believed in anything suddenly managed to find the enormous strength in the space of a few weeks to shake off the totalitarian system in a completely decent and peaceful way. We ourselves are also surprised at this, and we ask where the young people, in particular, who have never known any other system, find the source of their aspirations for truth, freedom of thought, political imagination, civic courage and civic foresight. How is it that their parents, the generation which was considered lost, also joined in with them? How is it possible that so many immediately grasped what had to be done?...

Of course, for our freedom today we also had to pay a price. Many of our people died in prison in the '50s, many were executed, thousands of human lives were destroyed, hundreds of thousands of talented people were driven abroad. . . . Those who resisted totalitarian government were persecuted, [as were] those who simply managed to remain true to their own principles and think freely. None of those who paid the price in one way or another for our freedom today should be forgotten. . . .

Neither should we forget that other nations paid an even higher price for their freedom today, and thus also paid indirectly for us, too. The rivers of blood which flowed in Hungary, Poland, Germany and recently in such a horrific way in Romania, as well as the sea of blood shed by the nations of the Soviet Union, should not be forgotten... it was these great sacrifices which wove the tragic backdrop for today's freedom or gradual liberation of the Soviet-bloc nations, and the backdrop of our newly charged freedom, too. . . .

This, it seems to me, is the great moral stake of the present moment. It contains the hope that in the future we will no longer have to suffer the complex of those who are permanently indebted to someone else. Now it is up to us alone whether this hope comes to fruition, and whether our civic, national and political self-confidence reawakens in a historically new way.

Newsweek *January 15, 1991*

PETE HAMILL
Who Cares About Eastern Europe?

Columnist Pete Hamill believed that the revolutionaries of Eastern Europe had a lot to teach America about foreign policy and human courage.

Year after year I'd see them in public places: on street corners in Chicago or in Washington parks or standing in the rain outside the United Nations in New York. It was always Captive Nations Week or some great date in a fading national history, and the exiles would chant their anguish and their protests in languages I could never know. The men were gaunt and moustached. The women were plump, with shiny pink skin. The languages in their leaflets had too many consonants, and in my life I was drawn more passionately to lands that were lush with vowels. Usually I sighed and walked on by.

After Hungary in '56, there was a brief time when their existence was recorded in the public prints. This man had fought a Soviet tank with a Molotov cocktail and that man's sister had died hurling a paving stone at a machine gunner; they made words and phrases like *sacrifice* and *freedom* and *in vain* sound like something more than Fourth of July oratory. But by the time we had plunged into our own anguished '60s, most of us had ceased to care. We could do something about Vietnam. It was our war, waged by our politicians, fought by our armies. We could do nothing about Eastern Europe except exchange missiles with the Russians.

The Reagan Right, of course, used Eastern Europe's plight to pander for ethnic votes; the fading American Left sometimes spoke wistfully about the Prague Spring. But neither seemed really to care very much. There were other matters to divert us: Watergate, abortion, Iran, drugs, various gurus, the religion of the LBO. Reagan railed at the Evil Empire, invented the contras (degrading the 1956 Hungarian resistance by calling these hired thugs "freedom fighters"), and directed the invasion of Grenada. But there was never any talk about "rolling back" the Red hordes in Prague or Warsaw, Sofia or Bucharest, East Berlin or Budapest; and places such as Lithuania, Estonia, Armenia, and Latvia had long ago vanished from the map. The attitude was brutally simple: Eastern Europe was "theirs"; Central America was "ours." *Realpolitik uber alles.* And every year or so, I'd pass the old exiled stalwarts holding weathered signs and chanting in the streets, occasionally producing one of their American children to do a dance in a folk costume from the old country.

There are lessons about what happened in Eastern Europe for all of us. The American Right, after an initial period of bafflement, is claiming a triumph of capitalism over communism. "But that's not what is going on here," said Rita Klimova, a woman I met in Czechoslovakia last year who lived in New York as a child from 1939 to 1946, returned to Prague, became an economics professor, was blacklisted after the fall of Dubcek, and then earned a marginal living as a free-lance translator for many years. "If people here had to choose a model, it would probably be Sweden."

Others noted that in the places where the United States did use physical force in the crusade against communism (Cuba, North Korea, Vietnam), Stalinism was still in power, its authority reinforced by the need (real or imaginary) to resist an outside threat. In Eastern Europe, the more pacific techniques of trade, cultural exchanges, and communications helped bring about the great change. Stalinism eventually fell of its own dumb weight. One Czech friend said to me: "There were two specific factors. One was Gorbachev, who made it clear that he wouldn't send the tanks. The other was the decision to stop jamming Radio Free Europe and the Voice of America. That allowed us to get hard news. We didn't care about the propaganda or the oratory. Just the news. That was *very* important."

He and the others were too modest to mention the one final factor: courage. Men like new Czech president Vaclav Havel, who began their lonely fight more than a decade ago, believed enough in their cause to place their bodies before the might of the state. They had no guns. They had no money. And in the end they won. They won for themselves and their families and their friends, for their country, for memory and history. But they also won for those lonely men and women who stood for so many years in the hard rain of strange cities. I wish I could find some of them and say that I am sorry for not listening to them in their separation and solitude. But they're gone now. And that might be the happiest ending of all.

Esquire *March 1990*

JOHN KENNETH GALBRAITH
What Sort of Capitalism is Best for Former Communist Nations?

As many in the West rushed to celebrate—and hasten—the arrival of freemarket Capitalism to the Eastern block, economist John Kenneth Galbraith warned that this was not what the Eastern Europeans needed—or wanted.

We are urging on Eastern Europe a kind of capitalism that we in the West would not care to risk. In the last century, when Marx wrote, and continuing on into this century and the years of the Great Depression, the survival of capitalism in its original and ideologically exact form was very much in doubt. The distribution of power and income between employer and employed was highly unequal. Workers, when unneeded, were discarded without income. There was cruel exploitation of women and children.

Most threatening of all, as Marx foresaw, were the recurring economic crises or depressions that swept millions into unemployment and deprivation. From all this came anger and alienation and, for many, the strong feeling, perhaps the near certainty, that the system could not survive.

The system did survive, however, because the welfare state mitigated many of the hardships and the cruelties of pure capitalism. Also, trade unions were legitimized and soon began to exercise countervailing power. And the Keynesian revolution gave to the state the responsibility—however imperfectly discharged—of smoothing out the business cycle and limiting the associated hardship and despair. The prevention of mass unemployment and the assurance of economic growth became the prime tests of government competence.

Let us be clear. What the countries of Eastern Europe see as the alternative to socialism, or, in the common reference, communism, is not capitalism. Were it capitalism in its classical form, they would not for a moment want the change. The alternative they see is the modern state, with a large, indispensable mellowing and stabilizing role for government.

I turn now to socialism. The economic and political structures under which Eastern Europeans have lived and suffered bear as little resemblance to the Marxian model as does the capitalism they are urged to embrace. Socialism, as it matured, had a task that Marx and Lenin did not foresee: the production of consumer goods in all their modern diversity of styles, designs, and supporting services. That was the model set by the non-socialist world. A centralized planning and command system could not contend with these demands. Nor could it contend with the special problems of agriculture, an industry that functions well only when blessed with the self-motivated energies of the individual owner and proprietor. A further and great misfortune of advanced socialist development was the increasing and eventually overriding role of organization, of bureaucracy.

Capitalism in its original, or pristine, form could not have survived. But under pressure it did adapt. Socialism in its original form and for its first tasks did succeed. But it later failed to adapt, and it nurtured an oppressive and repressive political structure. Having shed this last characteristic, how does it now adapt?

Two things are clear. First, those who speak, as so many do so glibly, of a return to the free market of Adam Smith are wrong to the point of mental vacuity of clinical proportions. It is something we in the West do not have, would not tolerate, could not survive. Ours is a mellow, government-protected life; for Eastern Europeans, pure and rigorous capitalism would be no more welcome than it would be for us.

Were I counseling the Eastern European countries, I would urge the release to the market of less urgent consumer goods and services. To facilitate this process, I would also urge loans from the state banks and any necessary steps to accommodate banks to this purpose. There should be no hesitation, as there now is in the Soviet Union, about having a private employer/employee relationship. This is a relationship, however identified with capitalism, that millions have survived and enjoyed.

I would be more cautious and gradual in releasing to the market basic foods, rents, and health services. Here hardship and suffering would be acute. All of the major industrial countries, after all, now heavily subsidize their agricultural production. As a result, farm prices are higher and/or consumer prices lower than they would be without such government intervention. All industrial countries also take special steps to provide lower-cost housing; nowhere does the free market alone supply good, inexpensive shelter. Health care, too, is only satisfactory where it is effectively socialized.

Nothing would be more disastrous in the West than a return to the economic order envisaged in early capitalist doctrine and still celebrated by its more devout theologians. The system has survived only because of its capacity, in a liberal political context, to adapt.

Socialism encountered revolt because it failed to adapt. What's needed now is adaptation and not a dramatic descent into primitive capitalism.

Harper's *April 1990*

BURTON YALE PINES
The Eighties: Ten Years of Triumph

As the new decade began, Burton Yale Pines of the Heritage Foundation, which had been at the forefront of the conservative revolution, looked back exultantly over what he saw as a decade of victories for the American Right.

W. H. Auden aptly called the 1930s a "low, dishonest decade." It would be just as appropriate an epitaph for the 1970s, a miserable time of pain and humiliation for Americans.

That those days now seem so distant, so incomprehensibly alien to us may be the grandest tribute to how marvelous the 1980s have been. As a nation, we have regained our self-confidence, our voice and our stride. We have become economically healthier, socially more mobile and militarily stronger.

It is in no small way thanks to what we have been doing that Iron Curtains have been lifting and Communist parties collapsing. Ronald Reagan's "It's morning again in America" has meant a new dawn for much of the world.

An appreciation of how far we've come requires recalling where we were just 10 years ago.

In the 1970s America was on the retreat on almost every front. We surrendered to high taxes, bracket creep, inflation, gas lines, coddling of criminals and falling educational standards.

We retreated in Vietnam, Angola, Ethiopia, Nicaragua and in the face of OPEC. We surrendered the Panama Canal, closed our eyes to Soviet treaty violations and at the United Nations apologized obsessively for being America and daring to have national interests. And we saw one president after another—Nixon and Ford and Carter—defeated by the problems they faced and turned haggard by the burdens of presidency.

It was a dreadful decade. We wanted to believe only the worst of ourselves and actually listened respectfully to leaders who told us what would have been hooted down by earlier American generations—that less is more, small is beautiful and yesterday was better than tomorrow will ever be.

The 1980s repealed all that. We cut taxes, began deregulating the economy and returned to a typically American strategy for economic growth that has unleashed individual initiative, restructured and repolished our old rusting industrial core and created hundreds of thousands of new enterprises and millions of new jobs.

By recognizing again that government is not the universal solution, we have reversed nearly a half-century of conviction that Washington knows best. Of course, in some cases it may; but now the burden of proof has been shifted to those who want government to meddle in our affairs.

In dealing with Moscow, the 1980s have restored a decade and a half of failure by shifting the correlation of forces and allowing us to bargain from strength. We rebuilt our military arsenal, dared Moscow to keep technological pace with our Strategic Defense Initiative and kept our promise to our allies (doggedly ignoring massive protests) to deploy medium-range nuclear missiles in Western Europe. We dared brand the Soviet Union "the Evil Empire," founded a National Endowment for Democracy to wage global battles for public opinion and proclaimed a Reagan Doctrine to help anti-Communist freedom fighters.

In doing so—in Nicaragua, Angola, Afghanistan and, poignantly, in tiny Grenada—we ended the free ride that the 1970s had given Soviet imperial expansion. With a price suddenly imposed on Moscow's adventurism, it was no wonder that Soviet leaders began pulling back their empire's frontiers.

We began the 1980s nearly paralyzed by mega-problems that affected nearly every American: inflation, high interest rates, economic stagnation, rusting industry, military weakness and geopolitical timidity.

By and large, these problems have been dealt with. This allows us to redirect our attention to such matters as education and the environment and also to those problems that, though serious, affect only some of us, like homelessness, child-care costs, catastrophic health care and welfare reform.

Our determination to do for these and similar problems what we have done for the mega-problems that we inherited from the 1970s will set our 1990s agenda—as will our need to craft with Moscow and our allies a new, stable international order.

These will be difficult challenges requiring our wisdom, energy and surely some sacrifices. But before we throw ourselves into these new tasks, we owe it to ourselves to uncork the champagne and indulge in a bit of celebration, of patting ourselves on the back, of savoring victory and of saying: "America, it's been a great decade. Job well done!"

The Minneapolis Star-Tribune *January 1, 1990*

CHRISTOPHER LASCH
The Costs of Our Cold War Victory

Not everyone saw the end of the Cold War as a cause for unqualified jubilation. Author Christopher Lasch argued that the "deep wounds" inflicted on the nation by forty years of "containment" would not be easily healed.

In 1947, George Kennan held out the hope that a policy of "containing" the spread of Communism, if it were vigorously pursued over several decades, would eventually lead to the "break-up or the gradual mellowing of Soviet power." Today the mellowing or break-up of Soviet power is taking place before our eyes.

It is taking place, moreover, as a direct result of American pressure, which has forced the Soviet Union into an arms race that ruined its economy, falsified its claim to be a workers' state and alienated those who once looked to it for moral and ideological leadership.

The Soviet Union has suffered a defeat the magnitude of which can hardly be exaggerated. By the same token, the West has won a diplomatic, military and ideological victory that appears to have vindicated advocates of containment and retrospectively discredited its critics.

It is important to remember, however, that critics of containment—and they included Mr. Kennan himself, after the mid-1950's—were concerned not only with its probable effects on Russian society but, above all, on our own. They may have underestimated the West's capacity to wear down the Soviet Union, but they were surely right in thinking that a protracted, single-minded, global struggle against Communism might cripple democratic institutions at home.

They warned us, in effect, that even if the West prevailed, it would pay dearly for its success and that the U.S., in particular, would pay most heavily of all.

At the beginning of the cold war, Walter Lippmann predicted that containment would force the U.S. to piece together a global network of client states, and that the clients would end up calling the tune. The need to sustain its credibility as a protector of anti-Communist regimes would lead the U.S. into police actions, even full-scale wars, that were inconsistent with its own national interests. The war in Vietnam, a national disaster from which the U.S. has never really recovered, bears out the accuracy of this insight.

Thanks to its willingness to support corrupt and repressive regimes in a global crusade against Communism—to ally itself with the most reactionary forces in the Third World—the North American colossus is now widely regarded as a colonial power whose verbal championship of freedom, democracy and social reform cannot be taken any more seriously than that of the Soviet Union.

Critics of American foreign policy also pointed out that containment would cause serious distortions in the American economy. Military spending would deflect investment from plan expansion and modernization, making the U.S. weak in exports and more and more vulnerable to imports.

Experience has confirmed this insight as well. Nations unburdened by large military expenditures, notably West Germany and Japan, have shot ahead of us in their productive capacity, taken over markets formerly dominated by American exports and invaded the domestic market—the final indignity.

The diplomatic and economic costs of containment merely scratch the surface. The cold war inflicted much deeper wounds on American society. Preoccupation with external affairs led to the neglect of domestic reforms, even of basic services. The development of secret police organizations, the erosion of civil liberties, the stifling of political debate in the interest of bipartisan consensus, the concentration of decision-making in the executive branch, the secrecy surrounding executive actions, the lying that has come to be accepted as routine in American politics—all these things derive either directly or indirectly from the cold war.

Their worst effect has been to undermine confidence in government, to weaken our public culture and to destroy the delicate fabric of trust on which civic life depends. If the West won the cold war, the U.S. can hardly be said to have shared in the fruits of that victory. It would be closer to the truth to say that the Soviet Union and the U.S. have destroyed each other as major powers, just as many critics of the cold war predicted.

The cold war now belongs to the age of political dinosaurs, when the earth was dominated by two overgrown empires each claiming to stand for rival principles of economics and politics, as easily distinguished from each other as black and white. The choice between them—even the abstract choice between socialism and capitalism—no longer interests the rest of the world.

The New York Times *July 13, 1990*

ALAN NAIRN
Notes and Comment (The Panama Invasion)

Deprived of its reliable enemy, the "Evil Empire" of the Eastern bloc, the Reagan-Bush doctrine continued to play itself out on a Central American stage. Military censorship had obscured many of the facts about the U.S.'s Christmas-week invasion of Panama. But Alan Nairn, in the New Yorker, *revealed both the hidden background and the bloody costs of Bush's first war.*

Last December 21st, as the United States invasion of Panama entered its second day, *El Diario-La Prensa,* a New York Spanish-language daily, carried a front-page photograph—under the headline "THE PRICE OF THE INVASION"—of eight bodies on the floor of a Panama City morgue. An article said that the hospitals were in "chaos." One hospital administrator reported, fourteen hours into the invasion, that he had so far taken in fifty bodies, forty-three of them civilian. The same day as the *El Diario* story, the *Times* carried a front-page news analysis concluding that George Bush had completed "a Presidential initiation rite" and had moved into the ranks of "American leaders" who "since World War II have felt a need to demonstrate their willingness to shed blood to protect or advance . . . the national interest." The *Times* said that Bush had thereby erased his image of indecisiveness, and shown himself "a man capable of bold action." That night, on ABC's PrimeTime Live, Colonel Ron Sconyers, the spokesman for the Pentagon's Southern Command, said, "If you have to fight and shed a little blood for democracy. . . it's great." Arthur Davis, the United States Ambassador to Panama, said that the costs of the invasion were justified, because it had "restored dignity to the United States."

On the fourth day of the invasion, Geoffrey Garin, a Democratic consultant, told the *Times* that "Panama was not as clean for George Bush as Grenada was for Ronald Reagan"—a reference not to the Panamanian and American dead but to the fact that General Manuel Noriega was still at large. Once Noriega sought refuge in the Vatican Embassy, even small tactical reservations began to fade from the Washington discussion.

In Latin America, by contrast, outrage was nearly universal, and was especially strong among those governments which Washington had long counted as its friends. Argentina decried the invasion as "a clear violation of the internationally enshrined principle of non-intervention." Peru noted that it had been a longtime critic of "the dictatorial regime of General Noriega," but nevertheless recalled its

Ambassador from Washington, on the ground that the invasion "constitutes an outrage against Latin America" and "evidences the most grotesque practices of imperialism."

In Washington, however, little attention was paid to the fact that an invasion ostensibly mounted—as Dan Rather announced on CBS—"to restore democracy to Panama" was being overwhelmingly condemned by the Hemisphere's democratic governments. Guillermo Endara, the man whom Washington installed as Panama's new President, was the apparent winner of the elections there last May, but there is reason to wonder what fate will befall him if he should decide in the future to steer a course independent of Washington's desires. The United States, after all, had helped overthrow elected Presidents in Guatemala (1954), the Dominican Republic (1963), Brazil (1964), El Salvador (1972), and Chile (1973), and Panama itself (1941), and is currently trying to do so in Nicaragua. In 1984, the United States recognized a fraudulent Panamanian election (so described in cables from the United States Embassy in Panama) and sent Secretary of State George Shultz to attend the inauguration of Noriega's handpicked candidate.

That, of course, was when Noriega was still working for the United States. He had been recruited by the C.I.A. in the late nineteen-sixties, while he was a junior officer, and eventually he collected an annual C.I.A. stipend of two hundred thousand dollars. And in 1983, with full United States support, he became Panama's de-facto ruler. Although the 1977 Torrijos-Carter Canal Treaties specified that American forces in Panama could be used only to defend the canal, Noriega in the early nineteen-eighties helped the United States turn Panama into an intelligence, training, resupply, and weapons base for the Reagan Administration's campaigns in Nicaragua and El Salvador. Along the way, he collected a sheaf of letters from the United States Drug Enforcement Administration thanking him for help in the fight against marijuana and cocaine. At no point was Noriega's relationship with our government impeded by the fact that Noriega was a drug trafficker himself. In 1976, after two drug-enforcement officials had gone as far as to recommend that Noriega be assassinated to stop his drug dealing, George Bush, who was then the director of the C.I.A., met with Noriega personally and took no action to remove him from its rolls. In 1983, after Noriega had joined forces with the Medellin cocaine cartel and Bush had become Vice-President and the coordinator of the Reagan drug war, Bush and Noriega met again, and Noriega's C.I.A. contract continued undisturbed.

President Bush justified the invasion as an effort "to combat drug trafficking," yet the cartel had shifted its business to other intermediaries after Noriega was indicted, in Miami, in 1988. The indictment followed a falling out with the United States which began in 1987, for reasons that are still unclear but apparently involved a cooling of Noriega's support for the Contras.

The President also said that the invasion was necessary "to safeguard the lives of Americans," citing the killing of an American soldier at a Panama military checkpoint. But the pre-invasion events claimed one American life, and the invasion itself claimed two dozen. Moreover, at least one American soldier is killed every month in some incident at one of our outposts around the world—often in an allied country—and the United States does not send in the Marines.

As the troops poured into Panama City, Dan Rather denounced Noriega as being "at the top of the list of the world's drug thieves and scums." Peter Jennings called him "one of the more odious creatures with whom the United States has had a relationship." Yet the uncomfortable truth is that, with the exception of Costa Rica (which does not have an army), Noriega's Panama had for years been the least violent and repressive member of Washington's Central American team. According to Amnesty International, Americas Watch, and the Organization of American States, Noriega's forces had been responsible for perhaps a dozen political killings from 1983 until the coup attempt last fall. In Honduras in the early eighties, just one military unit, the C.I.A.-backed Battalion 3-16, was implicated in at least a hundred and forty-two death-squad murders. The Nicaraguan Contras have murdered thousands, and more than seventy thousand civilians have perished at the hands of the American-trained Salvadoran Army since 1979. And in Guatemala, where in 1954 the C.I.A. overthrew a democracy and put the military in power, the Army, funded and trained by Washington, has wiped out six hundred and sixty-two rural villages, and killed more than a hundred thousand civilians since 1978.

In 1927, Robert Olds, an Under-Secretary of State, explained a United States invasion of Nicaragua (the last of four) by writing that "Central America has always understood that governments which we recognize and support stay in power, while those which we do not recognize and support fall." With the crucial—and, for the Reagan and Bush Administrations, maddening—exception of Nicaragua, the principle has held true to this day. General Noriega lived off the C.I.A. payroll for twenty years but thought that he could somehow survive when Washington told him it was time to go. What Noriega did not reckon on was the price that our government was willing to pay—a price consisting of Panamanian lives and ruined Panamanian property, and of American lives as well—in return for the restoration of American "dignity," and proof that a maligned American President was really a bold man after all.

The New Yorker *January 8, 1990*

ALEXANDER COCKBURN
U.S.–Backed Terrorism Won in Nicaragua, Not Democracy

Coming on the heels of the Panama invasion, Violetta Chamorro's February defeat of the Sandinistas in the Nicaraguan presidential election seemed to signify a total victory for Reagan-Bush policy in Latin America. But Nation *columnist Alexander Cockburn believed that the people of Nicaragua, casting their votes under the threat of U.S.-engineered violence and starvation, were not "hailing democracy," but rather "recognizing necessity for what it was."*

There was no victory for democracy in Nicaragua last Sunday. The victory was for violence and the lesson was that violence pays. After more than a decade of being bled dry by a powerful and relentless enemy—the United States—a majority of Nicaraguans chose realism over nationalism and said Enough.

It was appropriate that former president Jimmy Carter was in Managua as one of the chief foreign observers of the electoral process. He inaugurated the hostilities waged increasingly upon the Nicaraguan revolution by U.S. governments through the 1980s, and at the end was on hand to help broker the terms of surrender.

The Carter administration stretched its support for the Somoza dictatorship till almost the last. Even as the dictator fell, the U.S. government negotiated ardently for the survival in place of his national guard, and when the stratagem failed, it finally transported the top guardsmen into exile aboard a DC-8 plane illegally protected with Red Cross markings; thus did President Carter salvage the men who, under the tutelage of Argentinian torturers commissioned in this task by the CIA, became the Contra commanders.

Today, these crude agents of U.S. policy are left in the wings as the victors stride forth for their encores. Why mar triumph with tactless recollection of how it was achieved? Yet the Contra chieftain, Enrique Bermudez, should have been there beside Violeta Chamorro and Mr. Carter.

The function of the Contras was always to deny Nicaragua breathing space, compel its government to impose a military draft, to divert precious resources, to sustain, year after year, the burden of national emergency. Crucial to this function was terror.

On Aug. 30 last, in Abisinia, Jinotega, the Contras stopped a public-transport truck and captured an unarmed Sandinista union official. They broke his limbs, cut off his lips and tongue, gouged out his eyes and castrated him. The day after Christmas, in Pueblo Nuevo, Esteli, they kidnapped two poll watchers and three Sandinista activists. They shot one to death and cut the throats of the other three. One had his stomach cut open and his intestines ripped out. On New Year's Day, Contras murdered Sisters Maureen Courtney and Teresa Rosales.

What was the purpose of this terror? Former CIA officer David MacMichael takes the view that the Contras' sponsor—the U.S. government—was persuaded that the UNO coalition was losing and hoped that these attacks would prompt President Ortega to suspend the election. Maybe so. In my view these Contras had been ordered to inflict on every draftee's mother the simple message: "Vote for the Sandinistas and this killing will go on for another 10 years. Tomorrow it could be your son who is disemboweled."

The Contras inscribed this message on Nicaragua with knife and bullet, and George Bush drove the message home. At a November White House meeting between himself and Violeta Chamorro, the president said that the U.S. embargo would most certainly be lifted in the event of a Chamorro victory. Here, in counterpoint, was the message to every Nicaraguan mother: "Vote against the Sandinistas or watch your children starve."

How many times have we heard that "the Sandinistas ran Nicaragua's economy into the ground?" On the eve of the election, the Associated Press sent out to its subscribers some background information on Nicaragua containing the terse sentence, "But exports have declined sharply since 1979, when the Sandinistas seized power." Not a word of explanation; no suggestion that such a decline might have had something to do with the besieging of a tiny country by the mightiest power on earth, the imposition of an embargo in May 1985, and the blocking by Washington of all lending to Nicaragua by such institutions as the International Monetary Fund, the World Bank and the Inter-American Development Bank.

Is this then a triumph for freedom and democracy, that a country goes to the polls with its population clearly admonished that a vote for the Sandinistas means the certainty of continued war and continued embargo, whereas a vote for Chamorro the U.S. client means the likelihood of economic relief and the suspension of Contra attacks?

Thus did violence and the threat of continued violence duly reap their usual reward. Listen to Esmerelda Pareda, interviewed by the Boston Globe in a small town southwest of Managua as she waited to vote: "I have lost a son and a brother to the war. I have suffered enough. I am here to vote for peace." Is this the voice of someone exuberantly hailing democracy, or grimly recognized necessity for what it was?

Last week, the U.S. Congress cheered Czech President Vaclav Havel as he held forth upon the motions of the human soul and expounded upon the burden of his nation's postwar history that "taught us to see the world in bipolar terms as two enormous forces—one a defender of freedom, the other a source of nightmares."

Now it could be argued in Mr. Havel's defense that this performance was tongue-in-cheek, as a way of coaxing money from Congress for his country. How else can one explain, unless by the traditional flattery by an artist of a patron, Mr. Havel defying one very elementary feature of postwar reality, which is that in contrast to the tyranny and violence imposed by the U.S. upon Latin American nations, Eastern Europe under Soviet domination was benign indeed.

Where is the carnage in Eastern Europe, even including the terrible death toll in Hungary in 1956, to compare with the bloodlettings sponsored and condoned by the U.S. in this hemisphere? Since 1980, in El Salvador some 70,000 have been killed; Guatemala, some 100,000; Nicaragua, some 30,000. Contrast the indiscriminate bombing of Salvadoran neighborhoods and Salvadoran death squads murdering hundreds before Christmas with the death toll from the Soviet invasion in 1968 (92 dead, according to the present Czech ambassador to the U.S.), when the government of Alexander Dubcek was crushed. And this is just the start of the calculus. How many lives have been shortened or destroyed even as they began, ended by the hunger and disease endemic to systems sustained by U.S. arms and money?

Rather than flatter his audience, would it not have been more productive for Mr. Havel, in his evocation of bipolar rivalry, to have counted the price more frankly? As it was, he bolstered his audience in its own self-esteem, furnishing a fit overture in the paeans this week to "democratic renewal" in Nicaragua. The truer lesson he could have offered is that moral awakening begins with the construction of history as something more than merely the propaganda of the victors. The lesson that reached its climax in Nicaragua last Sunday was the same one taught by the U.S. in Guatemala in 1954 and Chile in 1973: violence pays and the more brainwashed the polity, the more vociferously will people cry "freedom" and "democracy" even as the violence is being consummated.

The Wall Street Journal *March 1, 1990*

EDUARDO GALEANO
Language, Lies, and Latin Democracy

The elections in Nicaragua seemed to lend credence to the accusations levelled by Uruguayan author and journalist Eduardo Galeano: that the Western "democracy meter" was a spurious means for judging the governments of the Third World.

I am a man from the South, and Latin American history teaches us to mistrust words. In 1965, the military dictatorship of Brazil, the military dictatorship of Paraguay, the military dictatorship of Honduras, and the military dictatorship of Nicaragua invaded Santo Domingo [in the Dominican Republic], together with the U.S. Marines, to save democracy threatened by the people. In 1961, in the name of democracy, those who longed for the dictatorship of Batista landed on the beaches of Cuba's Playa Girón. In the name of democracy, those who longed for the dictatorship of Somoza attacked Nicaragua's Sandinistas.

Latin America is a world where only rarely does the sound of words coincide with their meaning and where the vast majority of the people are condemned to the mute language of fear and solitude. Official language rants deliriously, and its delirium is the system's normality. "There will be no devaluation," say the ministers of economy on the eve of their currencies' collapse. "Agrarian reform is our principal goal," say the ministers of agriculture as they expand the plantations. "There is no censorship," rejoice the ministers of culture in countries where price and illiteracy make books inaccessible to the vast majority of the people. . . .

From the beginning, our ruling classes were inflicted with the belief that no one is better than he who copies best. Consequently, we had bourgeois constitutions without ever having had a bourgeois revolution or a bourgeoisie. The first constitution of Bolivia, personally drafted by the liberator Simón Bolívar for the country that bears his name, was a beautiful synthesis of the constitutions of the most civilized countries of that era. It suffered from only one defect: It had absolutely nothing to do with Bolivia. Among other things, it granted rights of citizenship only to those who knew how to read and write Spanish, leaving out 95 percent of all Bolivians.

The generals who won independence, and the traders and doctors who profited by it, acted as though the new countries could transform themselves into France simply by repeating French ideas, or could become England by consuming British goods. Today, their heirs act as though their countries could become the United States by virtue of imitating its defects. Bolivia has no coast, but it has admirals dressed up as Lord Nelson. Lima has no rain, but it has roofs with drain gutters. In Managua, one of Earth's hottest cities, condemned to boil perpetually, mansions were built with ostentatious fireplaces, and society ladies came to Somoza's parties draped in silver-fox stoles.

The dominant cultures, cultures of dominant classes dominated from abroad, reveal themselves pathetically incapable of offering either roots or wings to the nations they are said to represent. They are tired cultures, as though they had done a great deal. Despite their deceptive resplendence, they express the opacity of the local oligarchies, still able to copy but ever less able to create. After having covered our lands with fake Parthenons, fake palaces of Versailles, fake castles of the Loire, and fake cathedrals of Chartres, today our dominant classes deplete our national wealth by imitating U.S. models of ostentation and waste.

Far from an artificial import, democracy sinks its roots into the deepest of Latin American history. When all is said and done, Thomas More's Utopia was inspired by the indigenous American communities, which, through the centuries and the massacres and the scorn, miraculously have been able to perpetuate a mode of production and life based on solidarity, equal rights, and collective participation. But the Western "democracy meter" measures the greater or lesser degree of democracy in so-called Third World countries by their greater or lesser ability to imitate.

The democracy meter is located in the international centers of power—a handful of countries in the North where increasing wealth, in large part a result of the growing poverty of the rest of the world, allows for internal political freedom without risk of surprise attacks. In measuring underdeveloped countries, the democracy meter forces them to demonstrate a devotion to form, even though such devotion implies a betrayal of content. Little does it matter that the underdeveloped world's caricature of democratic institutions disguises a fear of real democracy, of any genuine expression of the popular will; little does it matter that almost all of the Latin American military dictatorships of the 20th century have been careful to pay taxes on their vices in order to finance the apperance of virtue. Nearly all of the dictatorships have held elections and financed parlia- ments, judges, political parties, and even an opposition press; they have paid homage to a tradition that places all importance on the husk and none on the grain. Thus the vigilant democracy meter rejected Sandinista Nicaragua, which reduced infant mortality by half during the year after its revolution. Yet it accepts, for example, Brazil, where the military dictatorship has been survived by a social dictatorship and where the economy annihilates ever more people than the police, who annihilate many.

The truth of the democracy meter, which is the truth of the system, can be a lie for the victims of the system. I don't think the eight million abandoned children who roam the streets of Brazilian cities believe in democracy. I don't think they believe in it, because democracy doesn't believe in them. Brazilian democracy wasn't made by them, and it doesn't function for them, even though it meets certain of the formal requisites demanded by the democracy meter before granting its approval.

Democracy is not what it is but what it appears to be. We live surrounded by canned culture, in which importance is given to what is said, not what is done. Canned culture: The marriage contract matters more than love, the funeral more than the dead, clothes more than the body, and Mass more than God. The spectacle of democracy matters more than democracy itself. The death penalty doesn't exist in Brazil, nor will it, according to the new constitution. But Brazil continuously applies the death penalty: Every day it kills a thousand children by starvation and who knows how many more by bullets in its violent cities and on its plantations invaded by desperate peons. Slavery supposedly has not existed for a century, but a third of Brazilian workers make little more than a dollar a day, and the social pyramid is white at the top and black at the base. Four years after abolition, around 1892, the Brazilian government burned all documents related to slavery, books and accounts of the slave companies, receipts, regulations, statutes, etc., as though slavery had never existed. . . .

More than half a century ago, a writer from the Dominican Republic, Pedro Henriquez Urena, asked that the blood spilled throughout the centuries not have been spilled in vain. He asked, or, rather, demanded, that the tragedy of Latin America be productive. "If our America is to be nothing more than a prolongation of Europe," wrote Henriquez Urena, ". . . if the only thing we do is offer new soil for the exploitation of man by man, if we haven't decided that this shall be the promised land for a humanity tired of seeking it in all climates, then we have no justification. It would be preferable to see our highlands and our pampas turned into deserts rather than let them serve to multiply human pain: not the pain born of love and death, which can never be avoided, but the pain inflicted by greed and arrogance."

The memory of pain is forcing us to struggle so that democracy shall be democracy, true democracy, and not the decorative mask of a system that sacrifices all other rights to the right of property and that only grants freedom of expression to those who can pay for it. And this democracy won't be any truer because it looks more like the European models. It will be a truer democracy to the extent that it unleashes the participatory will and creative energy of the people, which is an energy for the transformation of reality. Because that which copies best is not best; best is that which best creates, even when mistakes are made in creating.

And the process of creation, with its hits and misses, forebodes another time, a time in which laws to absolve the crimes of state terroism will not be written, but laws to absolve fear will; and no law shall require due obedience, but all laws will require due dignity; and the final word will not be said on justice until the final word has been said about the injustice that reigns in our sad lands. And then humiliation will disappear, not the men and women who fight against humiliation. This is our way of paying homage to these men and women, the thousands upon thousands who have disappeared in Latin America, and to the infinite number of combatants throughout the world who have fallen in the fight for human dignity. To create and to fight, against the powerful lie, against the powerful fear: This is our way of saying to each of them, to each of the disappeared, to each of the fallen: "When you died, your death was not."

Harper's *February 1990*
(Translated from the Spanish by Ed McCaughan)

JESSE JACKSON
Racism's Comeback is Destructive to All Men

On America's home front, race was increasingly at the center of conflict. As the facts became clear in a racially charged Boston murder case, the Reverend Jesse Jackson found more evidence that "racism is now so powerful in our domestic and foreign policy that it threatens the soul of our nation and our status as leader of the free world."

Police now believe that a cold-blooded murderer in Boston plotted two months ago to kill his pregnant wife, then produced an instant alibi by blaming his crime on an African-American man. Charles Stuart knew that pulling the race-cord would ring the bells of fear in a nation still tasting the lingering poison of a presidential campaign that played on racial anxiety. The police only discovered Stuart's suspected role in his wife's death when his brother turned him in. Then Charles Stuart, who understood how racism worked in America, jumped off a bridge.

This monstrous episode has much to teach us about the dynamics of racism in our country. The brutal ideology that was set back by the Civil War, Reconstruction and the civil rights movement has returned with tremendous force during the past decade. Racism is now so powerful again in our domestic and foreign policy that it threatens the soul of our nation and our status as leader of the free world.

Candidate Ronald Reagan sent the first deafening race-signal in 1980 with his transparent appeal to states rights in Philadelphia, Miss., where Michael Schwerner, James Cheney and Andrew Goodman, two Jews, and one African-American, were killed by white supremacists in 1964.

And so the racial agenda for the Reagan-Bush years was set: the diluting of the Civil Rights Commission; amid world protest, the laying of a wreath in a cemetery in Bitburg where some Nazi soldiers were buried; the attack on affirmative action; President Reagan's suggestion in 1983 that Dr. Martin Luther King was a communist; the retrenchment on civil rights and social justice; the Bush campaign committee that included members known for past anti-Semitic activities; and the shameful presidential campaign in 1988 that featured furloughed prisoner Willie Horton. As many have noted, President Reagan took the shame and guilt out of racism.

In foreign policy, too, racism made a comeback. The "constructive engagement" with the apartheid government in South Africa became the symbol of the Reagan-Bush approach to the human rights of nonwhite people. The arming of rampaging guerrillas in Angola and Nicaragua showed a shocking indifference to life in the Third World, as did the military invasions of Grenada and Panama. Would we be so quick to invade these nations and so cavalier about the death of their people if those dying were, say, Europeans?

Even the good news of walls tumbling down in Eastern Europe contains a dark lining for the people of Africa. For, as the Congress hurried to approve millions more for Eastern Europe, African experts noted the total U.S. aid to the countries of sub-Saharan Africa was likely to fall as a result.

Closer to home, it was shocking to watch the misplaced priorities over the last few weeks as letter-bombs exploded in the hands of judges and NAACP leaders across the South while President Bush placed a bounty on the head of Gen. Manuel Noriega. Where are the bounties on the heads of the white supremacists terrorizing citizens and public officials in America?

The racism that still contaminates public policy today must be overcome. The war on drugs, for example, will go nowhere as long as we accept the myth that the average drug user is an African-American male. The reality, according to the National Parents' Resource Institute for Drug Education, is that the average drug user is a white male, and drug problems are "significantly worse" among white youth than African-American youth. The least likely drug user is an African-American female.

And yet the police arrest African-Americans at a rate far higher than they arrest whites. While African-Americans constitute only 12 percent of those who abuse drugs, according to the National Institute on Drug Abuse, they make up 38 percent of drug arrests. This means that African-Americans constitute a small minority of drug users but a vastly disproportionate percentage of prisoners taken in the war on drugs. That is not right.

Meanwhile, the African-American middle-class is shrinking, hanging on the precipice. While college-educated white men earn an average $35,701 a year, African-American male college graduates earn an average of $26,550. As *Money* magazine concluded in a study of the eroding African-American middle class, "As long as today's pattern of discrimination continues, blacks will never become fully integrated into the American economic mainstream—and both races will continue to pay the high price for living in different worlds."

So we have much work ahead of us to take down our own wall the wall of racism and hatred. As the deceitful Charles Stuart showed us before his leap from the bridge, it is far too easy in America to blame African-Americans.

As we celebrate the birthday of Dr. Martin Luther King, we must remember that the wall of racism keeps *all* Americans apart, incomplete and down. Racism is good neither for the racist nor the victim. It is personally destructive, politically divisive, economically exploitative, and theologically a sin. Racism is contempt for God because it assumes that God made an error in creating a world of difference.

As Dr. Martin Luther King said, "All life is interrelated. All humanity is involved in but a single process, and to the degree I harm my brother, to that extent I harm myself."

The Los Angeles Times *January 18, 1990*

RALPH WHITEHEAD, JR.
Class Acts: America's Changing Middle Class Faces Polarization and Problems

For author and University of Massachusetts professor Ralph Whitehead, Jr., the economic disparities between blacks and whites were only one facet in the new, polarized class structure of 1990s America, typified by the extremes of "Donald Trump in his penthouse and the homeless people in the subways."

As we enter the 1990s, American society exhibits a vastly different social and economic make-up from the one that we grew accustomed to in the 30 years that followed World War II. The gap between the top and bottom is far greater now, of course, but the economic position of people in the middle is changing, too. This new social ladder is seen most vividly in the lives of our younger generations, the baby boom and the later baby bust. Because the new ladder is so much steeper than the old one, it's creating an alarming new degree of polarization in American life.

As it held sway for roughly the first three decades after World War II, the old social ladder was shaped largely by the continuing expansion of the middle class. For the first time, many people could afford to buy a house, a car (or two), a washer and dryer, an outdoor grill, adequate health coverage, maybe a motor boat, and possibly college for the kids. And for the first time, a growing number of blacks and Hispanics could enter the middle class.

Within this expanding middle class, there were a couple of fairly well-defined ways of life: white-collar life and blue-collar life. White-collar life was typified by TV characters like Ward and June Cleaver and later Mike and Carol Brady. Blue-collar life was typified by characters like Ralph and Alice Kramden and later Archie and Edith Bunker.

At the top of the old social ladder stood a small number of rich people. A larger but declining number of poor people stood at the bottom, and the rest of the ladder was taken up by the middle class. The old social ladder looked roughly like this:

THE RICH

THE EXPANDING MIDDLE CLASS:
White collar
Blue collar

THE POOR

The new social ladder is markedly different. Within the baby boom and baby bust generations, the middle class is no longer expanding. Therefore the new social ladder is shaped by—and at the same time is helping to shape—a new polarization between the haves and the have-nots. The social ladder of the 1990s looks roughly like this:

UPSCALE AMERICA
The Rich
The Overclass

THE NEW MIDDLE CLASS:
Bright collar
New collar
Blue collar

DOWNSCALE AMERICA:
The Poor
The Underclass

The rich are still on top, of course. But the new generation of rich people is typified by Donald Trump, the billionaire developer of luxury buildings for the newly rich, rather than by someone like his father, Fred Trump, a developer who made millions building modestly priced postwar homes and apartments for the expanding middle class—the kinds of homes in which the Kramdens and Bunkers lived.

The poor are still with us, of course, but they're no longer at the bottom. It's not because they've risen to the middle class but rather because some of them have fallen into the underclass. Because definitions of the underclass vary, so do estimates of its size. However, it does include at least two million people who lead lives that aren't even typified in America's popular culture. To belong to the underclass is to be without a face and without a voice.

Just as an underclass has emerged, so has an overclass, which occupies the rung just below the rich. Located chiefly in a dozen metropolises and heavily concentrated in lucrative management and professional jobs, the overclass is roughly the same size as the underclass. Its significance lies not in its numbers, however, but in its immense power throughout American society. The overclass holds the highest level positions in the fields of entertainment, media, marketing, advertising, real estate, finance, and politics. It's pursued for its consumption dollars and cajoled for its investment dollars. It is crudely typified by the media stereotype of the yuppie.

What clearly stood out on the old social ladder that shaped American society during the '50s and '60s was the dominant presence of an expanding middle class. What is noticeable about the new social ladder is the unmistakable emergence of distinct upper and lower rungs, and the vast social, economic, and psychological distance between them. Together, the rich and the overclass form Upscale America. Together, the underclass and the poor form Downscale America.

The expanding middle class, with its white and blue collars, has given way in the baby boom and baby bust generations to a new middle class. It consists largely of three kinds of workers:

• **Bright collars.** Within the ranks of managerial and professional workers a new category of job has emerged. The white-collar worker is receding and the bright-collar worker is advancing. The bright collars are the 20 million knowledge workers born since 1945: lawyers and teachers, architects and social workers, accountants and budget analysts, engineers and consultants, rising executives and mid-level administrators. They earn their livings by taking intellectual initiatives. They face the luxury and the necessity of making their own decisions on the job and in their personal lives.

Bright-collar people lack the touchstones that guided white-collar workers like Ward Cleaver in the 1950s and '60s. The white collars believed in institutions; bright collars are skeptical of them. The corporate chain of command, a strong force in white-collar life then, is far weaker for bright collars today. They place a premium on individuality, on standing out rather than fitting in. Although the older white collars knew the rules and played by them, bright collars can't be sure what the rules are and must think up their own. The white collars were organization men and women (mostly men); bright collars are entrepreneurs interested in building careers for themselves outside big corporations.

Three quarters of the managers and professionals of the 1950s were men. Today half are women. Seven percent are black or Hispanic or Asian. Bright collars make up a third of the baby boom work force. They're typified by figures like *LA Law's* Grace Van Owen, Mike Kuzak, and Victor Sifuentes.

• **Blue collars.** Within the manufacturing workplace, blue-collar work endures, but on a much smaller scale. Thirty years ago almost 40 percent of the adult work force did blue-collar work. Today, after the relative decline of American heavy industry, it's done by less than 25 percent of baby boom workers. During the '50s and '60s, blue-collar wages rose steadily, thus helping fuel the expansion of the middle class. In the past 15 years these wages have been relatively flat. Young blue collars often must live near the economic margins.

The blue-collar world is still a man's world. Roughly three quarters of today's younger blue collars are men—the same percentage as in the 1950s. Twelve percent are black, Hispanic, or Asian. Within a growing number of innovative manufacturing workplaces, new models of blue-collar work have begun to emerge, but they haven't yet advanced enough to trigger a new category of American worker. In the popular culture the new generation of blue collars finds a voice in Bruce Springsteen, but it still hasn't found a face.

• **New collars.** These people aren't managers and professionals, and they don't do physical labor. Their jobs fall between those two worlds. They're secretaries, clerks, telephone operators, keypunch operators, inside salespeople, police officers. They often avoid the grime and regimentation of blue-collar work, but without quite gaining the freedom of bright-collar work. Two thirds of the new collars are women. More than 15 percent are black, Hispanic, or Asian. The new collars make up at least 35 percent of the baby boom work force. They're typified by figures like Lucy Bates and Joe Coffrey of *Hill Street Blues*.

Federal Express truck drivers are typical new-collar workers. They design pickup and delivery routes, explain the company's services and fees, provide mailing supplies, and handle relatively sophisticated information technology in their trucks. They aren't traditional truck drivers so much as sales clerks in offices on wheels.

The rise of the new social ladder has helped to drive a number of changes in American life, but one of them, already evident, should be underscored: the dramatic shift of power within both the middle class and the society as a whole.

As members of the expanding middle class of the postwar years, blue collars once held considerable leverage. In the electorate, for every vote cast by the white collars in 1960, the blue collars cast two. In the workplace, they acted through powerful unions. In the marketplace, they were valued as consumers. As a result, blue collars dealt with white collars as equals. In the '50s and '60s, whatever class lines still divided the two groups seemed to be dissolving.

Within the new middle class today, the balance of power is much different. In the electorate, for every vote cast by younger blue collars in 1988, bright collars cast two. In the workplace, younger blue-collar workers are losing union power, while bright collars exert the power of their knowledge and the privilege of their status. In the marketplace, blue-collar consumers are written off as too downscale, while the bright-collar consumer is courted as an aspiring member of the overclass. Deep divisions have sprung up between bright collars and blue collars. They look a lot like class lines.

The rise of an overclass throws the decline of blue-collar life into sharper relief, and vice versa. Upscale yuppie haunts spring up: the health club, the gourmet takeout shop, the pricy boutique, the atrium building. Downscale blue-collar haunts wither: the union hall, the lodge, the beauty parlor, the mill. The guys with red suspenders began showing up in the beer commercials right about the time the loggers and guys with air hammers began to disappear. The overclass' stock portfolios began to get fat just as blue-collar families were losing their pensions and health insurance. Condo prices were climbing in Atlanta just as bungalow prices fell in Buffalo. It seems that there's a battle here, a zero-sum game, whereby the rise of one comes at the expense of the other.

The contrast between the rich and the underclass is sharper than ever. If you look at the new social ladder in New York, you see Donald Trump in his penthouse and the homeless people in the subways.

This situation intensifies the shift of power in society as a whole. With the middle class divided, the center cannot hold. The dominant forces in society become Upscale America and Downscale America—or, more precisely, Upscale America *versus* Downscale America. Upscale America uses its power to secure privileges such as proposed cuts in the capital gains tax. Downscale America strikes back blindly through rising rates of crime. Through the old social ladder, the expanding middle class acted as the nation's glue. With the new social ladder, the new middle class is merely caught in the crossfire.

The Utne Reader *January/February 1990*

STUART BUTLER
A Conservative Agenda for a War Against Poverty

Heritage Foundation analyst Stuart Butler offered up a popular conservative solution to the problems of America's growing underclass: the abolition of the "poverty-industry bureaucracy" which served to keep the poor "on the liberal welfare plantation."

If the United States took all the money spent each year on anti-poverty programs—about $130 billion—and divided it by the number of Americans categorized by government as poor—about 32 million—each poor person would receive about $4,000, and each family of four more than $16,000. Even after reasonable administrative costs, there would still be more than enough to lift all welfare families above the poverty income threshold—$12,091 for a family of four in 1988.

So why isn't this happening? The reason: Most of this money does not reach the poor. It goes instead to finance the industry "helping" the poor.

Some one-half million poverty-industry bureaucrats administer special education programs for the disadvantaged, manage public housing projects, and provide day care, food, and special medical services for low income families. In addition, an army of doctors, hospitals, farmers, real estate developers and other private interests prosper by producing goods and services paid for by government programs and intended for the poor. It is the middle-class members of this industry, and not the poor, who truly are most dependent on welfare spending.

To liberal paternalists like Massachusetts Sen. Ted Kennedy, the poor cannot be trusted to look after their own lives. They must be carefully managed: Don't let them choose a school for their child—they might pick one we don't approve of. Don't give them housing vouchers and let them decide where they want to live—build public housing for them so we can segregate the poor into one place and look after them. Keep them on the liberal welfare plantation.

There will never be a successful war on poverty until the poverty industry is cut down to size and made to serve the poor, not live off their problems. That will take several steps. And those steps can only be spearheaded by conservatives. The liberals do not believe in empowering the poor, and are afraid of offending their traditional allies in the industry.

First there must be a concerted attack on those regulations which protect nobody except professional service providers. Tight regulation of day care, for instance, has done little to curb child abuse. Local, informal centers, on the other hand, are under the watchful eyes of parents and neighbors. Yet the bureaucracy frowns on such day care providers.

It's time to streamline rules to break the poverty industry cartel and to stimulate inexpensive neighborhood services.

Second, government should try to select service providers from the community, even if they don't have "paper" qualifications. Many local groups have done wonders compared to the anti-poverty professionals. The tenant managers at the Kenilworth-Parkside public housing project in Washington,D.C., for instance, have put professional housing managers to shame. And in its first year of operation, the volunteer Homes for Black Children in Detroit placed more black children for adoption than the 13 official city placement agencies combined. The reason local groups succeed where the professionals fail? Because they are neighbors helping neighbors. They want to help because they also reap the benefits; and they want to solve problems, not draw paychecks just to treat problems.

Finally, it is time to push ahead with vouchers for the poor: in housing, education, and other services. Nothing frightens the poverty industry more than the prospect of allowing poor people, through vouchers, to decide where they will live, or which schools their children will attend.

Conservatives are the natural allies of the poor in the quest for such reforms. And conservatives believe in the innate good sense of ordinary people—poor as well as rich—when it comes to running their own lives. Conservatives are naturally antagonistic to government-paid professionals who want to run people's lives. Conservatives are far more inclined to trust local neighborhood organizations to understand what is needed to solve local problems.

Of course, some conservatives have a lot to live down if they are to form a coalition with the poor to defeat the poverty industry and the welfare dependency it perpetuates. For one thing, they need to spend more time explaining their own strategy, and less time simply grumbling about the cost of liberal programs. For another, some need to state loudly, and unequivocally, that they were wrong in opposing the bedrock civil rights legislation of the 1960s.

Conservatives are making good progress in this. They have been visibly on the side of inner-city mothers who demand the right to choose a school, of public housing tenants wanting to run their own projects, and of local groups battling welfare dependency. And with

Jack Kemp winning plaudits from the poor for turning his Department of Housing and Urban Development into the command center for a conservative war on poverty, we may at last see an effective challenge to the poverty industry.

The San Diego Union *February 25, 1990*

RALPH NADER
Corporate Welfare State is on a Roll

Consumer advocate Ralph Nader argued that it was wealthy corporations, not the poor, who benefited from government "welfare" payments—forcing taxpayers to foot the bill for everything from spurious subsidy programs to environmental cleanups to the massive S&L bailout.

Raiding taxpayer assets is the big game in Washington, but not everyone can play. From bailouts to outright givaways and from military procurement fraud to bloated subsidies, our national government has become a golden accounts receivable for hordes of organized, corporate claimants who lobby daily to get something for nothing or a lot for a little.

Taxpayers and their lobbying groups focus on tax rates and loopholes, paying insufficient attention to misappropriation of their dollars by corporate welfarists. One reason for this inattention is that the laws shut taxpayers out—they may not petition the offending agencies and departments or take them to court for the arbitrary and capricious transfer of taxpayer assets to corporate use and control. The stakes are enormous for both present and future generations of Americans.

Four areas of abuse are booming.

Bailouts. The prominent bailouts of the 1970s—the $250-million Lockheed loan guarantee and the $1.5-billion Chrysler loan guarantee—were legislated after public hearings and now look like small change. The taxpayer bailout of the wreckage caused by fraud and speculation in the savings and loan industry will reach at least $300 billion before the dust settles. Estimates of cleanup costs for U.S. nuclear weapons plants, managed by private firms such as DuPont and North American Rockwell, range from $50 billion to $150 billion.

Bailouts are increasingly being shaped and decided with fewer and fewer congressional standards. In December, 1988, in a secret frenzy of round-the-clock give-aways, the Federal Home Loan Bank Board unloaded the assets of dozens of S&Ls into the laps of financiers who had to invest comparatively tiny amounts of their own capital, while the board assumed open-ended liability for these failing institutions. The board obligated the taxpayers for more than $40 billion in this feeding frenzy, without any congressional authorization. Congress turned down efforts to reopen these deals (whose full texts are still secret) and instead retroactively ratified the board's wildcat indebtedness.

To illustrate the lucrativeness of these back-room bonanzas: One financier, Ronald Perelman, recouped 80% on his investment in a Texas S&L in just the first 90 days after concluding his deal with the board.

It is not corporate taxpayers who must endure the bailout burden of these corporate scandals; it is primarily the small taxpayer, who neither caused nor benefitted from the scandals.

Resource depletion. Public lands make up one-third of the United States. The laws declare them to be commonwealth: They are owned by the people in trust for posterity and managed largely by the Departments of the Interior and Agriculture. For a century, in a trend that accelerated under the Ronald Reagan-James Watt regime, rich mineral rights, timberland and other wealth have been taken from the commonwealth and leased at bargain-basement prices to corporations. The cost to taxpayers to facilitate private cutting of virgin timber lands is more than 10 times what they get back in royalties. One Alaskan pulp mill paid $2.12 for a 100-foot-high spruce, while taxpayers footed the bill for roads to make the cutting possible. Third World nations demand tougher royalty agreements from U.S. oil companies than our own government does. The under-reporting and under-payment of royalties, and the longer-range depletion and destruction of public natural resources, erode these taxpayer assets.

Taxpayer-funded research and development. This giveaway also expanded rapidly under the Reagan Administration. The prevailing practice is to give exclusive patents on government-financed inventions to private contractors. Even inventions generated by government laboratories are being given over to private business. The National Cancer Institute, which developed the application of the drug AZT against AIDS, allowed Burroughs Wellcome, Inc. to obtain an exclusive patent to market the medicine without any price restraints or royalties. A year's treatment with AZT costs from $6,000 to $10,000. Under Medicaid, the taxpayers are paying twice for a drug their taxes developed for clinical use. Total federal and state purchases of AZT from Burroughs Wellcome between 1982 and 1987 are estimated at $2.4 billion.

The federal government funds nearly half of the nation's R&D. Taxpayers, who provide the roots for this work, are denied the fruits, which mostly flow into corporate coffers.

Subsidies to profit-making businesses. Perhaps the most grotesque example of corporate welfare is the millions of dollars in Urban Development Action Grants and other subsidies given to General Motors in 1981 to build an automated Cadillac plant in Detroit. There are many examples of UDAG grants going to profitable companies, along with a large menu of other direct grant and subsidy programs. There are even subsidies for exporting nuclear power plants and tobacco. The overall value of these corporate welfare payments is easily more than $100 billion a year.

There are simply no open administrative procedures, as there are with environmental and consumer regulations, for taxpayer participation in the use and disposition of such public wealth. The Supreme Court has ruled that federal taxpayers cannot appeal to the courts to stop waste, fraud and unlawful conversion of taxpayer assets because they have "no standing to sue." The usual argument by the court is that a taxpayer's interest is shared with millions of others and is comparatively minute and indeterminable. When Richard Nixon's White House aides were openly using their time and government facilities to advance his reelection campaign in 1972, a federal court refused to admit a taxpayer's suit to enjoin such unlawful behavior because of the standing issue. Even 50 million taxpayers in a class action would not have made a difference to the court.

Many states give taxpayers standing to sue state government. Some explicitly authorize taxpayers to sue as private attorneys general to uphold the laws that officials are ignoring. If President Bush and Congress really are serious about preventing taxpayer assets from being looted, mismanaged or converted to private parties, legislation is needed to protect the public's property from giveaways, as in the patent area; to establish procedures that will assure more open and accountable government policy-making regarding taxpayer assets, and give taxpayers standing, under what constitutional lawyers call a "participant-review provision," to defend their interests in federal courts.

Hundreds of billions of dollars in taxpayer assets have been squandered. It is time to give taxpayers the means to correct these injustices. After all, they pay the bills.

The Los Angeles Times *March 5, 1990*

STEPHEN P. PIZZO
S&L Scam: Deeper and Deeper

As the year progressed, the taxpayers' bill for the S&L scandal continued to rise, and Washington continued to scramble for explanations. Stephen P. Pizzo, co-author of Inside Job: The Looting of America's Savings and Loans, *wrote that "the reason for all the pussyfooting around the real causes of the thrift crisis" was "the legion of unclean hands" in high places.*

How much longer does Washington believe it can fool the American public into believing that the estimated $300 billion lost in the meltdown of the thrift industry was the result of a few ill-conceived laws and a slump in the Texas real estate market?

Few failed thrifts died of natural economic causes. Most of them were murdered, sucked dry by the small army of financial vampires Congress unleashed on the industry in 1982 with deregulation.

Washington's fictional account will become harder to maintain as the pieces of the picture emerge daily. The recent collapse of CenTrust Savings in Miami is linked to the financial alchemy of Michael Milken, the indicted junk bond king. Milken used thrifts as dumping grounds for tens of billions of dollars of junk bonds issued by his company, Drexel Burnham Lambert, which declared bankruptcy last month. The bonds were purchased with federally insured deposits.

Federal investigators are probing the web of transactions between CenTrust and Charles Keating's Lincoln Savings in California. The failures of Lincoln and CenTrust alone will cost taxpayers at least $4 billion. Meanwhile, their former owners, and Milken, left the field very wealthy men.

Thrifts also became favorite watering holes for organized crime. Coast to coast, mob families and their associates bellied up to thrifts and sucked out hundreds of millions of dollars. One New York mob associate turns up in the records of 130 thrifts; 125 of those went belly up. Another mobster, now in jail, was in the federal witness protection program while he defrauded several thrifts of tens of millions of dollars. The longer list of those who showed up at now-dead thrifts reads like a Mafia Who's Who.

And many of those who abused thrifts also defaulted on millions of dollars of federally backed loans from the Department of Housing and Urban Development. Last week, HUD's new secretary, Jack Kemp, clipped the wings of a HUD official who was doling out contracts to a former Keating insider. It's increasingly clear that the thrift and HUD crises are sides of the same corruption coin.

Thrift deregulation not only attracted swindlers and crooks, but created them by the gross. Prestigious accounting firms routinely cooked the books for client thrifts to hide the larceny. Appraisers grossly inflated appraisals to fatten their own fees, allowing crooks to walk away with huge loans they never intended to repay.

Law firms held off regulators for months at time while crooked thrift owners continued their looting. Members of each of these professions sold their ethics for a juicy piece of the thrift action.

Deregulation created enough confusion at thrifts to offer a cover for just about anything—maybe even CIA covert operations. A freight airline flying guns to Central America in 1983 funded its operations with nearly $1 million in loans from two failed Kansas institutions. A U.S. attorney said that when he tried to investigate, he was waved off by the CIA.

Court records show that in the failure of a Denver institution, a witness testified that the defendant was a contract CIA employer—on an approved mission to use federally insured deposits to fund covert operations. A Houston Post reporter claims to have connected 22 failed thrifts to individuals with mob and CIA connections.

If money is the mother's milk of politics, deregulated thrifts became the cows. Some of the sleaziest thrifts became the biggest contributors to congressional campaign coffers. In return, critical legislation and strict new regulations were stalled, and federal regulators were taken to the Capital Hill woodshed when they stepped on the wrong contributors' toes.

Meddling by five senators on behalf of Lincoln Savings and Loan resulted in delays that will cost upward of $2.5 billion. Just last week, the House Banking Committee released the desk diaries of CenTrust's former owner, David Paul, showing that he'd huddled privately with two of the same senators in late 1988, just as regulators were trying to rein him in.

The crisis continues and deepens. A federal judge has now ruled that the director of the Office of Thrift Supervision, M. Danny Wall, was unconstitutionally appointed to his job, since he was not confirmed by the Senate. Confirmation hearings were avoided because they threatened to air everyone's dirty thrift laundry.

Thanks to that thrift abusers across the country can demand in court that their "unconstitutionally seized" thrifts be given back—further gumming up the government's efforts to stem the losses. As Congress and the administration continue to fiddle, the price tag for the bailout rises by $29 million a day.

The reason for all the pussyfooting around the real causes of the thrift crisis is the legion of unclean hands. Thrift deregulation, and the money it made so easily available, triggered a catastrophic collapse of ethics at every level of business, sweeping Washington into its grasp. Now, instead of legislating and investigating bravely, too many are prowling Washington like Lady Macbeth, trying to wipe the stain from their hands.

Santa Rosa (California) Press Democrat *March 3, 1990*

LESLIE SAVAN
The Face of the People

Village Voice *"Op Ad" columnist Leslie Savan pointed out that, like the president, corporate advertising seemed determined to project the image of a kinder, gentler, rosy-futured world for the 1990s: "This is capitalism with a happy face."*

Companies are airing ads and odes to the new decade as if they were hyping a miniseries, perhaps one called *The '90s: A Return to Values.* Already the '90s means global, hope, green—it's a people decade. *Good Housekeeping* magazine has taken out ads declaring the '90s as the "Decency Decade" (as if the last one had exposed itself). Sure, there's human wonderment over what the future will bring, but the rush to name that decade is also fueled by the urge to package *something*—a new and improved *feeling*—in order to sell it, or at least its T-shirt. Greed is out—it no longer boosts profits.

But that's cynical. People 'round the world do say "om" together, i.e., they say "Coke." As the most recognized brand name in the world, Coca-Cola has a lot at stake in promoting Trekkie fantasies of one-worldism: we'll come to recognize our common destiny through the brands we have in common. And so Coke says it decided "to usher in the 1990s" with a new version of its 1971 "Hilltop" commercial, in which hundreds of teenagers from 30 countries dressed in native togs, stood on an Italian hill, and sang "I'd like to buy the world a Coke!" Only this time, the 400 or so folks include some of the original cast, now grown and singing with their children. The spot begins with the same blond British female, only 19 years later and with a teen of her own, warbling, "I'd like to buy the world a home and furnish it with love." (The five-month search by a detective agency to locate the original caffeine kids cost $25,000 alone.) "Hilltop Reunion" debuted on the Super Bowl in "QSound," which is supposed to be like 3-D sound if you have a stereo TV (for the last Super Bowl the company hyped a 3-D commercial, which turned out to be as flat as most diet sodas).

Coke has used the big, bountiful humanity gambit before: three years ago, more than a thousand adolescents sang for the arms summit; earlier, Coke was a major sponsor of Hands Across America; and in 1977, a phalanx of kids aligned themselves in the shape of a Christmas tree and sang of Coke. The important thing for peace-loving corporations is to herd in *lots* of humans, of many colors, and for the finale, pull back with an aerial shot from God's p.o.v.

In this, British Airways out-Cokes the cola. Like its '83 spot in which the island of Manhattan seems to land in London, BA's is this year's whammo ad.

Four hundred people in ruby-red bathing caps and suits swim out of what looks like an ocean, form into a pair of lips, and march across a desert like a kiss-shaped army of red ants. On a city street, people in blue compose a huge eye. Eyes, lips, and nose meet in a Picassoesque jumble on the Salt Flats. Like earthworks art or the giant symbols etched into the desert floor by the Anazi Indians, the sight, filmed at remarkable locations throughout Utah, is entrancing, and is backed beautifully by Delibes's opera "Lakme," remixed by Malcolm McLaren. but the sales hook is less Sex Pistols than Hallmark, as hundreds of folks of all ethnicities embrace each other as if the desert were an airport waiting room; a matron kisses a Chinese toddler, a black man hugs a blond cheerleader (she must represent America). "Every year, from all around the world British Airways brings 24 million people together," says narrator Tom Conti.

At the end, the facial features come together to form a 2000-person large face—it smiles and winks and, at the last second, it becomes a globe.

This is capitalism with a happy face—and, global schmobal, a particularly blue-eyed one at that. What are the '90s? They're a corporate-sponsored '60s: product-enhanced peace and environmental wisdom and never a logo far away. Sixties values are now safe for corporate America. Antiecology then, multinationals are now "green." They're rejoicing over revolution in Eastern Europe (British Airways's ad agency itself, the largest in the world, hung a billboard on the Berlin Wall that read, "Saatchi & Saatchi: First Over the Wall"), but you didn't see 16-ounce Coca-Colas handed out during Kent State—which exploded the year before Coke's first "Hilltop" spot aired. What's gnawing at the heart of these nurturing-'90s spots is the feeling that the '60s failed. But if we follow the sponsors' lead, we can have the '60s sans fear or any rough bumps at all. That's their job—to make life go down smoothly. BA's big face was dreamed up in the first place in order to "bring warmth and humanity to the airline's professional and technical image." (But sometimes the workers need to remind the big people to be warm: When *Chariots of Fire* director Hugh Hudson had the high school students who made up the face working long past mealtime, the kids got together and spelled out the word "lunch.")

Are the '90s going to be as people-friendly as these Hands Across Your Wallet ads would have us hope? The real theme, of course, is not bonding between humans, but between humans and brands. Despite all the hugging of ethnically diverse peoples in these spots, it's the homogenization of diversity that makes global marketing work. Though the face spot is pricey—approximately $2 million for the production alone—considering the 600 million people in 38 countries it will eventually reach, it's "one of the most cost-effective worldwide advertising campaigns ever mounted," BA says. That's the prime goal of global advertising: to use the same promotion for the same product in different countries, with possibly some minor tinkering. Selling product, not '90s enlightenment, is the name of the game. In certain British Airways markets "some scenes will be changed," a Saatchi & Saatchi exec told me. "In some countries, you can't show blacks and whites together."

Peace.

The Village Voice *February 6, 1990*

BRUCE ANDERSON
A Plague on All Your Houses

In America's small towns, the future often looked less than rosy. For Bruce Anderson, editor of the Anderson Valley Advertiser *of Northern California, the 1990s promised further invasions by "a plague of locusts."*

I thought Mike Gentella's Sunday story in the PD [*Santa Rosa Press-Democrat*] accurately summed up the transition of Anderson Valley. The area is going over to an economy based on tourism—an awful nexus of wine tasting rooms, inns and restaurants. The old sheep ranches are being parcelled off and sold to rich people. Anderson Valley is very fast becoming a place dominated by the very wealthy. If these people were stone age savages suddenly blessed by pounds of gold bullion and thrust into the twentieth century we'd have a comparable phenomena. The lords and ladies of yesteryear occasionally commissioned some good art, some good music, some good plays. The American rich of the subspecies invading Anderson Valley are a plague of locusts, devouring everything, wrecking the rest. They have no redeeming virtues, none.

There seems to be some confusion abroad as to the position of this newspaper on the Valley's transformation. Let me make myself clear. I am opposed to logging. It's over. It can be done well and unobtrusively, but the economics of the industry, as established by mammoth corporations, dictate destruction in favor of short term profit taking. We won't talk about what logging has done to the rivers, the fish, the rainfall, the planet. We're clearly doomed. It's over for them, it's over for us. The local gyppos will soon be stuffed and propped up in our little museum as the last logger's exhibit.

But I've never seen any of the opponents of Charlie Hiatt's logging projects at the Mendocino Environment Center nor have I ever heard a single word of protest from any of them about L-P or G-P [Louisiana Pacific] or [Georgia Pacific]. Charlie Hiatt is not a mammoth corporation. He is not the problem. I contribute about thirty bucks a month to the MEC in newspaper sales. I've been opposed to prevailing logging practices for a long time because these practices mean the end of employment for people I like. I don't have druidic attachments to trees though I like them vertical better than I like them horizontal. Yes, I hope the Albert Elmer parcel stays as it is. I hope Charlie Hiatt sells it intact. But if he doesn't, that's free enterprise, folks. It's your system, not mine. As they say in Russia, "Tough shitski."

Hell, no, you don't need to cut trees down to build houses or for toilet paper or for newspapers. Houses can be made out of all sorts of stuff. Half the people of the world wipe their arses with their left hands and water. If you find yourself in any part of the Arab world, don't touch anybody with your left hand or place your chewing gum behind your ear with your left hand. Your left has one purpose and one purpose only! Paper can be made from all sorts of plants, most notably hemp. Nobody really needs to cut down a tree.

All the loggers I know, tell me privately they understand they will soon need a new line of work because of the radical forest overcut of the last several years. They don't say it publicly because they don't want to be identified as the allies of unemployables and loons which is how they view much of the environmental movement. The environmental movement does in fact harbor a disproportionate number of nuts just as the timber industry harbors a large number of crankers, drunks and woman beaters. Nobody's perfect while mental illness seems equitably and generously distributed among the American population generally. I plan to personally participate in the physical occupation of corporate logging sites this summer. Logging has gone too far. If on-the-ground loggers have any sense of self-preservation they will join us in the fight against the corporations. Got me so far? Get my drift?

As for tourism, permit me to say I regard it as almost as pathetic and sad as street prostitution. It has transformed the village of Mendocino into a medium sized cash register. Children are legislated against to prevent them and their skateboards from disturbing the cash customers. Families can't afford to live there. Horrible liberals from Los Angeles have bought all the houses and made them into expensive overnight stops for wealthy visitors. New Mendocino tourism is causing downtown Boonville to be tarted up in a most unseemly way, sort of like dressing gran up in a miniskirt and pushing her out onto the street with a begging bowl. Boonville used to be simply a place on the way to another place. The yups didn't even slow down. It was better that way.

Tourism depends entirely on people having large amounts of discretionary income to spend. People who have discretionary income tend to be the wrong kinds of people by AVA social standards. Every time I see a middleaged man in designer jeans with his designer sweater tied around his tidy little shoulders and his designer glasses perched in his designer hair, I resist an impulse to ultra violence. Tourism jobs pay minimum wage. It's an exploitive, dumb, ugly, dishonest way to make a buck. It's almost as bad as the newspaper business or journalism. Whenever people call this paper asking about places to stay or eat or visit I advise them, "I wouldn't come up here if I were you. We're having a terrible outbreak of pellagra, or genital warts, or consumption. When the wind's blowing the right way, we have trouble with all three." Logging makes money the old fashioned American way by raping the earth and selling the babies to the highest bidder. The British are shopkeepers. We are destroyers! Let's keep it that way.

I went to a B&B once with my wife. I won't say where. Anyway, the place was pathologically clean. Every time I turned around I knocked some kind of expensive knick-knack off a shelf. My wife kept whispering to me to be careful. I asked her why she was whispering. She said she didn't know. I told her she was giving me the creeps, the place was giving me the creeps. I ripped a loud fart to try to make her laugh. The guy who owned the place ran in to ask if we were ok. My wife asked me when I was going to grow up. I said I didn't think I would ever make it. The other guests were these antiseptic-looking jogger-type people. I asked one guy if I could dance with his wife. He said he didn't care. I said I didn't know how to dance. He said not to let that stop me. He asked me if he could dance with my wife. I told him if he even looked at her I'd kill him. I finally fell asleep about two in the morning. The quiet and the clean made me tense. I woke up at five. "Don't let me die in this place," I begged my wife. She said, "You always do this when we go to nice places and meet nice people." This isn't a nice place and these aren't people, I insisted. I told her I had to get out right away. We left at 5:15am. I put all the croissants in my jacket pockets as we went out the door of the kitchen. They turned out to be bitter and stale. "I'm never going anywhere with you again. Ever," my wife said. She's been saying that for twenty-five years. Boonville was like regaining the gates of paradise after the B&B horrors.

Worst of all is the wine industry. For pure swinishness, the wine people are the equals of the staffs of the Santa Rosa *Press Democrat* and the Mendocino County Farm Bureau combined. In a twelve dollar bottle of the stuff, there is perhaps thirty cents worth of grape juice prepared by Mexican serfs. Without these serfs there would be no wine industry. There wouldn't be American agriculture either, but that's another matter. The typical wine consumer is the kind of idiot who falls asleep wishing he'd been born a European aristocrat. He's spent thousands of hours learning the difference between grapes, but he'll always be a shmuck. The wine industry is the most purely exploitive enterprise I can think of. I'm glad the French imperialists are buying up grape land in Anderson Valley. The French at least bring good food, attractive and stylish women, and a general elegance with them whereas our wine homeboys are a half step ahead of pure savagery. Americans should make beer, not wine. We're not ripe ourselves.

To summarize: Let's put an end to logging, tourism, and the wine business. Freeze frame Anderson Valley at 1970 when we were young and it was beautiful and there was some hope.

The Anderson Valley Advertiser *March 10, 1990*

PART TWO

A NATION DIVIDED

APRIL–JUNE 1990

AS THE IDEOLOGICAL DEBATES OF THE COLD WAR slipped away, the environment emerged as the focus of a new international debate. This new debate often found nations divided not into the traditional blocs of East and West, but into North and South—the so-called First World and Third World. It appeared that the roots of future conflicts would be found not in ideology, but in struggles to control increasingly scarce resources amidst an increasingly fragile environmental landscape.

It was not always easy to understand the terms of the environmental debate. On the surface it seemed that people were at last beginning to take environmental issues seriously. A 1990 Gallup poll showed that a full 75 percent of Americans considered themselves to be environmentalists. Politicians and even corporations also affected concern over the environmental crisis. But this concern was seen by many as little more than a public relations front for polluters. "Companies are using concern for the environment as a marketing tool to sell pollution," said Peter Dykstra of Greenpeace, the environmental group with five million members worldwide. "Instead of cleaning up their act they are cleaning up their PR by wrapping themselves in the green flag. Companies that are green on the outside and dirty on the inside are peddling eco-pornography."[1]

This sort of disgust bubbled everywhere just below the serene surface of preparations for April's Earth Day, the multinational, multimedia extravaganza intended to raise America's collective consciousness and herald a new worldwide crusade to clean up the environment. One ad put out by the U.S. Council for Energy Awareness, a lobby for the atomic power industry, read: "Every Day is Earth Day with Nuclear Energy." As more and more corporations scrambled to climb aboard the Earth Day juggernaut, committed environmentalists began to wonder—whose movement is it anyway?

In fact, Earth Day 1990 represented an epochal ideological shift in the ecology movement, away from confrontational protest and toward environmental advocacy based on consumerism. Like most events in post-Reagan mass politics, Earth Day depended more on imagery and packaging than on any traditional notion of political organization—and that in itself marked how far the terms of the debate had shifted. While 1970s environmentalists had waged court battles against strip-mining and offshore oil-drilling, the promoters of the twentieth-anniversary Earth Day focused on breaking through the clutter of the nightly news with surreal eco-tableaux, attention-grabbing flares that were designed "to raise your awareness." The emphasis shifted from macro- to micro-pollution, from shaming industry to exploring personal guilt, from government policy to family policy. The earnest tips that took up much of the "in-depth" coverage of Earth Day, like the exhortations to recycle household garbage, car pool, and put a brick in your toilet tank, could hardly be expected to have a significant impact on the most serious environmental problems, which are global in scope.

Furthermore, Earth Day was catching the curl of "Third Wave" environmentalism, which sought negotiated settlements with industry. By the 1990s, environmentalists sat on boards of major polluters, and big business often helped finance environmental groups. The National Wildlife Federation, for example, has a corporate council—designed to help captains of industry schmooze with environmentalists—that companies can join with a $10,000 gift. The National Audubon Society, as Eve Pell reported in *Mother Jones,* received a mere $150,000 in corporate contributions in 1986, but picked up nearly $1 million from industry groups in 1989. And where some environmentalists once argued that the government should run the energy industry, most welcomed the 1990 Clean Air Act, which allows utilities to trade vouchers conferring the right to pollute.[2]

Over the last decade, the Reagan administration had systematically dismantled existing environmental laws—throwing open the public lands and coastal waters to oil exploration, sabotaging auto emission controls, and abandoning the first stirrings of an alternative energy movement. Although George Bush was a major player in this sagebrush rebellion, by the time of his 1988 campaign he had positioned himself as an environmental candidate—the man who indicted Exxon for its role in the Alaskan oil spill, pledged himself to elevate the EPA to cabinet status, and was prepared to sign a Clean Air Act that had been blocked for years by industry-friendly Democrats John Dingell and Robert Byrd, and offered to help the countries of Eastern Europe in rebuilding their ravaged environments while guiding them down the path toward freemarket capitalism. But as events would show, the administration's real commitment was to the polluters, not the environment.

Even at the local level, America's self-proclaimed environmentalism was not always borne out. Just how conservative the nation remained on environmental matters would be made clear during the fall battle over California's Proposition 128, the so-called Big Green initiative. Big Green would have required a tax on oil companies to pay for the cleanup of offshore spills, preserve the redwoods, and try to reduce greenhouse gases. But the key provision—which had its roots in the struggle by United Farm Workers to protect grape and vegetable pickers from pesticide poisoning—required that any pesticide already determined by the government to cause cancer or reproductive damage be phased out of use in California over the next five years.

The state's powerful farm interests, joined by the big oil and chemical firms that make pesticides, fought Big Green, spending over $10 million—as opposed to just over $4 million spent by supporters of the proposition. The University of California, which is deeply involved in agriculture through research, took steps to curtail the activities of the California Public Interest Research Group (CALPIRG), the most agressive arm of the pro-Big Green lobby. And, in their most successful ploy, the anti-Big Green forces brought in the nation's former chief public health officer, C. Everett Koop, to campaign against the proposition. Koop reinforced the industries' claims as to the safety of the food system from pesticide residue.

The proposition would be defeated in the November election, and environmentalists would once again be reminded how far they had to go before every day would become Earth Day.

Beginning with the Rushdie affair of 1989, Americans found themselves facing the issue of free speech with renewed ambivalence, and early 1990 brought a series of new debates over First Amendment issues. In January and February of 1990 the question became whether beggars in the subway were protected under the First Amendment. This was followed by the flag burning controversy, and free speech actually began to look "un-American." Then, in April, the National Endowment for the Arts issued its annual grants, and recipients found themselves having to sign a clause stipulating that they would not put forward any work which might be considered to be obscene "in the opinion of the NEA." This was Congress's compromise with North Carolina's Senator Jesse Helms, who had earlier led the attacks on the "homosexual pornography" of Robert Mapplethorpe and the "sacrilegious" photographs of Andres Serrano. Many people on both sides thought the compromise was a poor one: Some artists and arts organizations gave up their funding rather than sign away their right to complete freedom of expression, while Helms sought to have the NEA abolished altogether.

Harvard law professor Kathleen Sullivan referred to the "chilling effect" of the obscenity clause on innovative artistic expression,[3] while First Amendment lawyer Marvin Garbus saw evidence that under the guise of eliminating obscenity, government sought to limit free speech nationwide by an increased number of federal and state prosecutions.[4] Indeed, in April, Cincinnati Contemporary Arts Center director Dennis Barrie, who had just opened a retrospective of Robert Mapplethorpe's photographs, was indicted for pandering obscenity. In June, members of the rap group 2 Live Crew—as well as a retailer who had sold their records—were arrested in Florida for the obscenity of their lyrics. And in July the FCC placed a ban on "indecent broadcasting" except in cases where the broadcaster could prove the absence of children in the audience—a virtual impossibility.

Such government actions were bolstered by private sector efforts to control the content of films, television shows, and rock lyrics, spearheaded by groups like Donald Wildmon's American Family Association and Tipper Gore's Parents Music Resource Center. A broad-based movement toward censorship—rooted, perhaps, in what Tom Wicker called "fear of difference"—was becoming more and more evident.

Artist and writer Richard Bolton, writing in the *New Art Examiner* in June, argued that while "these attacks on the art world seem to have come from out of nowhere, they are actually part of a larger pattern of control that has been developing for over a decade. . . . The conservative attack on art is part of a much larger attempt to regulate public expression and identity, and so diminish challenges to the government's authority. Censorship is far more than the work of a few narrow-minded people. It indicates a much larger crisis within American democracy—the failure of democratic institutions to manifest and defend the complexity and diversity of the American public."

Bolton asserted that "censorship is not only the repression of an utterance; it is an attempt to impose order, to limit social experience. . . . Those currently in power wish to deny the emerging complexity of our society. They want to halt the development of a heterogeneous, multiracial, multisexual public because they fear their own power will not survive the arrival of such a public."[5]

Commentary from conservatives themselves seemed to support Bolton's ideas. Illinois congressman Henry Hyde wrote that the controversy over NEA funding showed that America was in the midst of "a *Kulturkampf*—a culture war, a war between cultures and a war about the very meaning of 'culture,'" which demanded that "those who believe that the norms of . . . classic Jewish and Christian morality should form the ethical basis of our common life" shore up the barricades against "thoroughgoing moral relativism."[6] Patrick Buchanan warned that "the arts crowd is after more than our money, more than an end to the congressional ban . . . It is engaged in a cultural struggle to root out the old America of family, faith, and flag, and recreate society in a pagan image."[7]

In September, Congress would renew the NEA, but only after weakening its peer review procedures. And on Christmas Day, in what would seem an anticlimactic conclusion in light of the great importance the literary community had first attached to the issue, a beleaguered Salman Rushdie would choose to throw over the idea of freedom of speech—as it pertained to his own case, at least—for the language of "reconciliation" and "good will" toward his Islamic would-be assassins.[8] Still, the underlying issues involved in the controversy—ranging from America's identity as a "multicultural, multisexual" society to government control of information and expression—would resurface throughout the year in debates over everything from immigration to gay rights to college curricula to war news censorship.

KIRKPATRICK SALE
The Environmental Crisis is Not Our Fault

America's April celebration of Earth Day focused on "simple things" that ordinary citizens could do to "save the planet." But author and environmentalist Kirkpatrick Sale argued that the massive ecological crisis demanded not recycling and string bags, but "nothing less than a drastic overhaul of this civilization."

I am as responsible as most eco-citizens: I bike everywhere; I don't own a car; I recycle newspapers, bottles, cans, and plastics; I have a vegetable garden in the summer; I buy organic products; and I put all vegetable waste into my backyard compost bin, probably the only one in all of Greenwich Village. But I don't at the same time believe that I am saving the planet, or in fact doing anything of much consequence about the various eco-crises around us. What's more, I don't even believe that if "all of us" as individuals started doing the same it would make any but the slightest difference.

Leave aside ozone depletion and rain forest destruction—those are patently corporate crimes that no individual actions can remedy to any degree. Take, instead, energy consumption in this country. In 1987 (the most recent figures) residential consumption was 7.2 percent of the total, commercial 5.5 percent, and industrial 23.3 percent; of the remainder, 27.8 percent was transportation (about one-third of it by private car) and 36.3 percent was electric generation (about one-third for residential use). Individual energy use, in sum, was something like 28 percent of total consumption. Although you and I cutting down on energy consumption would have some small effect (and should be done), it is surely the energy consumption of industry and other large institutions such as government and agribusiness that needs to be addressed first. And it is industry and government that must be forced to explain what their consumption is for, what is produced by it, how necessary it is, and how it can be drastically reduced.

The point is that the ecological crisis *is* essentially beyond "our" control, as citizens or householders or consumers or even voters. It is not something that can be halted by recycling or double-pane insulation. It is the inevitable by-product of our modern industrial civilization, dominated by capitalist production and consumption and serviced and protected by various institutions of government, federal to local. It cannot possibly be altered or reversed by simple individual actions, even by the actions of the millions who took part in Earth Day—and even if they all went home and fixed their refrigerators and from then on walked to work. Nothing less than a drastic overhaul of this civilization and an abandonment of its ingrained gods—progress, growth, exploitation, technology, materialism, anthropocentricity, and power—will do anything substantial to halt our path to environmental destruction, and it's hard to see how life-style solutions will have an effect on that.

What I find truly pernicious about such solutions is that they get people thinking they are actually making a difference and doing their part to halt the destruction of the earth: "There, I've taken all the bottles to the recycling center and used my string bag at the grocery store; I guess that'll take care of global warming." It is the kind of thing that diverts people from the hard truths and hard choices and hard actions, from the recognition that they have to take on the larger forces of society—corporate and governmental—where true power, and true destructiveness, lie.

And to the argument that, well, you have to start somewhere to raise people's consciousness, I would reply that this individualistic approach does not in fact raise consciousness. It does not move people beyond their old familiar liberal perceptions of the world, it does nothing to challenge the belief in technofix or write-your-Congressperson solutions, and it does not begin to provide them with the new vocabulary and modes of thought necessary for a true change of consciousness. We need, for example, to think of recycling centers not as the answer to our waste problems, but as a confession that the system of packaging and production in this society is out of control. Recycling centers are like hospitals; they are the institutions at the end of the cycle that take care of problems that would never exist if ecological criteria had operated at the beginning of the cycle. Until we have those kinds of understandings, we will not do anything with consciousness except reinforce it with the same misguided ideas that created the crisis.

The Nation *April 30, 1990*

VIRGINIA I. POSTREL
Greens Want to Make Peasants Out of Us All

Not everyone was ready to jump aboard the Earth Day bandwagon. Libertarian Virginia I. Postrel denounced the underlying ideology of the environmental movement as "dangerous to individual freedom and human happiness."

If there is one popular cause in the 1990s, it is the environment. Motherhood and apple pie, baseball and the flag—all may be subjects of controversy. But the environment is beyond debate. As *Time* magazine puts it, "Our stand on the planet is that we support its survival." Could any cause be more humane, or less questionable?

But beneath the rhetoric of survival, behind the Sierra Club calendars, beyond the movie-star appeals lies a full-fledged ideology—an ideology every bit as powerful as Marxism and every bit as dangerous to individual freedom and human happiness. Like Marxism, it appeals to seemingly noble instincts: the longing for beauty, for harmony, for peace. It is the green road to serfdom.

The green idea is dangerous precisely because it appeals so strongly to deep longings shared by many people. It evokes a world of natural beauty and human scale, in which people will fully understand the tools they use and will provide for themselves without depending on experts or specialists. It speaks of slowing life down and of viewing life whole. It offers a sense of place, of rootedness.

In a sense, green ideology is a *cri de coeur:* "Stop the world, I want to get off!" Technology is too complicated, work too demanding, communication too instantaneous, information too abundant, the pace of life too fast. It is a vision that can be made remarkably appealing, for it plays on our desire for self-sufficiency, our longing for community, and our nostalgia for the agrarian past. Back to a life we can understand without a string of Ph.D.'s.

"In living in the world by his own will and skill, the stupidest peasant or tribesman is more competent than the most intelligent workers or technicians or intellectuals in a society of specialists," writes Wendell Berry, an agrarian admired by both greens and cultural conservatives. Berry is a fine writer; he chooses words carefully; he means what he says. We will go back to being peasants.

But people don't want to be peasants. The cities of the Third World teem with the evidence.

The greens want people to give up the idea that life can be better.

They say "better" need not refer to material abundance, that we should just be content with less. They may indeed convince some people to pursue a life of voluntary simplicity, and that is fine and good and just the kind of thing a free society ought to allow.

But I do not want to give up 747s, or cars, or private washing machines, or tailored clothing, or long workweeks spent at a computer I could never build. Yet these are all things that at least some greens say I will have to live without.

Many ordinary human beings would like a cleaner world. They are prepared to make sacrifices—*tradeoffs* is a better word—to get one. But ordinary human beings will not adopt the Buddha's life without desire.

Reason *April 1990*

ANDRE CAROTHERS
The New Pitch of Battle

As Greenpeace's Andre Carothers noted, the "amiable era" represented by Earth Day was short-lived, and environmentalists who pressed for serious, substantial changes in policy found themselves facing an often savage backlash from government and industry.

How quickly things change. Almost before all the trash had been picked up from the celebration of Earth Day, the short and amiable era that April 22 represented was gone, and a new earnestness had taken over the environmental movement. Signs of the transformation are everywhere.

A year ago, the heads of state who attended the Paris economic summit of the seven leading industrialized nations, graced by that Great Green Hope, EPA chief Bill Reilly, issued a few slim planetary platitudes and jetted home. The mainstream environmentalists cooed in delight. This year, Reilly wasn't even invited, and the whole spectrum of environmental groups appeared at the Houston economic summit to slam the United States for its criminal environmental record. Even the normally stodgy National Wildlife Federation took its gloves off, accusing the Bush administration of "killing our world."

President Bush, who two years ago said he was an "environmentalist," dubbed the assembled environmentalists' modest complaints "absolutely absurd." He would not be moved, he declared, by those on "the environmental extreme," which, using his air pollution positions as a benchmark, means every visiting head of state (save perhaps Italy), well over half the U.S. Congress and the dozens of established environmental groups in attendance.

It's a new decade, and there's an uneasy feeling in the air. Two years ago on this page, I wrote that the summer of 1988, by virtue of its natural tumult (oppressive heat and drought, marine mammal plagues and massive forest fires), had managed to get the public's attention. Well, it did. Now, after two years of unprecedented public involvement, it appears the environmental movement has also gained the attention of those sectors of government and industry that are less sympathetic to the plight of the earth. And they are not pleased.

In small communities around the nation, members of the thousands of environmental citizens' groups have discovered that defending their environment could mean being jailed, held without bail or even charges, losing a job or being branded a criminal. In the last year, the FBI has spent $2 million to infiltrate a group of activists and build a conspiracy case against one man, Earth First! founder Dave

Foreman. It has trampled the civil rights of perhaps a dozen citizens in its zeal to incarcerate Earth First! activists Judi Bari and Darryl Cherney.

Meanwhile business and government have latched onto Cold War imagery to attack ordinary citizens. "Americans did not fight and win the wars of the 20th century to make the world safe for green vegetables," Bush's budget director Richard Darman crowed cryptically last May. Environmentalism, he claims, "is a green mask under which different faces of politico-economic ideology can hide." Environmentalists have replaced communists as the species to be watched for under the bed at night.

From one perspective, we can credit ourselves for the shift. Those in business and government who support growth at any cost are discovering that their formerly safe platform is suddenly under attack. The environmental movement as a whole has finally admitted that business-as-usual cannot continue if we are serious about preserving the ecological integrity of the planet. This explains their new attention to forums like the economic summit—environmental groups that used to concentrate their efforts on preserving prairie potholes have steeled themselves to the fact that local habitat, national policy and the corporate boardroom are intimately linked. There is no point in saving the pothole if the planet it rests on is drying up.

So now we face the inevitable backlash. Environmentalists, for the most part, can take the heat. It's part of their job. What is troublesome is the effect that the new climate could have on citizen participation. When administration officials equate caring for the planet with anti-Americanism, a huge sector of the patriotic public is suddenly without a country. The rhetoric does not serve the administration; on the contrary, such tactics will lead slowly but inexorably to public disenchantment with its policies. But certain institutions, as well as the more volatile comers of public sentiment, will respond to the rhetoric, making life difficult for people who are simply trying to protect their homes.

We have to remind each other and the media of who the real patriots are and where our loyalties should lie: not to the prerogatives of business, but to the security of the home and the family; not to some vague notion of personal freedom in the marketplace, but to our communities and to the ecological integrity of the planet.

Greenpeace *September/October 1990*

JUDI BARI
The COINTELPRO Plot that Failed

Earth First! organizer Judi Bari fell victim to a new level of violence in the backlash against environmentalists. In May, Bari's involvement in a campaign to save the California Redwoods left her crippled by a bomb—and under attack by the FBI.

On May 24 a car bomb exploded under my seat as I drove through Oakland, California. This attack followed a series of death threats against me, and occurred as I was travelling to organize for Earth First!'s Redwood Summer, a series of non-violent protests against liquidation logging of the redwood forest. My injuries are painful and severe, and will leave me permanently crippled. But the unspeakable terrorism of this ordeal does not end there. For rather than conducting a fair and impartial investigation into this assassination attempt, the FBI and the Oakland police immediately concluded that I was responsible for bombing myself, and attempted to charge me with the crime that nearly took my life.

There is nothing in my personal history to make the FBI think I would carry a bomb. I am a single mother of two small children, ages 4 and 9. I have a 20-year history as a non-violent organizer, including activism in the labor, peace, and environmental movements. My role in Earth First! has been to promote the use of non-violent civil disobedience as a primary tactic. I have forged alliances with loggers and millworkers and led Northern California and Southern Oregon Earth First!ers to renounce the tactic of tree-spiking.

The behavior of the police and FBI in this case raises serious questions about the role of these agencies in suppressing domestic dissent in the 1990's. Within hours after the bombing, they declared that my companion Darryl Cherney and I were the only suspects in the case. They based this charge on an FBI agent's statement that the bomb was on the floor in the back seat of the car, therefore we should have seen it, therefore we knew we were carrying it. Later they admitted that the bomb was hidden well under the seat and could not have been seen. But based on the FBI's original misstatement about the bomb's visibility, Cherney and I were arrested.

During the next eight weeks police and FBI searched unsuccessfully for evidence against me. They raided my house twice, and even pulled finishing nails from my window trim in a vain attempt to link me to nails found in the bomb. Meanwhile a letter was received claiming credit for the bombing, explaining why the letter writer wanted to kill me for my political activities, and describing the bomb in such detail that police had to admit that the writer had personal knowledge of it. But instead of searching for the letter's author, the police concluded that, since I was presumed guilty, the letter writer must be my accomplice, and I remained the only suspect.

Throughout these eight weeks, while I lay in the hospital too weak to respond, the police and FBI carried on an orchestrated media campaign against me. Using selected leaks and innuendos they kept the issue in the news and continued to imply my guilt. Yet the filing of charges against me was delayed twice then finally dropped on July 18 for lack of evidence. In spite of this the FBI was successful in damaging my reputation and discrediting the non-violent movement I was helping to organize.

A clue to the inappropriate behavior of the FBI in this investigation can be found by looking at who is in charge of the case. Richard W. Held, the head of the San Francisco FBI and a spokesperson for the investigation against me, is best known for his work with COINTELPRO. This program of FBI covert operations was formally suspended in 1971 after Congressional investigations and media exposes revealed the crimes the FBI engaged in to discredit and disrupt legitimate movements for social change in this country. This included a 10-year secret war against Dr. Martin Luther King and outright assassinations of members of the Black Panther Party and American Indian Movement.

Richard W. Held's personal involvement in COINTELPRO included the orchestration of a dirty tricks campaign against the Los Angeles branch of the Black Panthers. Held also directed a campaign against Puerto Rican Independentistas involving warrantless searches and seizures of private property and the assassination of two of the leaders. He was involved with his father Richard G. Held in the reign of terror at Pine Ridge, South Dakota in 1975, in which American Indian Movement members were framed and murdered.

Although COINTELPRO was formally suspended, a former agent, Wesley Swearington, has testified that its activities have continued without the acronym. We know that the FBI has spent $2 million to infiltrate Earth First! over the last few years, and used agent provocateur Michael Fain to set up Earth First!ers for arrest in Arizona. Considering this history, it seems wildly improper for the FBI to be conducting any investigation of the bombing attack on me in Oakland.

Earth First! is not a terrorist organization, although the FBI has done its best to present us as one. Our primary campaign right now is Redwood Summer, a series of non-violent protests designed to stop the destruction of the redwood forest. Participants must take non-violence training and agree to a non-violence code including no use of provocative language and no destruction of property. Our largest demonstration so far has drawn 2000 participants, and we have been successful both in bringing attention to the problem and maintaining our non-violence, sometimes in the face of hostile opposition.

If the FBI can succeed in framing and discrediting us, then domestic dissent is not safe from COINTELPRO-type disruption in this decade. The right to participate in social change movements without fear of harassment is a cornerstone of a free society.

Congressman Ron Dellums has called for a Congressional investigation of the FBI and Oakland Police Department's handling of the car bombing case. We must push forward with this investigation or we will find ourselves at the mercy of police agencies who have no respect for our democratic principles

The Anderson Valley Advertiser *August 22, 1990*

H. JACK GEIGER
Generations of Poison and Lies

Some ordinary citizens were paying a devastating price for environmental pollution, while the government concealed or ignored its dangers. H. Jack Geiger of Physicians for Social Responsibility revealed the massive human and ecological costs of the radioactive waste released by one rural weapons plant.

Never have so many human beings been exposed to so much radiation over so long a time—while so few knew about it. Now, more than 40 years after it began, we are just beginning to learn what the U.S. government's Hanford nuclear weapons plant in Washington state has done to thousands of citizens who unwittingly drank radioactively contaminated water, breathed radioactively contaminated air, and fed milk laced with radioactive iodine to their children.

The first results of a five-year, $15 million scientific study of radioactive emissions from the Hanford plant are shocking. From 1944 to 1947 alone, the nuclear weapons factory spewed 400,000 curies of radioactive iodine into the atmosphere. The bodily absorption of 50 millionths of a single curie is sufficient to raise the risk of thyroid cancer. For years thereafter, Hanford poured radioactive water into the Columbia River and leaked millions of gallons of radioactive waste from damaged tanks into the groundwater.

Of the 270,000 residents of Washington, Oregon and Idaho at risk, some 13,700—one in 20—absorbed an estimated dose of 33 rads to their thyroid glands some time during the last 40 years. This is the rough equivalent of having a diagnostic nuclear scan of the thyroid—but for these thousands there was no diagnostic or therapeutic purpose. No one told them; there was no informed consent.

And for a small but still undetermined number of infants and children among the 20,000 babies born in the area between 1944 and 1960—the age group most vulnerable to radiation damage—the dose to the thyroid gland may have exceeded 2,900 rads: an appallingly dangerous figure, the rough equivalent of 100 thyroid nuclear scans for each. This irradiation of children similarly was a Government secret, concealed in the name of "national security."

The same self-serving obsession with secrecy by the Department of Energy, its predecessor agencies and their contractors generated two decades of lies that denied the risk—now a clear and present danger—of devastating explosions in Hanford's waste tanks, stuffed with lethal, radioactive waste.

When the data on the appalling safety violations and environmental contamination first began to surface two years ago, a task force of Physicians for Social Responsibility, of which I am a member, called the situation a "creeping Chernobyl." The menace involved not only Hanford but a dirty dozen other facilities: Rocky Flats near Denver, Fernald near Cincinnati, Savannah River in South Carolina, the Nevada Test Site and other installations in the South and Southwest.

But there's a difference. Chernobyl was an accident. Hanford was deliberate. Chernobyl was a singular event, the product of faulty reactor design and human error. Hanford was a chronic event, the product of obsessive secrecy and callous indifference to public health.

The official cover-up at Chernobyl lasted a few weeks; at Hanford, it went on for four decades. The total damage wrought by Chernobyl, at 7 million curies released, will be far greater, but at least it was not purposeful.

There is a double tragedy playing itself out at Hanford. The Government knowingly risked the health of thousands of innocent civilians and then lied to them until forced by Freedom of Information lawsuits to disclose some of the facts. At the same time, by refusing to release to independent investigators the vast storehouse of data on the health records of its workforce, the Department of Energy and its predecessor, the Atomic Energy Commission, obstructed scientific progress in understanding the biological effects of low-level radiation, knowledge that is essential to the public health in a nuclear age.

The radiation releases were not made out of ignorance. You don't have to be scientifically sophisticated to understand that 400,000 curies might be dangerous. The exposures were the result of policy decisions that gave nuclear weapons production, at any cost, priority over the lives of the citizens whom the bombs were supposed to protect. In one official experiment, 50,000 curies were released into the atmosphere in order to test the Government's radioactive fallout monitoring system.

The medical consequences of 40 years of irresponsibility include underactive thyroids and thyroid growths and cancers. Thousands with no apparent symptoms live with the fear that they are carrying a ticking biological time bomb. It will be years before we know with any certainty how much illness and death resulted at Hanford. Current studies to determine how much radiation went where and the consequent occurrence of disease may take decades.

We can take only small comfort from the fact that we are beginning to get at the truth, for Hanford is only one of dozens of risk areas. There are no adequate studies under way at any other weapons production site. Such studies should be undertaken as soon as possible; even then, given the difficulty of this research—and of prying the relevant data out of secret files—a whole generation may pass that does not know the truth.

But we don't have to wait that long to make some long overdue policy changes. The first of these should be the immediate, complete and unqualified release to independent scientific investigators of all Department of Energy records on worker health, and on radiation releases at all its nuclear weapons facilities.

The next step should be to end the conflict of interest inherent in the Department of Energy's jealous insistence that it be responsible both for weapons production and health protection. It is stubbornly trying to maintain its control over the research agenda. The Radiation Research Reorganization Act, now in Congress, would mandate the transfer of all health research on nuclear plant workers and surrounding populations from the Department of Energy to the Department of Health and Human Services, where it belongs.

Finally, the Government should accept full responsibility for the harm it has already done to people—and the dangers still posed to them—around Hanford, Rocky Flats, Fernald, Savannah River, Oak Ridge, Tenn., and all of the other nuclear weapons production, research and testing facilities. It must assume responsibility for the harm it has done in science by withholding data, collected at public expense and crucial to the public interest, from the scrutiny of independent researchers.

The decades of anguish that surround Hanford demonstrate that secrecy is the ultimate crime. It blocks the principle of open scientific inquiry that is the only sure road to truth. It violates cardinal principles of medicine: to do no avoidable harm, and to assure informed consent. It denies the right of free people to control their governments. And it permits—and conceals—all the other crimes committed in pursuit of the dubious proposition that an endless, ever-growing supply of nuclear weapons will make us safe.

The New York Times *August 5, 1990*

TOM WICKER
Home of the Brave?

By mid-year, free speech issues had heated up, with the proposed flag-burning amendment, the Florida arrest of 2 Live Crew, and renewed efforts to control NEA funding to controversial artists. Underlying these events, wrote New York Times *columnist Tom Wicker, was the real threat to freedom of expression in America: a growing "fear of difference."*

This week the President of the United States proposed an amendment to limit the First Amendment to the Constitution, the American guarantee of freedom of speech, assembly and religion.

This same week, a Federal judge in Florida found that the words of a rap hit (1.7 million albums sold) were obscene, whereupon police arrested a retailer for selling it and members of the group 2 Live Crew for singing it.

This week, too, Senator Jesse Helms, who is running for re-election in North Carolina, and other protectors of the public complacence continued their efforts to abolish or restrict the grants of the National Endowment for the Arts.

Thus, at the highest level, in all three of its branches, officials of the Federal Government sponsored efforts to diminish a fundamental American right: freedom of expression.

The most threatening of these efforts to limit freedom is President Bush's renewed assault on the First Amendment. The constitutional amendment he proposed ostensibly would outlaw nothing but burning a flag; but that might restrain not just free speech but free assembly, in the event more than one person should join in the attempt, and possibly even free religion, if a church group should be involved.

Besides, once the First Amendment is opened to restriction, as it never has been in American history, who can say what others of its magisterial provisions might fall before fearful and passionate majorities? Freedom of assembly, for example, might well have been endangered during the difficult years of protest against the Vietnam War had Presidents Johnson or Nixon surrendered to political temptation as abjectly as has George Bush in the puerile case of flag-burning.

Mr. Bush is playing politics with the Bill of Rights, assuming that Republicans will support his disreputable amendment and that in the fall elections the public will punish any Democrat with the courage and patriotism to oppose it.

But most Americans who applaud Mr. Bush against the mighty danger of flag-burning, as well as those who support the attempt in Florida to suppress 2 Live Crew, and those who agree that "there ought to be a law" against Federal grants to sexually explicit or anti-religious art—most of these Americans are motivated by nothing more elevated than fear.

Fear of sex? Hardly. Not when Eddie Murphy concert films, Andrew Dice Clay performances, shelves full of skin magazines can flourish as they do—even in Miami, where 2 Live Crew felt the force of the law. Not when advertising, television, movies are drenched with sex, and no one in authority lifts an eyebrow.

Fear of the overthrow of the Government? Ridiculous. A flag-burning in every city every day might signal much discontent, but not even that would threaten Mr. Bush's power. A few flags burning occasionally threaten literally nothing; the exploitation and demeaning of the flag by sleazy merchants is more obnoxious to many Americans.

Fear of a threat to religion? Not likely. Not in a country where an overwhelming percentage of the population professes, if it does not always practice, a faith; and where the phrase "under God" can be inserted into a supposedly secular Pledge of Allegiance with something like unanimous consent.

Fear of art? This gets closer to a truth, as the likes of Senator Helms proclaim their anxiety that the morals of youth be protected from certain photographs and paintings; but museums, movies, the theater, orchestras—demonstrate that it's not art itself but only some art that arouses the protectors.

Fear of race? That's even closer, since 2 Live Crew is a black group singing quintessentially black lyrics. But Eddie Murphy is black, too, and so is Richard Pryor, and they also offend many sensibilities. The artists whose work most specifically brought criticism on the N.E.A. are white.

All those fears may be at work, to some extent, as are the overwrought emotional appeals of Mr. Bush, Mr. Helms and other clever politicians. But what really threatens freedom of expression in America, now only more visibly than usual, is the persisting fear of difference, and the willingness to be different, even to be despised.

Political dissent, provocative or outrageous art and expression, social protest, an insistence on the rights of the individual—all at some point strike fear into the hearts of many who loudly extol the land of the free. But that land cannot exist if it is not also the home of the brave.

The New York Times *June 14, 1990*

PATRICK BUCHANAN
Mission to Destruct?

For conservatives like Pat Buchanan, the battle over NEA funding also had high moral stakes. He saw restrictions on grants to artists as a line of defense against "a cultural struggle to root out the old America of family, faith, and flag, and recreate society in a pagan image."

"The flaw is not with a public that refuses to nourish the arts. Rather, it is with a practice of art that refuses to nourish the public," writes Frederick Hart in the fall issue of Arts Quarterly.

Speaking of the blazing controversy over new funding for the National Endowment for the Arts, Mr. Hart adds, "The public has been so bullied intellectually by the proponents of contemporary art that it has wearily resigned itself to just about any idiocy that is placed before it . . . But the common man has his limits, and they are reached when some of these things emerge from the sanctuary of the padded cells of galleries and museums and are put in public places, when the public is forced to live with them and pay for them."

The "limits" of the common man may have been reached with news that NEA, directly, through a $60,000 grant, and indirectly, through the New York State Council on the Arts, subsidized Chelsea's Kitchen Theatre, whose winter sensation was Annie Sprinkle.

Miss Sprinkle, a veteran of 150 porn films, conducted for the Kitchen 12 live sex shows, at the end of each of which she urinated on stage. Midway in the show, she stopped masturbating with a sex toy to declare, to the hoots of the audience, "Usually I get paid a lot of money for this, but tonight it's government-funded."

Your tax dollars at work.

For most Americans, the natural reaction is: Let the sickos sculpt, paint, print, whatever they please, so long as my dough isn't involved, and I don't have to look at the garbage.

But I'm afraid we're not going to get off that easy.

For, as Mr. Hart adds, there is a hidden agenda. Behind the "baiting and taunting" of a tolerant nation lies the "current philosophy and practice of art, which . . . thrives on a belief system of deliberate contempt for the public. . . . Underneath its outrage, the art world can barely contain its secret delight at this publicity bonanza featuring a heroic scenario of free spirits vs. troglodytes."

In short, they are not going away; they are not going to leave us alone. An alienated arts crowd is going to continue to provoke the American people, to get the attention of a public that has ignored it, to force us to react in anger, so it can then cast itself in the self-satisfying role of victim and martyr in a fascist Amerika.

But, we ought not to minimize what is at stake here.

"Cult and culture go hand in hand," writes art critic Hamilton Reed Armstrong. "Just as Indian art reflects its Buddhist or Hindu underpinning, and Romanesque and Gothic art project Christian faith and hope, and Renaissance art reflects the humanism of the day, so also much of 20th-century art reflects underlying currents of what can only be described as the occult worldview."

Art manifests belief; and, before a new faith is established, the old must be torn down. Andreas Serrano's photo of a crucifix dipped in urine, Martin Scorsese's "The Last Temptation of Christ," Madonna's "Like a Prayer," are cut from the same bolt of cloth. Each was done to mock, shock, denigrate.

The arts crowd is after more than our money, more than an end to the congressional ban on funding obscene and blasphemous art. It is engaged in a cultural struggle to root out the old America of family, faith, and flag, and recreate society in a pagan image.

The maneuvering in America's Kulturkampf is over, the forces are now engaged; and, a bewildered defensive Christian society is absorbing one blow after another.

The desecration of churches in Los Angeles, the homo-fascist assault on St. Patrick's Cathedral, the non-negotiable demand that all schoolchildren be instructed in the use of condoms, the drive to down-grade Western culture in college curricula—all are part of an offensive visible as long ago as the '50s, with the drive to remove all Christian practices, symbols and beliefs from public education.

Hollywood, having successfully defended "The Last Temptation of Christ" as a film of great art, has become more aggressive.

A week ago, The New York Times ran a full-page ad for "The Handmaid's Tale," a new film about an America taken over by fascist and hypocritical Christian fundamentalists. Critic Joseph Farah's depiction of it as "bigoted and inflammatory" is understatement. The same paper ran a two-page ad for "Nuns on the Run," described as "The Funniest Anti-Clerical Transvestite Comedy of the Decade."

With its demand that the NEA be funded at the higher level, that all restrictions on what recipient artists may do with the money be removed, that congressional oversight be ended, America's artists are demanding the prerogatives of a new priestly class. Public money without accountability. The right to dictate what is art. The right to bait and taunt with impunity.

The new militancy was on display in this city last week, during Cultural Advocacy Day.

The NEA is under attack by a "homophobic cabal," railed Joseph Papp, as Andreas Serrano signed autographs. "This is no longer a fight about obscenity," declaimed Dr. Mary Schmidt Campbell, New York City commissioner of cultural affairs. "This is about the very principles of democracy and the fundamental values of this country."

The lady is right. This *is* a war about the fundamental values of this country; and, to see the White House endorse an increase in money for NEA, and removal of any constraints on the recipients is to suggest, that, in the battle for America's soul, the administration plans to be something less than a fighting ally.

The Washington Times *March 26, 1990*

SARAH SCHULMAN
Is the NEA Good for Gay Art?

Many commentators extended the parameters of the ongoing censorship debate to encompass issues involving what Tom Wicker had called "the threat of difference" in an increasingly diverse America. For writer Sarah Schulman, the NEA controversy took place within a "broader political context" of resurgent racism, sexism, class-bias and especially homophobia, in which "thousands are systematically excluded from support because they don't fit the profile for privilege."

The government is using homophobia again as an instrument of social control. We need to focus on homophobia and not on "saving the NEA." Of course, museums and boards of directors find it easier to articulate "Save the NEA" than to engage in fighting the oppression of gay people. This euphemism might even make the fight more palatable, but when the crisis over the NEA is resolved one way or another, no political impact will have been made on our behalf.

At the same time, the organized arts community has a lot of soul-searching to do about its own history of exclusion. Before Helms, many other biases existed in the funding and presentation of artwork. Historically, the reward system in the arts has been reserved primarily for white people from the middle and upper classes whose work fits the aesthetic agenda of critics and arts administrators. Yet the majority of artists previously admitted to the reward system never spoke up about the institutionalized discrimination until it affected us. Obviously, it is not acceptable for artists who are gay (or whose work has explicit sexual content) to be excluded from federal funding. Nor is it acceptable for rewards to be demanded by one group at the expense of another.

For any minority artist, part of being admitted to the reward system is that while the benefits are great for the individual, the price for the community is tokenism. I know this first-hand, having personally benefitted from the "exception" distortion because I fit the criteria for tokenism. It is important to remember that people get rewards, like grants, gigs and reviews, not necessarily because they are the "most deserving" but also because of things like personal connections and how well they play the art-game. Of course, recognition doesn't always equal betrayal, but I think that it is important not to blindly accept someone as our representative simply because she or he has been selected by a government agency, publishing company or corporate-funded art venue.

Up until about five years ago, lesbian artists were almost completely excluded from the reward system. In fact, some of the gay men currently involved in the NEA scandal participated in that exclusion. Lesbians were not reviewed in mainstream publications, were not presented in prominent art venues and almost never received funding for explicitly lesbian projects. As a result, the work remained invisible, and many women were unable to develop their talents, while others could, and their work thrived. This is still the case, with the small exception of the 30 or so out lesbian artists, across all genres, who have access to the new tokenism. However, before funding, work was supported by the audience and determined by the lives, needs and experiences of the community.

Now, through the new tokenism, a few political and apolitical sensibilities are permitted to be contained within the dominant culture. Individuals are even easier than political movements to contain. As a result, a single style is declared to be representative of a hugely diverse community that it cannot represent. At the same time, racism, class bias and the emphasis on trendy, marketable genres (like detective novels and stand-up monologues) keep other voices from the public arena. When the frustrated community pressures the token to be more accountable to its needs for expression, she often declares herself "independent," puts down the community as "p.c.," or "narrow," and disengages herself for her own artistic and career development. In the end, the permitted aesthetics encourage new artists to work in precisely the same styles so that they, too, can be rewarded. In this manner, much of the development of lesbian arts are taken out of the hands of the audience and given instead to a small group of critics and administrators. This year, the NEA panel that recommended the artists whose grants were later rescinded was composed of six arts administrators and one artist.

Media reporting on the NEA scandal further distorts the picture. A *Village Voice* cover story by critic Cindy Carr entitled "The War on Art" focused only on the exclusion of artists whose work she had previously supported. Although I deeply respect and admire the work of Karen Finley, there are entire communities of artists who have been systematically silenced. They too deserve C. Carr's attention, even if they don't meet her aesthetic agenda. Attaching the "censored" label to artists whose NEA experience is bringing in publicity and audiences far beyond what they might have naturally achieved takes the underdog position away from everyone who really is. It accepts the distortion that the art world is *the world.* When Karen Finley stands up at a national press conference and says, "A year ago I was in a country of freedom of expression; now I'm not." there is a refusal or ignorance about the history of this country in which most people have been systematically denied expression. I find a disturbing subtext to some of these arguments that white artists "deserve" to retain our race and class privileges even though we're gay. Artists could, instead, use this attention on funding as an opportunity to discuss a real democratization of the reward system, as well as the passive complicity with the state that has dominated North American arts.

The *Village Voice* ran photos of the four artists whose grants were rescinded over the caption "Defunded," even though they receive more funding, exposure and institutional support than 99 percent of the artists in this country. When Cindy Carr said, in a second article, that she "may now be forced to conceive of a new demimonde—a bohemia of the unfundable," I got really angry. Doesn't she know that 99 percent of the artists in this country already live in the world of the unfundable? And that this invisibility is due, in part, to the role played by critics like her? I certainly think that these artists should receive the grant money that they were rewarded, but I do object to a kind of fetishized egomania that depoliticizes the events. We are living in a city of 90,000 homeless people. No one is getting the service and funding that they need. I wish that these artists could see themselves in relation to their own society and place the NEA event in a broader political context.

While we must support lesbian and gay arts, we must also refuse the distortion of calling "censorship" of the rewarded while ignoring the thousands who are systematically excluded from support because they don't fit the profile for privilege. Every out gay artist loses grants, gigs and opportunities and faces bias and limitations throughout her or his career for being gay. This needs to be addressed politically with a recognition of how homophobia works on all levels, not only in the case of the most visible.

Obviously artists want recognition. I apply for grants, and I like getting approval. But the NEA scandal is giving us all an opportunity to rethink the values we've created as well as the ones we've been handed. At the same time that we won't lie down for a homophobic, anti-sex NEA, neither can we roll over for elitist exclusionism in our community. The fact is that there is a huge backlash going on against the gay visibility generated by AIDS. This includes increased street violence, restrictive immigration and continued negligence in the face of the AIDS crisis. In response, a variety of grass-roots, community-based movements like ACT UP and Queer Nation are arising. Despite the historically apolitical stasis in which many artists have festered, we can still rise to the occasion and participate as activists in these movements, working in community to end the oppression of gay and lesbian people, instead of working to maintain an exclusive, tokenizing NEA.

OutWeek *August 8, 1990*

RANDOLPH RYAN
U.S. Role in a Civilian Massacre

The issue of censorship also had broad implications for U.S. foreign policy, which was often carried out behind the backs of the American public and the American press. The details of more recent covert operations often remained murky, but, as Boston Globe *columnist Randolph Ryan recounted, the persistent investigations of journalist Kathy Kadane uncovered twenty-five-year-old evidence of the CIA's involvement in "one of the worst mass murders of the 20th century."*

The Japanese emperor apologizes to Koreans for having "inflicted unbearable suffering and sorrow." Germans try to atone for the Holocaust. Soviet leaders rue the slaughter of Polish officers, and admit the invasion of Afghanistan was wrong.

Fortunately, being American means never having to say you're sorry. Yet as the Cold War fades, a jarring account of a US role in a civilian massacre—the liquidation of the Indonesian Communist Party in 1965—comes into view.

A 1968 CIA study summarized: "In terms of the numbers killed, anti-PKI massacres in Indonesia rank as one of the worst mass murders of the 20th century."

The circumstances of the slaughter have been clarified in a report by Kathy Kadane, of States News Service in Washington. Kadane stumbled across the subject in the late '70s and pursued it for nearly a decade. She obtained corroborating statements from embassy and CIA officials that they prepared a death list of 4,000-5,000 top party officials and then gave it to the Indonesian army. For months, they checked off names as they were killed.

The role of US officials has been suspected, but not confirmed. The US list, and encouragement, imparted momentum to butchery that killed 250,000 by CIA estimates; upward of 500,000 by others.

A CIA spokesman denied involvement, but it is evident from statements Kadane obtained from involved officials, including former CIA director William Colby, that a shooting list was compiled by as many as six CIA and embassy officials.

"It really was a big help to the army," said one. "They probably killed a lot of people and I probably have a lot of blood on my hands, but that's not all bad. There's a time when you have to strike hard at a decisive moment."

The event must be understood in the context of the times. President Sukarno helped galvanize the Third World movement toward neutralism. In refusing to take sides in the US-Soviet contest, he put himself at odds with Washington, which was slouching into the Vietnam War.

Alienated from Sukarno, the US cemented close ties with the Indonesian military. Meanwhile, the embassy team compiled the list for "operational planning," as Colby put it. The team pooled names from CIA sources, and from newspaper accounts and photos of PKI functions. The list included provincial and local officials and leaders of organizations such as labor, women's and youth groups. It extended from the national leadership to the village level.

The PKI was the third largest communist party in the world, with 3 million members and 14 million more in labor and youth groups. Its aim from the Washington perspective was that it reinforced the neutralist tendency in Sukarno; it rivaled the army which US planners hoped would take over when Sukarno died.

On Oct. 30, 1965, several top army generals were killed in a mutiny. The origins of the mutiny remain murky, but army chief Suharto blamed the PKI and commenced the purge. As firing squads commenced, the US Embassy fed in the names and provided communications gear to facilitate the army's sweeps across the country. Security agency eavesdroppers monitored the progress of the liquidation. As persons listed were killed, US officials checked off their names, and added new ones.

In less than four months the PKI had been destroyed. Hundreds of thousands of "sympathizers"—meaning anyone fingered as communist—fell.

Based on this elimination of a huge, popular movement, Colby, who was then director of the CIA's Far East division, set up a similar system in Vietnam—the Phoenix Program—to destroy the communist party cadre. Lessons seem to have been applied on a modest scale in Chile in 1972.

Howard Federspiel, in 1965 the Indonesia specialist at the State Department Bureau of Intelligence and Research, told Kadane: "No one cared, as long as they were communists, that they were being butchered. No one was getting very worked up over it."

To have spotted this story in the bin of lost memories, pursued it for a decade, and finally to have nailed it down, is something for which a reporter can be proud.

The Boston Globe *May 29, 1990*

ANDREW LAM
Why We Eat Dogs

Pacific News Service editor Andrew Lam observed that in an America that had become "an ethnically filled landscape where mainstream culture is an abstraction," acceptance of diverse cultures was the only path to common ground.

"Eat a dog, fricassee a cat, go to jail. So demands California assemblywoman Jackie Speier, in a bill she has introduced in the state legislature. The very necessity of such a bill implies that the yellow horde is at it again, that the eating habits of Southeast Asians, specifically the Vietnamese, are out of control and need to be curbed."

This is how I began an opinion piece that recently ran in a number of U.S. newspapers. The response: nearly a thousand letters, most of them startlingly hostile. "Go back to where you came from, or change your ways. You are in my country now," urged one reader. Others echoed: "No Vietnamese is worth a dog's life!" "Get back on your boat!" "You all should be treated as criminals!"

In making my case against the bill, I could have argued soothingly and accurately that the number of dogs eaten by my fellow Vietnamese in this country is minuscule (the documented number of dogs slaughtered for food in the United States in the last decade comes to four). But mine was a different point. It had to do with being a people rooted in peasant culture. And it had to do with a new definition of pluralism that America must grope toward. I wrote:

"Why, you may wonder, eat a dog when there are other meats available in America? Is it out of hunger that a refugee resorts to slaying man's best friend for consumption? The answer to both lies deep in Asian provincial culture. Dog meat, to those few who dare eat it in America, is a passage to the homeland. A few Vietnamese men gather together, veterans of war perhaps. They drink whiskey and tell stories of brave battles, or they remember their rural life, while dog meat, spiced with lemon grass and garlic, sizzles on a kiln. They are bound together, these men, in another time, another world. As they reminisce over what's lost in their life, they share the rare delicacies, daring to eat the loyal animal."

I made the point that Americans are perhaps unsentimental about eating beef or pork because few Americans ever see the inside of a slaughterhouse. For the Vietnamese refugee, the ritual of killing the animal is as significant as the eating. The actual slaying, the clubbing, the skinning of an animal, is part of our Third World culture. It is a "hands-on" experience, and it reminds the refugee of a way of life that was simple and earthy.

"God help this country, lamented one letter writer. "[After the dog] who is second? The youngest child?" "Stay away from American dogs!" an angry reader warned me over the phone. Advised a certain Ms. Victor: "When in Rome, Mr. Lam . . ."

The problem may be that Ms. Victor and I can't come to the same definition of Rome. She assumes that there is one dominant culture and everyone should adhere to it. Yet the San Francisco area where I live is an ethnically filled landscape where mainstream culture is an abstraction. Instead of a unifying official culture, I see pockets of thriving ones that challenge the concept of melting-pot assimilation. The Chinatowns, Japantowns, Koreatowns, and other towns that have mushroomed across the United States indicate we are in fact heading for a pluralistic society where you and I share a thinning cultural bond. A few decades ago, who would have thought raw fish would have become such a hit? Fish sauce can now be found on aisle 3. On a Los Angeles freeway an exit sign reads: LITTLE SAIGON.

There's also me. I come from one of those little Saigons. An "upstart" to some, I question U.S. legislation over the private culinary practices of my people. As I wrote in my newspaper piece, in Vietnam dogs are both expensive to keep as pets and don't perform work like horses or oxen. In a country hardened by famine and war, the dog is the first animal to be sacrificed when times are lean. Coming from such a pragmatic culture, the Vietnamese refugee in America is thus often baffled in America by the existence of dog-training schools, pet cemeteries, and even cosmetic surgery for dogs and cats. So yes, some of us dare to eat dogs on rare occasions. That habit, however, has caused many in the Vietnamese community to feel shame, while others are inclined to deny that such practices even exist.

As a Vietnamese, though I have never tried dog meat, I feel as though my culture's practices and traditions are now forced to stand trial. Other Americans eat rabbits, pigeons, turtles, and even swallow live goldfish for a prank. But with the lawmakers' approval, our culture would be pruned and corrected to conform to the dominant taste. "Are we to be treated as criminals," I asked, "for keeping some remembered part of ourselves alive in this new land?"

"I'll pit my eighty-pound Samoyed wolf with you," replied one letter writer, who attached a picture of a quite large and adorable dog. "May the victor eat his fill!" A columnist for the *San Jose Mercury News,* which serves an area populated by a large number of Vietnamese, accused my article of "setting off a firestorm" and "giving hostile people an easy excuse to hate 'foreigners.'" But I think otherwise. Anti-Asian sentiment in this country has always been deep rooted. Yet to keep silent does not dispel those sentiments. They get worse. Did it help, I wonder, for the parents of those slain Cambodian and

Vietnamese children gunned down in a Stockton schoolyard to have kept quiet their intimate family life, their very different culture?

America is changing profoundly, and there is hope to be found in the "firestorm" around my little article. Ten years ago, I doubt any newspaper would have run it. Ten years ago, I doubt any politician would have paid attention to Vietnamese protest, as Jackie Speier has now. (She amended her bill to include all household pets, which made it a less specific cultural attack. It passed.) What I wrote helped lift a corner of a dark cloth, one that covers unspoken hostility born of fear. The fear is that others' exotic lifestyles today might be familiar and accepted ones tomorrow. Conflicts between different groups are inevitable in a country so diverse as ours, and so they must be brought out into the open.

Here then, is a riddle for Ms. Victor: If the melting pot is obsolete, what then, is Rome? Answer: There isn't any Rome. Rome is more like a cacophonous zoo where each group is seemingly caged, for few of us care to venture out and confront and ask each other questions. We hear only the screeches of those in neighboring cages, but we haven't yet a clear picture of what everyone looks or acts like. And unless we strain to watch and listen, it will be impossible to imagine what we "Romans," as un-Roman and dissimilar as we've all become, can do to find common ground to walk on.

Mother Jones *July/August 1990*

IKE ADAMS
Ike's a Hillbilly and Proud to Be One

In 1990s America, diversity—racial, ethnic, social, and even regional—was a reason for both conflict and pride. According to columnist Ike Adams of the Whitesburg, Kentucky Mountain Eagle, *it was an issue which had relevance even for the hill people of the Cumberland.*

I was at a staff training conference last week and the leader of one particular session requested that every person in the room write down one word that best described him- or herself. Of course when trainers do that sort of thing you know that their next step is to ask you to announce to the rest of the crowd what you think of yourself.

I studied on it for quite a while and even after the teacher commenced going around the room asking folks to 'fess up, I still hadn't quite got down to one word. What I really wanted to say was about three sentences long and I was trying to see if I could get that down to one sentence by using a bunch of commas. He'd already let a couple of folks get away with using two words, and my frank opinion of myself was just too damn complex to even narrow down to a simple phrase.

Finally I wrote down "Proud, honest, opinionated native of eastern Kentucky." I figured when it came my turn I'd just spit that out as fast as I could and insist that all things were equally important to my notion of who I am and if he didn't like it I'd just tell him that his rules wouldn't fit me.

Most other people in the room weren't having a bit of trouble. Some thought themselves simply "honest" or "caring" or "committed" or "intelligent." One fellow said he was "good" and I breathed a sigh of relief because his was the first answer that somebody had given that I couldn't also lay claim to.

And then the teacher called on me.

And it came to me like a flash.

"Hillbilly!!!!" I yelled out like a contestant on Wheel of Fortune who figures out the puzzle half a second before the time runs out. I can't remember the last time I was as pleased with myself.

Harry Caudill is a proud, honest, opinionated native of eastern Kentucky. Call him up and ask him if you don't believe me. I, on the other hand, am a hillbilly and no single other word could come close to describing me as inclusively and as accurately.

Harry would probably get mad if you called him a hillbilly. Not me. I'm studying about having it tattooed on my forehead. Maybe some of us could talk to Harry and see if he'd settle for being called a Mountain William. That's what they call Hoover Dawahare in Lexington.

The point is that people from the hills—particularly the hills of eastern Kentucky—deserve an ethnic identification and I think it's high time we restored a little self pride in who it is we are. Hillbilly pride. Hillbilly endurance. Hillbilly hospitality. It starts to sound poetic when you say it a few times.

But the problem is that most hillbillies are ashamed of it. There's a fight in Hamilton, Ohio, every night because someone called someone else a hillbilly. When eastern Kentuckians move up north, the first thing they do is start mimicking the locals. Deetroit becomes Duhtrt. School becomes scoouuuoul. My becomes myiaaah. They stop saying "ain't" altogether, and they'd never admit in public that their children are youngens. They move to Ohio. They come home from Ohighya.

I heard a feller explaining to a store clerk in Cincinnati that he was from "just outside of Lexington" and me knowing full well that the farthest he'd been from Doty Creek in Letcher County before he was 18 years old was a trip he'd made with the basketball team when Letcher High played Jackson at their place.

When they ask me where I'm from they get "Blair Branch." Every time. And if they want to know where Blair Branch is I tell 'em halfway between Spring Branch and Isom. How close to Lexington is what they want to know next, and I ask them where Lexington is. If people up north started thinking I was from Lexington, that's when I'd start getting embarrassed.

I think we ought to make up bumper stickers, "Hillbilly on Board." If you're from the mountains and you now live in Ohio, you ought to have one on each side of your license tag. I ran into a man I went to high school with at a Bluegrass festival last summer and I asked him where he was living. "Oh, I'm a Hoosier now," he said.

"I'll ask the whole congregation to pray for you in church tomorrow," I told him. "You might get over it."

Speaking of music and hillbillies at the same time, if you're not too busy this week end and you live within a few hours' drive of Whitesburg, let me suggest that you make the trip. My friends at Appalshop are throwing the bash they do every year called "Seedtime on the Cumberland."

Things get under way on Thursday evening (May 31) and run through Saturday night. There'll be all kinds of old-time fiddling and banjo picking, a theatrical performance of *Pretty Polly* that is getting rave reviews from yankees and hillbillies alike and all kinds of displays. If you aren't proud of being a hillbilly now, just go to Whitesburg this week end and find out why I'm getting so stuck up on myself. I'm gonna be there.

The Mountain Eagle *May 30, 1990*

SARAH FERGUSON
Us Against Them

Intolerance was an issue not only in America's legislative chambers, but "in streets and doorways across the country"—where, reporter Sarah Ferguson observed, a "class war" involving the homeless was heating up.

In streets and doorways across the country, a class war is brewing between angry indigents and disgruntled citizens forced to step out of their way.

Tompkins Square, the Manhattan park that spawned New York's first love-in in the '60s has become symbolic of what happened when a liberal community loses patience with the homeless. It was neighborhood tolerance that allowed the encampment of homeless men and women to swell to a shantytown of more than 300 indigents last summer. But it was the rising outcry from neighbors who claimed that the homeless had "taken the park hostage" that forced the city to finally tear the mess down.

Police raids on Tompkins Square Park over the past year, however, have done nothing to abate the flood of homeless people camped out in public spaces. Because, of course, the homeless keep coming back.

In Tompkins Square, construction crews have already plowed away the patches of scorched earth that remained after last December's raid, when many of the homeless burned their tents in open defiance. But you can still find a dozen or so homeless people, mostly black, huddled around the Peace, Hope, Temperance and Charity cupola. Another 15 are sprawled on piles of sodden blankets in the band shell, and maybe 20 more jammed in the bathrooms, sleeping in the stalls and sometimes charging fifty cents to move their bedding before you can enter.

Fed up with such seemingly intransigent masses, cities across the nation—budgets squeezed dry by the Reagan Revolution—are starting to adopt a closed-door attitude toward the displaced.

In Washington, D.C., the city council just slashed $19 million from the homeless budget and is seeking to roll back Initiative 17, the referendum that required the city to provide shelter to all those in need.

In Atlanta, Mayor Maynard Jackson has proposed a policy of licensing panhandlers as part of an intensified campaign to drive the homeless out of the center city business district.

In Berkeley, the University of California has ordered repeated police sweeps of People's Park, long a holdout for vagrants and the dispossessed, and has evicted the People's Cafe, a soup kitchen set up this winter by an organization called the Catholic Worker.

Of course, there have been periodic outcries against the homeless since the media first discovered the "problem" in the early 1980s. But today's growing disfavor bodes ill at a time when the economy worsens, and the line between the middle class and the poor becomes ever more precarious. The need to maintain an "us versus them" mentality seems all the more pressing.

"The tension level is definitely rising," says Wendy Georges, program director for Berkeley's Emergency Food Project. "With more homeless in the streets, people are starting to lose patience—even in Berkeley. If a city like this successfully attacks homeless people and homeless programs, it will set precedents. The homeless backlash will become a popular thing—so that nobody has to feel guilty about it."

Part of the reason for the growing backlash is simply sheer numbers. The U.S. Conference of Mayors' annual survey found that the demand for emergency shelter in 27 cities increased an average of 25 percent in 1989; by comparison, in 1988, the demand increased 13 percent. Some 22 percent of those requesting emergency shelter were turned away.

Public disfavor may also be spurred by changes in the makeup of the homeless population. Although figures are scarce, anyone who looks can see that the homeless population has grown younger. A 1960 survey of Philadelphia's skid row by Temple University found that 75 percent of the homeless were over the age of 45. And 87 percent were white. In 1988, 86 percent were under the age of 45, and 87 percent were minorities.

As the population shifts, the sterotypical image of the old skid row bum meekly extending his palm for change has been replaced by young African-American and Hispanic men, angry at the lack of well-paying jobs, often taking drugs or selling them—or demanding money with a sense of entitlement that passers-by find enraging. . . .

The sometimes belligerent attitude of street people goes along with a growing shelter and welfare rebellion. In New York, the growth of a Tent City in Tompkins Square reflected the refusal by many homeless to enter New York's degrading shelter system. As many as 1,000 people are housed each night in armories where diseases such as AIDS and tuberculosis run rampant. Moreover, a substantial number of homeless people refuse to sign up for welfare and other entitlement programs, preferring to fend for themselves on the streets rather than get caught up in a "dependency mentality" and suffer the degradation of long welfare lines and condescending case workers.

Instead, homeless people have begun banding together in support networks and tent encampments, demanding political recognition, and fighting back when they don't get it. Their resolve is seen in Santa Cruz, where a dozen vagrants have been arrested repeatedly for sleeping outside the local post office, or in San Francisco, where more than 100 people continue to camp in front of City Hall, adamantly protecting their belongings as police patrol the area daily to sweep away unguarded possessions.

"I see this as a form of anarchy," says Jake, a 30-year-old blond woman with tattoos decorating her chest, lying back in a bed of blankets and heavy metal tape cassettes next to her two companions, Red, 29, and Gadget,24. "We're not going to hide somewhere. Just us being here is a protest." When pressed as to why they don't go out and get jobs, Gadget responds, "I'm not going to go flip burgers at some McDonald's so I can share a tiny apartment with a bunch of crazy a———s. I've got friends and family here."

Such comments are grist for newspaper columnists, who are increasingly taking a hard-line approach toward the homeless, arguing that little can be done for people who don't want to help themselves. "Enough is enough," proclaims the editorial board of the Philadelphia Inquirer, which has called for a law to ban people from camping out in public places. The San Francisco Examiner recently ran an editorial calling for the "benign incarceration" of street people.

Even those cities that have made significant strides to shelter or house their homeless populations have begun to adopt closed-border policies. Although officials admit they cannot constitutionally restrict people from receiving assistance, both Philadelphia and Washington, D.C., have regulations stating that they need not provide shelter to people who come to their cities just for that purpose. . . .

On Manhattan's Lower East Side, a group of merchants called BEVA, Businesses in the East Village Association, formed last year to respond to the growing number of street people and peddlers clogging the parks and sidewalks. "All of us are liberal people," says BEVA president Kathleen Fitzpatrick, owner of a local cafe. "Our doors are open. But many well-meaning acts, when they go unregulated, turn sour. Look at Tompkins Square—it's the only park without a curfew and that (allows) open fires (fire barrels). But look at what's happening. It's uncontrolled. It's a toilet. The other day they found 20 needles in the playground area."

"You can't say all homeless people are drug users—we know that," Fitzpatrick continues. "We want to do something to re-establish a community presence in the park—not to kick the homeless out—to try and regulate it. I'm a victim of this. What happened to all the government programs? The states say they don't have any money; the cities don't have the money. It all filters down to the community—to me at Life Cafe or Bob at the bookstore—all of us little people who are now forced to contribute our income, our time, our energy and money to finally do something. I guess that's what Reagan wanted."

The San Francisco Chronicle *May 6, 1990*

ROBERT RAFSKY
AIDS Research: It's Killing Us

The handling of the AIDS epidemic, a public health crisis, often reflected the struggles over power in a divided society. Ralph Rafsky of ACT UP believed that irresponsibility and the misdirection of government research funds had allowed thousands to die—most of them, not coincidentally, "gay or people of color or poor."

An AIDS vaccine within a few years? And drugs that could make AIDS manageable like diabetes? Yes, say the scientists. It sounds like good news for the 6 million people, myself included, who are already infected with HIV, the virus believed to cause AIDS. But it only sounds like good news. For those of us actually confronting the disease, it's more like a cruel joke.

Unless there is a major change in the way this epidemic is handled, most of us will die before that vaccine, or other drugs that could turn AIDS into a chronic, manageable disease like diabetes, are made available.

The U.S. government has spent $1 billion on AIDS research during the 10 years of the epidemic. But that money has produced virtually nothing which can prolong life or health beyond a short period of time.

I know. I just carried a friend in a coffin from a small church in Brooklyn. I'm reading newspaper articles into a cassette recorder for another friend who's going blind.

A third friend just went through his address book from a couple of years ago; it was equally divided between the names of the living and the dead.

As for myself, I'm okay—for now. But I have to watch my immune system like a hawk. My friends and I follow our T4-cell counts—a key measure of immune system health—with the passion that other people reserve for batting averages.

There's also a long list of AIDS symptoms, and we know them all. Our bodies have become battlefields of the imagination. *Is that a lesion—or just a bruise? Is that a swollen gland—or just some tender flesh?* We joke about it to keep the panic away.

I'm scared. And angry. I'm angry because the more I learn about the continuing sickness and death, the more I realize that it can be stopped.

How could our government spend so much money on AIDS and save so few lives?

Could it have something to do with the fact that most of the people dying are gay or people of color or poor?

It's hard to believe that business would be going on as usual if white heterosexual men were dying in large numbers.

But with AIDS, business has gone on as usual for an entire decade.

Scientists have pursued the most interesting AIDS research, the kind that brings fame and Nobel Prizes.

Drug companies, often working with those scientists, have been relentless in their search for profits.

Politicians, from the President on down, have made speeches, although the President waited for the second year of his administration to even make a speech about AIDS.

No one is in charge of saving lives.

The National Institutes of Health, the government agency in charge of AIDS research, has spent 75% of its AIDS budget on one drug—AZT.

AZT attacks the AIDS virus directly, and does so in a scientifically interesting way. It's an area of work that's familiar to the virologists and other scientists who run the AIDS research effort.

Also, AZT was an available drug—it had been tried previously, and failed, as an anti-cancer agent. It promised enormous profits for its manufacturer, the British drug company Burroughs Wellcome.

But AZT has been a problem drug from the beginning. At first it was prescribed in such large doses that half the people who took it got sick.

Now, at lower doses, there are fewer side effects, though everyone who takes AZT worries about what harm it may cause in the long run.

I took AZT for a while. I'm not sorry I did, though it's hard to say if it really helped.

I know the thing that felt best about AZT, both physically and psychologically, was getting off it.

But if my T4 cells, which have been stable, start to drop again, I'll probably go back on AZT. There is very little else out there.

And that's scary, because no one believes AZT or any other available drugs work indefinitely. Someday my immune system will be depleted and I'll be vulnerable to the infections that actually kill people with AIDS.

The infection that has killed most people with AIDS is a form of pneumonia called PCP. Statistics on death from AIDS are notoriously bad, but the best information we have is that in the late '80s, while the government debated what to do about PCP, more than 16,000 people died from it.

And their deaths were horrible—shrunken young bodies with contorted faces, groaning while respirators pumped their lungs. For most, death was a relief.

Finally, in desperation, doctors and their patients in New York and San Francisco began their own drug trials—the first time that has ever happened.

They found a drug called aerosolized pentamadine, which prevents PCP and which, unlike other PCP treatments, most people can tolerate.

They forced the government to approve it.

Now, if you have access to decent medical care, you don't have to die from PCP.

But there are so many other infections to die from. My friend who is going blind has an infection called CMV. New statistics (flawed, but the best we have) show a slight drop in cases of PCP but a sharp rise in CMV and other infections.

The House of Representatives just approved a $400 million program for testing and early treatment of AIDS.

Maybe it will actually pass Congress and be signed by the President.

But unless there are drugs to prevent the *infections* that kill people with AIDS, it will be a $400 million joke.

That's why I and a thousand other people stormed the campus of the National Institutes of Health in Bethesda, Md., a few weeks ago, demanding that someone give priority to saving our lives.

All we got was a press release announcing 12 trials of drugs that may prevent AIDS infections, to begin at some unspecified time in the coming year.

Twelve trials aren't nearly enough to test all of the promising drugs we've heard about, nor to slow down the dying—if they happen at all.

Many of us greeted President Bush with loud protest when he came to New York last week. His leadership could fix the government's response to AIDS. But we haven't much hope.

Though he's been in the White House, first as vice president and then as President, for the entire epidemic, George Bush hasn't shown any real understanding or taken any decisive action.

The AIDS speech he finally made was compassionate. But compassion won't keep us alive.

I've signed petitions. I've sent telegrams. I've shouted and screamed. I've been arrested—three times.

What else can I do?

My friends and thousands of others are disappearing, like swimmers carried out beyond their depth.

Their bodies slip beneath the water one by one and, though I struggle, I fear mine is next.

The lifeguards are in their chairs, but they don't seem to see us.

People sit on their blankets and point at us, but no one cries out that something should be done.

The drowning goes on, and on, and on.

The New York Daily News *July 29, 1990*

JUAN GONZALEZ
The Best Heroes are Distant Ones

As the nation momentarily united to celebrate a June visit by Nelson Mandela, who had been jailed in South Africa for twenty-seven years, New York Daily News *columnist Juan Gonzalez reminded Americans of "the scores of political prisoners hidden and forgotten in the jails of our own country."*

Darryl Joyner never heard of a ticker-tape parade before yesterday.

Darryl, 9, and his classmates from Public School 137 in Ocean Hill-Brownsville were on lower Broadway with their teacher, Miss Hatchet, waiting for Nelson Mandela. While they waited, they giggled at the endless showers of shredded paper flying out from the buildings and fluttering down over the crowd.

"He's a freedom fighter who fought for his people," Darryl said.

"When he was in jail, his wife spoke for him," said 8-year-old Cheryl Booker.

Yet, when it comes to knowing the difference between a common criminal and a political prisoner, third-graders at PS 137 know as much as the mayor of New York or, for that matter, as much as most American grown-ups.

And as our leaders trip over each other to praise this 71-year-old-man and unroll a red carpet for him, we must never forget that just a short time ago he was considered a criminal and a terrorist in his own country.

They tried and convicted him and threw him in jail for 27 years for insisting that South Africa's blacks were as human as its whites, and for plotting a revolution to topple apartheid. While he was in jail, only a tiny few of those who now fawn over him ever lifted a finger of protest for his release or for an end to the barbaric treatment of his people.

Still, it was a grand and wonderful thing to see New Yorkers like Daniel Dugas cheering the world's most famous political prisoner. Dugas is a banker who lives on the upper East Side, and he held his 5-year-old daughter, Nicole, aloft on his shoulders so she could catch a glimpse of the man he called the "Gandhi of our times."

But I couldn't help thinking, as I watched the cheering crowd, of people like Dylcia Pagan, Susan Rosenberg, Elmer Geronimo Pratt, Joe Doherty and the scores of political prisoners hidden and forgotten in the jails of our own country.

It doesn't take much bravery to support someone in jail halfway around the world. Bring the issue home and watch the excuses surface.

Let us not dwell solely on the gross paradox of the mayor of this city calling Irish nationalist Doherty a "political prisoner" and Puerto Rican nationalists Lolita Lebron, Rafael Cancel Miranda and Irving Flores "assassins."

Mayor Dinkins last week named a city square after Doherty, who is already convicted of killing a British Army captain of killing a British Army captain and who has been in a New York jail for seven years fighting extradition. Meanwhile, Dinkins criticized a planned meeting between Mandela and the three Puerto Rican freedom fighters who spent 25 years in jail for wounding five congressmen in 1954.

Our government says it has no political prisoners, just criminals, in its jails, which is what South Africa used to say. Human rights groups say the number of U.S. political prisoners is between 100 and 300.

Take Dylcia Pagan, for instance. She used to be a television producer in this city. This month she and 14 other Puerto Rican independence supporters completed 10 years in federal prisons. All were convicted of "seditious conspiracy" against the U.S. government and sentenced to from 36 to 90 years in prison. The government claims they were members of the terrorist FALN organization, though they weren't convicted of any actual bombings.

Then there are Susan Rosenberg and Timothy Blunk, white leftist radicals convicted in 1985 of possessing explosives. They got 58 years with no recommendation for parole. That same year, anti-abortionist Michael Donald Bray was convicted of bombing 10 abortion clinics. He received only 10 years. Dennis J. Malavasi, who admitted one abortion clinic bombing and another attempt, got seven years.

Geronimo Pratt, a former Black Panther leader, has been in jail for 20 years for a murder conviction that many groups, including Amnesty International, insist was engineered by the FBI.

Katya Komisaruk, an anti-nuclear activist, was sentenced in 1987 to five years in prison for destroying a missile guidance computer at Vandenberg Air Force Base.

Jean Gump, Larry Morlan and three other Plowshares activists are serving seven or more years after being convicted of hammering and pouring blood on Minuteman missile silos in Missouri.

In case after case, people convicted of politically motivated crimes get much stiffer sentences than common criminals and often are treated worse in jail than the regular prison population, says Ronald Kuby, a lawyer with the Center for Constitutional rights, which has represented dozens of these activists.

Thus, American courts penalize people for their political beliefs, but the government refuses to recognize them as political prisoners.

As Nelson and Winnie Mandela's truck passed along Broadway on its way to City Hall, you could see Gov. Cuomo and Dinkins smiling and waving. Beside them Winnie held up a clenched fist to the crowd.

During the coming days, many eloquent words will come from the mouths of our leaders about this former "political prisoner" named Mandela.

But they will never mention America's own political prisoners, for they have no idea what the words actually mean nor what constitutes the real courage of a Nelson Mandela.

The New York Daily News *June 21, 1990*

ROGER WILKINS
With Mandela

Nelson Mandela's tour of the United States became the most celebrated public event of the year. The tour's national coordinator, writer Roger Wilkins, observed Americans' reactions to Mandela, later suggesting that "Nelson Mandela makes white cops weep and black kids cheer because he . . . expands, before our very eyes, the limits of what a human being can be."

When I was about nine years old, Joe Louis fought Billy Conn on the old Polo Grounds in Harlem. A lot of us who lived in the neighborhood couldn't afford the price of a ticket. So we gathered on Coogan's Bluff to get a glimpse, through a gap in the old stadium's structure, of a corner of the ring and to hear the actual roar of the crowd as we listened to the contest on our portable radios.

I've been thinking about Joe Louis recently. When I traveled earlier this year with Nelson Mandela, a former fighter himself, Mandela spoke of Louis as a hero and a role model for South African boys who wanted to be fighters in Joe's championship days. "We fought flat-footed," Mandela observed at a fund-raiser one night, just after he had met and embraced former heavyweight champion "Smokin' Joe" Frazier. "We fought flat-footed because Joe Louis fought flat-footed. Nobody could have convinced us to try to get up on our toes."

On that night against Conn, Louis was surely fighting flat-footed. We, who had gathered so gleefully expecting an early knockout, sadly began drifting back to our apartments as the rounds continued and Conn moved in, peppering Joe with punches and dancing away again. At the end of the twelfth, with Joe losing his crown to the cocky Irish challenger, Coogan's Bluff was nearly empty, and Harlem grew silent.

Then it happened. In the thirteenth, Joe blasted Conn into oblivion and Harlem exploded. People erupted back onto the streets, screaming, singing, hugging strangers, and dancing through the night. Though it happened forty-nine years ago, the memory is still laser vivid. I didn't see anything like it again until Joe Louis's fan, Nelson Mandela, came to the United States.

There were similarities in the reception to these two men. Joe flattened strong white men with his fists in an age when, in certain parts of the country, other black men could be killed for trying such a thing. Nelson Mandela brought an arrogant and racist government to the negotiating table with his moral grandeur at a time when other black men in his country *were* being killed for using other means in trying to achieve the same end.

But there were differences, as well, differences both striking and instructive. In Harlem in 1941, Joe's fans had all been black. But on the Mandela trip, from one end of this country to the other, I saw whites as well as blacks lose all restraint in celebrating the man. Middle-aged white cops in New York turned in toward the motorcade, wiping tears from their eyes and waving.

The attributes that lifted Joe above the crowd were fairly narrow. He was an athlete—a superb champion, but an athlete. Mandela's attributes, on the other hand, are as broad as humankind. As we traveled across the country together, I found him as attentive to children as to statespersons. The first people to greet him in the United States were tiny South African children. He bent down deeply in order to hear their offerings of song and poetry, focusing his full attention on them while the governors of New York and New Jersey, the mayor of New York, movie stars, millionaires, and other notables stood in the background, waiting their turns. During the rest of our trip, I found Mandela to be strong and gentle, firm and patient, prickly and wise, serenely self-contained, a fighter still. In his blackness, he has a surpassing dignity.

Joe ripped from blacks a primal response: he splattered our foes. Nelson Mandela makes white cops weep and black kids cheer because he lifts us up above our primal selves and expands, before our very eyes, the limits of what a human being can be. This hardworking African politician forged, in his twenty-seven years of incarceration, spiritual qualities that touched us in deep, wondrous, and sometimes even quite depressing ways.

In a real sense, the responses to both of these black heroes reflected needs—emptinesses—buried deep inside ourselves. In Joe's case, it was our need to strike back at people whose oppression included the power to make striking back an impermissible and dangerous violation of the nation's cultural codes. In a deeper sense, Joe's successes in the ring helped fill—if just for a little while—that place that might have contained our pride as a people, had the nation not twisted our sense of ourselves into an ugly and shame-filled thing.

It is surely true that for most if not all African Americans, and for some white Americans as well, Mandela filled the soul with pride. Beneath this celebration, though, there was apparent in city after city an almost frightening intensity of desire to be near him. One man wondered "what it would take" to persuade me to have Mandela make a stop at his home. Another noted American stayed in my hotel room into the wee hours, pleading shamelessly for me to bring Mandela by his office.

As Mandela moved through crowded fund-raisers, people whom I have known to be sensible would take on frenzied looks, clutch for the man, attempt to spin him around to face cameras together, and insinuate personal intimacy with the first syllables they had ever exchanged with him. It became clear that, for many people, the effort to gain proximity to Mandela, even briefly, became a quest for self-validation.

In crossing the country with Mandela, the depth and pervasiveness of this phenomenon was puzzling. It struck me that we are a country filled with cardboard celebrities, whose heads appear briefly on television for no discernible reason, only to be replaced with sets of equally undistinguished heads. Real heroes here—William J. Brennan, Jr., Eudora Welty, and Thurgood Marshall, for example—are rarely celebrated. So, there's no good measure of the real thing. In the United States, everybody can yearn to be a pygmy-somebody, and feel cheated if momentary celebrity is not achieved.

Mandela *is* the real thing. His strengths and wisdom appear to come from places inside him, sources so deep that they surely have no counterparts in our own poor, ragged psyches. His simple presence dramatized our spiritual emptiness, just as the strength of Joe's punches underscored our powerlessness a generation ago. Mandela's visit demonstrated that in our made-for-television culture, not everything and not everyone is shallow. Our yearning for something better still runs very, very deep.

Mother Jones *November/December 1990*

PART THREE

QUESTIONS OF JUSTICE

JULY–SEPTEMBER 1990

BY MID-1990, THE PUBLIC HAD BECOME PRIVY TO THE details of a financial scandal that promised to ravage the nation's economy and destroy the American dream of home ownership. Since the days of the Great Depression, the government had sought to provide, through loans and other financial guarantees, a means for lower income people to borrow money to build or buy their own homes. The savings and loans were established to provide financing to working-class and middle-class borrowers. But beginning in the late 1960s, the savings and loans came under increasing strain. At first, they found it impossible to compete with other financial institutions which, at a time of rapid inflation, could offer far higher interest rates to attract investments than could the S&Ls, whose rates were circumscribed by Congress. Then, in 1980, legislation freed the S&Ls, and they joined in the speculative race for funds, offering higher and higher interest rates. Next the housing industry collapsed, leaving the thrifts exposed. Friendly federal examiners looked the other way and clever accountants papered over the S&Ls' increasingly desperate situation. But ignoring or disguising the crisis could not make it go away, and by 1990 over one thousand S&Ls had collapsed.

The American taxpayers' bill for deregulation and subsequent abuse in the thrift industry will be massive: Congress provided $80 billion to the bailout in 1989 and 1990, and is expected to supply at least another $50 billion in public funds, making this the costliest financial scandal in American history.

George Bush was temporarily rescued from the crisis in domestic economics by Iraq's invasion of Kuwait in the early morning hours of August 2. The president reacted quickly, freezing Iraq's foreign funds, dispatching rapid deployment forces to the Gulf, and urging the United Nations to impose economic sanctions against Saddam Hussein. Undeterred, Iraq formally annexed Kuwait and began detaining Westerners as "guests."

Saddam Hussein's invasion of Kuwait was not entirely unexpected. Saddam had issued a series of signals during the first six months of the year, heralding a new and more bellicose policy toward the Gulf nations. The U.S. had apparently ignored these signals, choosing to think Saddam was all bluster.[1] The Bush administation had even pursued various business and farm deals with Iraq during this period, despite continuing protests in Congress against Iraq's human rights policies. Members of Congress worried about Saddam's threats to unleash chemical weapons on Israel and remembered his past use of poison gas against the Kurds, but the administration appeared determined to think of Saddam as a reformed despot—until he proved otherwise.

The crisis in the Gulf breathed new life into the debate over energy policy, which had been quiescent since Ronald Reagan's election in 1980. President Reagan and later President Bush had led the attack on Jimmy Carter's modest efforts at improving energy conservation by blocking them and arguing for deregulation. Attempts at counter-measures in Congress came to nought: Efforts to extend so-called CAFE standards, which would require auto manufacturers to make motor vehicles that used less gas, were blocked by a coalition of Republicans and Democrats in both the Senate and the House. Now the U.S. faced the possibility of going to war to sustain its oil-dependent way of life.

The struggle in the Gulf centered on the trade in oil: Saddam Hussein had unilaterally tried to interfere with the system of production and distribution, and as a result he faced opposition and isolation. But he was only the most notable example of the liabilities of the United States' trade policies. International trade had become the dominant foreign policy issue of the future, and the central job of Bush's presidency would be a general effort to harmonize, coordinate, and police the rules of world trade. In the summer of 1990, the centrality of trade issues could also be seen in debates over the U.S. role at the Houston economic summit, the revamping of domestic farm policies, and the nascent negotiations for a free trade agreement with Mexico.

Domestic attention turned, in August, to the vacancy left by retiring Supreme Court Justice William Brennan, long a champion of civil and First Amendment rights. President Bush, no doubt intent on avoiding a rehash of the 1989 battle over Bork, nominated New Hampshire Supreme Court Judge David Souter, a "strict Constitutionalist" whose chief virtue seemed to be his relative silence on controversial legal issues—the absence of a "paper trail" of written judicial opinion which would be open to attack by liberals and interest groups.

This same absence, however, was cited by some of Souter's critics, who felt that his unremarkable twelve years of service in the sleepy New Hampshire court system hardly qualified him for a position on the highest court in the land. Other opponents noted that Souter had, in the course of his career, ruled in favor of the prosecution in 90 percent of the cases before him. His record implied that he would be a willing ally in what many saw as a broad-based effort to narrow the Fourth Amendment rights of the accused being led by Chief Justice William Rehnquist. And many pointed to Souter's disconcerting record on rape, privacy, church and state, and labor issues.

But what progressives feared most was simply that the loss of Brennan, and his replacement by any nominee hand-picked by Bush—in this case, evidently at the behest of his chief of staff, former New Hampshire governor John Sununu—would give the already tipped Court the solid majority it needed to begin overriding decisions that had been settled for a decade or more.

Nan Aron of the Alliance for Justice wrote that "though Conservatives attacked the Warren Court as overreaching, the Rehnquist Court has been one of the most activist in the nation's history. It has reopened settled law on the questions of abortion, employment discrimination, and capital punishment. . . . Constitutional law experts warn that where the Court is unwilling to overturn precedent by a five-to-four majority, having a six-vote majority will embolden the conservatives to overturn precedents that most Americans have come to take for granted."[1]

Souter sailed through the Senate confirmation hearings to take his place on the bench. Conservative appointees now held a solid six-vote majority on the Court (soon to increase to seven with the mid-1991 retirement of Justice Thurgood Marshall).

Among those constituencies with the most to fear from the new Supreme Court were pro-choice women. Since the 1989 *Webster* decision, new state restrictions had been consistently chipping away at American women's free access to abortion, and 1990 brought new losses.

Early in the year, the battle had focused on RU 486, the "abortion pill" that had just been placed on the market in France. RU 486 offered women a new level of safety and privacy in ending unwanted pregnancies, and also had other significant medical uses. But threats of a boycott and backlash from antiabortion groups kept any manufacturer from taking steps to secure the testing, approval, and sale of the drug in the U.S. In March, Guam's Governor Joseph Ada signed into law a bill criminalizing advocacy of abortion and prohibiting nearly all abortions. Only vetoes by Idaho Governor Cecil Andrus and Louisiana Governor Charles Roemer prevented passage of similar laws in those states (and in 1991 the Louisiana legislature would override a second governor's veto, and Utah too would pass a highly restrictive law). In June, the Supreme Court reviewed a Minnesota statute that required pregnant teenagers to notify both parents before having an abortion, and upheld the constitutionality of such laws provided they allowed teenagers to seek a court waiver of the notification requirement. (One Indiana sixteen-year-old had already died, in 1989, as the result of an illegal abortion.)

The passage of such laws was in tune with new rhetoric employed by many in the antiabortion movement. Seeking to position themselves as "moderates," antiabortion forces stated that they were seeking laws only to prohibit abortions used as "birth control"—in reality, all abortions except in cases of rape, incest, or life-threatening medical necessity. Other efforts targeted the most vulnerable women: teenagers and the poor. In addition to parental consent laws in several states, there was a federal regulation prohibiting the release of any information on abortion to patients at federally funded clinics—a regulation which would, in 1991, be reviewed and upheld by the Supreme Court in *Rust v. Sullivan*.

The Supreme Court and state legislators were joined by the White House in what seemed to many a broad-based effort to roll back women's progress toward social and professional equality. In June President Bush vetoed the 1990 Family and Medical Leave Act, a piece of legislation that would have provided job security for workers who took time off to care for a newborn or a sick child, spouse, or parent. Although literally gender-neutral, the law would, of course, have had the greatest practical impact upon women, particularly single working mothers. In addition, Bush's fall veto of the 1990 Civil Rights Bill denied an improved line of defense against job discrimination to women as well as people of color. It appeared that a *de jure* movement to return women to their "rightful" place in the home, held more or less at bay throughout the Reagan years, was winning new ground in the nineties.

MARK SHIELDS
The Neil Bush Case: Talk About Teflon!

Washington Post columnist Mark Shields observed that the runaway S&L crisis had been fueled not only by corrupt practices in the industry, but also by a widespread tolerance of corrupt practices by both the government and the press. As a case in point, he offered the kid-glove treatment afforded to Neil Bush.*

Aneurin Bevan, the late British Labor Party leader, did not try to conceal his contempt for what he judged to be his country's unaggressive press corps. Once, when asked about proposed measures that could raise the threat of press censorship, Bevan responded: "You don't need to muzzle sheep."

That same putdown could today be used to characterize the outrageously submissive deference shown by both opposition Democrats and most of the Washington press corps toward the First Family of President George Bush. Politically, Bush has been granted a nonstick coating that makes Ronald Reagan's vaunted Teflon look like Velcro by comparison.

Here are the facts. Neil Bush, 34, President and Mrs. Bush's third son, is under investigation for possible conflicts of interest as a director of the Silverado Savings and Loan of Denver, which one year after its own auditors found it insolvent and just weeks after the 1988 presidential election, was closed by federal authorities, at a projected cost to American taxpayers of $1 billion.

No one is blaming the younger Mr. Bush for the collapse of Silverado. But Neil Bush is being asked to explain a couple of truly unusual relationships he had with two Colorado businessmen, both of whom first invested in Neil Bush's own company and then later defaulted on millions of dollars of loans from Silverado.

Take Neil Bush's unorthodox relationship with developer Ken Good. In 1984 Good made a loan of $100,000 to Neil Bush to invest in a high-risk venture. The terms were that Neil Bush did not have to repay the $100,000 to Ken Good unless the investment was successful. That's right, this may have been the first completed loan in financial history in which the *creditor* defaulted.

In testimony before the House Banking Committee, Neil Bush was recently asked about this special relationship with Good. In a masterpiece of understatement, the president's son responded, "I know it sounds a little fishy, but I've heard this happen before."

Not in my neighborhood you haven't, Mr. Bush. There, such transfers are usually made in cash inside an unmarked No. 10 business envelope. In fact, the fishy-sounding Good-Bush transaction may qualify as a gratuity, as gravy, as grease, or worse. But it was not by anybody's definition a loan.

Even though he was required to disclose his relationship with Good and *failed to do so,* Neil Bush said he abstained from voting, as a director, on loans Good sought from Silverado. But the House committee released a letter written by Neil Bush, as director, to the Silverado chairman requesting a $900,000 line of credit for Ken Good, who had earlier bought a 25 percent interest in Neil Bush's own oil and gas exploration company for $10,000. That $10,000 made Good a lot bigger investor in Neil Bush's company than Neil Bush himself, who put up just $100.

But Good was a small fish compared to Denver real estate developer William Walters who had purchased for *$150,000* a *6.25 percent* share of Neil Bush's company. You figure it out.

As a director of Silverado, Neil Bush did not disclose his relationship with Walters. Nor did Neil Bush abstain from voting to approve $106 million of loans to Walters, *all of which went into default.*

Nor was Bill Walters just a borrower, either. Walters was a lender, too, through the Cherry Creek National Bank, which Walters controlled. Among those to whom Bill Walters' bank made loans was Neil Bush, who was able to borrow $1.75 million from Cherry Creek National.

About that $106 million in defaulted loans: the bill for all that and the rest of Silverado's billion-dollar tab will be picked up by the working men and women of America who pay their bills, raise their families and pay their taxes—and who not surprisingly never had anyone say: Here's a hundred grand. Pay me back only if your ship comes in; otherwise forget it.

What truly is surprising is the failure of the political press and the political opposition to confront the Bush involvement in the savings and loan scandal. Would George Bush be given the same Teflon treatment if his name were Carter or Nixon or Cuomo or Reagan?

Does anyone remember the public pummeling Billy Carter took for openly accepting $5,000 to appear at a stock car race? Howard Hughes' loans to Richard Nixon's brother, Donald, became a permanent campaign issue. Yet no presidential relative before has been personally involved in a failed enterprise that left American families as co-signers liable for a billion-dollar default.

Maybe it's Andover or Yale, or Greenwich or Kennebunkport that exempts the Bushes from ordinary criticism. Maybe it's just the moral superiority of the Mayflower Compact descendants as heard in the words of Massachusetts Republican William Weld, who, when asked where his 1990 gubernatorial campaign got the money for a large TV buy, told The Boston Globe: “We don’t get money. We have money.”

The Washington Post *June 6, 1990*

JIM WRIGHT
Seek Solutions, Not Scapegoats, in S&L Industry Collapse

Former House Speaker Jim Wright of Texas, himself forced to resign over his involvement in the S&L scandal, had his own take on the crisis. As he assessed its causes, he denounced the "mindless cannibalism" that made "scapegoats" of individual players like Neil Bush.

The glee with which some of my fellow Democrats have seized upon the involvement of President Bush's son Neil in a failed Colorado savings-and-loan company is symptomatic of a sickness in our political society. That malady is contagious. It has invaded both of our political parties. It is every bit as pervasive and destructive as the human weaknesses that underlie the virtual collapse of the nation's thrift industry.

The most prominent symptom of the illness is the incessant search for scapegoats—not for causes and solutions, but for villains in order to personalize the blame. A year ago, I called this tendency "mindless cannibalism." We see it in the growing eagerness of party flaks to scandalize leaders in the opposition party by attacking not their philosophy but their personal character.

We see it also in the prevalence of negative campaign advertisements that pollute the airwaves and degrade the political process. Slander begets slander, and this begets public disgust. One obvious result is a marked decline in voting. The Texas gubernatorial primaries last spring drew an all-time low turnout.

Of Neil Bush's problems, I know very little. From all I have read, I infer that his sins, if any, were mainly of omission rather than commission. Gullibility rather than culpability. Inattentiveness rather than fraud. If his name were Neil Jones there would be no public outcry and surely no call for a special prosecutor.

Perhaps I can sympathize with Mr. Bush better than most. While House speaker, my name became a target for various charges in the finger-pointing frenzy involving the S&L industry. While most of those charges were either untrue or grossly exaggerated. I do hold myself to account that I, like many others, failed to see the scope of the looming crisis in time to head it off.

The obsession with scapegoating is worse than childish. In this case, it is dangerously distracting. It diverts attention from the economic failures and policy misjudgments that caused the savings-and-loan industry's downfall.

People understandably resent the gargantuan price tag of bailing out millions of innocent depositors. Much of that cost, now estimated at $500 billion, will have to come from the pockets of taxpayers. But it is escapist folly to suppose that any major part of this tragic cost is due to "crooks" and political charlatans in either party. For all our human greed, Americans did not set out to steal half a trillion dollars from fellow Americans.

In truth, the causes of the monumental collapse were more economic than moral. There were plenty of human errors and mistakes on all sides. Lenders and borrowers made flawed business judgments. Public officials in both political parties erred in policy judgments.

The most obvious error was the headlong rush in both the administration and Congress to deregulate an industry whose deposits are insured by the public and to cut it loose from its fundamental public purpose. The thrifts were created to perform a very basic and necessary service: to make home loans to American families at interest rates they could afford.

In 1982 when interest rates rose to an unhealthy level and S&Ls were stuck with a lot of old mortgages paying traditional rates, both White House and Congress took the easy way out. At the enthusiastic urging of President Reagan, and by the vote of big majorities in both parties, Congress deregulated the thrifts. The new law openly encouraged them to abandon their historic mission to family homeowners and look instead for speculative borrowers who would pay them higher rates of interest.

The result should have been predictable. Spurred by 40 years of steadily rising land values, speculators borrowed and thrifts scrambled to lend at high interest rates on every sort of land and real-estate ventures—office buildings, shopping centers, high-rise apartments, commercial subdivisions. Then came the fall.

My state of Texas was the first to feel the pinch. For the first time in 50 years, land prices dropped. Office buildings stood vacant. Rentals fell. Entrepreneurs who put the deals together could not meet their payments. Bankruptcies rose to the highest level since the Great Depression. Lending institutions held paper based on old, inflated values. Foreclosures would no longer pay off the debts. Most of this was not the result of fraud but of greed and over-reaching by business people and bad judgment by public officialdom. We should not have deregulated the thrifts.

Another major factor was the skyrocketing increase in home foreclosures that began in the mid-1980s. An epidemic in foreclosed homes was precipitated by the adjustable rate mortgage and its pernicious handmaiden, negative amortization. The Home Loan Bank Board should never have permitted it! For sitting by and letting this happen, people in both parties are guilty.

A lot of naive borrowers, particularly young families, were lured into the quicksands of insolvency by deals with low down payments and graduating rates of interest. Disillusioned purchasers discovered to their dismay after a couple of years that they owed more than when they started. Their monthly payments meanwhile had escalated far beyond their ability to pay. Left no alternative, they walked away from their obligations in great numbers, leaving the once-eager lenders holding their abandoned properties.

There was some outright fraud, to be sure. The guilty must pay the price of their misdeeds. But most of the loss was not due to theft or fraud or criminal activity, and it is a great disservice to the public to pretend that it was.

Most of the bailout cost for which the public will have to cough up money is the result of bad policy judgments. The taxpayers will be served not by a strident political finger-pointing contest but by a rectification of those policy errors.

Government can start by putting a premium on solvency and setting the example. It should show the courage to raise taxes and to pay as we go.

With a balanced budget, government can and should insist on steadily declining rates of interest. The goal must be to make it possible for people to get out of debt.

The thrift industry should return to the historic role in which it and the taxpayers suffered no losses for 50 years: helping American families own homes.

And surely we must put brakes on the mania to deregulate. If government is to guarantee deposits, it owes it to the citizens to make sure that publicly insured institutions are serving the public weal.

The Fort Worth Star-Telegram *August 2, 1990*

ALEX MOLNAR
"If My Marine Son is Killed . . ."

Saddam Hussein's August invasion of Kuwait, and the White House's response to it, raised the spectre of a long-term U.S. war for the first time in over fifteen years. One of the most personal—and most powerful—early statements against the war came from Alex Molnar, a University of Wisconsin professor and the father of a young Marine just dispatched to the Persian Gulf.

Dear President Bush:
I kissed my son goodbye today. He is a 21-year-old marine. You have ordered him to Saudi Arabia.

The letter telling us he was going arrived at our vacation cottage in northern Wisconsin by Express Mail on Aug. 13. We left immediately for North Carolina to be with him. Our vacation was over.

Some commentators say you are continuing your own vacation to avoid appearing trapped in the White House, as President Carter was during the Iran hostage crisis. Perhaps that is your reason. However, as I sat in my motel room watching you on television, looking through my son's hastily written last will and testament and listening to military equipment rumble past, you seemed to me to be both callous and ridiculous chasing golf balls and zipping around in your boat in Kennebunkport.

While visiting my son I had a chance to see him pack his chemical weapons suit and try on his body armor. I don't know if you've ever had this experience, Mr. President. I hope you never will.

I also met many of my son's fellow soldiers. They are fine young men. A number told me that they were from poor families. They joined the Marines as a way of earning enough money to go to college.

None of the young men I met are likely to be invited to serve on the board of directors of a savings and loan association, as your son Neil was. And none of them have parents well enough connected to call or write a general to insure that their child stays out of harm's way, as Vice President Quayle's parents did for him during the Vietnam War.

I read in today's *Raleigh News and Observer* that, like you, Vice President Quayle and Secretary of State Baker are on vacation. Meanwhile, Defense Secretary Cheney is in the Persian Gulf. I think this symbolizes a Government that no longer has a non-military foreign policy vision, one that uses the military to conceal the fraud that American diplomacy has become.

Yes, you have proved a relatively adept tactician in the last three weeks. But if American diplomacy hadn't been on vacation for the better part of a decade, we wouldn't be in the spot we are today.

Where were you, Mr. President, when Iraq was killing its own people with poison gas? Why, until the recent crisis, was it business as usual with Saddam Hussein, the man you now call a Hitler?

You were elected Vice President in 1980 on the strength of the promise of a better life for Americans, in a world where the U.S. would once again "stand tall." The Reagan-Bush Administration rolled into Washington talking about the magic of a "free market" in oil. You diluted gas mileage requirements for cars and dismantled Federal energy policy. And now you have ordered my son to the Middle East. For what? Cheap gas?

Is the American "way of life" that you say my son is risking his life for the continued "right" of Americans to consume 25 to 30 percent of the world's oil? The "free market" to which you are so fervently devoted has a very high price tag, at least for parents like me and young men and women like my son.

Now that we face the prospect of war I intend to support my son and his fellow soldiers by doing everything I can to oppose any offensive American military action in the Persian Gulf. The troops I met deserve far better than the politicians and policies that hold them hostage.

As my wife and I sat in a little cafe outside our son's base last week, trying to eat, fighting back tears, a young marine struck up a conversation with us. As we parted he wished us well and said, "May God forgive us for what we are about to do."

President Bush, the policies you have advocated for the last decade have set the stage for military conflict in the Middle East. Your response to the Iraqi conquest of Kuwait has set in motion events that increasingly will pressure you to use our troops not to defend Saudi Arabia but to attack Iraq. And I'm afraid that, as that pressure mounts, you will wager my son's life in a gamble to save your political future.

In the past you have demonstrated no enduring commitment to any principle other than the advancement of your political career. This makes me doubt that you have either the courage or the character to meet the challenge of finding a diplomatic solution to this crisis. If, as I expect, you eventually order American soldiers to attack Iraq, then it is God who will have to forgive you. I will not.

The New York Times *August 23, 1990*

WENDELL BERRY
Unfair Trade for Farmers

For years, American family farmers had been losing ground to multinational agribusiness corporations, and in 1990 they faced further threats from the Bush administration's efforts to reorganize agricultural production through international trade agreements. Writer and farmer Wendell Berry warned that the administration's policies would have dangerous consequences for local economies, the environment, and even personal freedom.

After World War II, the United States and 95 other nations entered into the General Agreement on Tariffs and Trade (also known as GATT) for the purpose of regulating international trade and resolving international trade disputes. The Bush administration is now attempting, mostly in secret, to make changes in this agreement that would have dire economic and ecological effects upon the member nations, and would significantly reduce the freedom of their citizens as well.

The Bush proposals originally drafted by Daniel Amstutz, a senior vice president of Cargill, and backed by other large corporations, aim to eliminate all agricultural price supports and production controls, and could require member nations to conform to health and safety standards that would be established by Codex Alimentarius, a group of international scientific bureaucracies in Rome.

If these proposals are adopted it will mean that every farmer in the member nations will be thrown into competition on the so-called "free market" with every other farmer. And this will be a competition that will not be won by any farmer, but rather by the international agribusiness corporations that are well positioned to profit from the unprotected produce and the further cheapened labor of all farmers. American farmers, who must buy their expensive labor-replacing machines, fuel and chemicals on markets entirely controlled by the suppliers, will be forced to market their products in competition with products of the cheapest hand labor of the poor countries. And the poor countries, seeking to feed their own people, may see the food literally vacuumed off their plates by a lucrative export market.

How these proposals might affect all of the 96 countries involved is probably too complicated a question to be answered even by Amstutz, but it is clear that their effect on American farmers and American agriculture will be ruinous. These proposals are part of a long-standing ambition of certain parties in the agribusiness establishment to cheapen food here in order to use it as a weapon abroad. They wish to increase American control of foreign countries by causing them to become dependent on cheap American food. And they wish to use these increased exports of food to balance the American trade deficit.

But of course American food can be cheapened only by continuing and worsening the economic and agricultural practices by which we are destroying our farmers, our farm communities, and our farm land, and by which we are diminishing the quality and the healthfulness of our farm products. To increase the volume of our food exports at such a cost, obviously, will sooner or later require a greater volume of food imports—if, in the meantime, such policies will not have ruined the food economies of other nations.

Furthermore, the adoption of the Bush proposals will mean that no member nation, and no local government in any member nation, will be permitted to impose regulations on the use of pesticides or other toxic substances on imported food that are stricter than the regulations set by Codex Alimentarius.

These proposals, which would deny to the people of 96 nations any choice in the matter of protecting their land, their farmers, their food supply, or their health, have not been drafted and, if adopted, would not be implemented, by anybody elected in any of the 96 countries. The effect of the proposals, in short, would be to centralize control of all prices and standards in the international food economy, and to place this control in the hands of the few powerful corporations best able to profit from it. The amended GATT would thus be a license issued to a privileged few for an all-out economic assault on the land and people of the world. We are witnessing here the work of an international capitalism as insidious, ambitious, totalitarian and destructive as international communism, and as deserving of the same fate.

The Bush proposals offend against democracy and freedom; they offend against any intelligent concern for bodily ecological health; they offend against every wish for a sustainable food supply. Apart from the corporate ambition to gather the wealth and power of the world into fewer and fewer hands, they make no sense, for they ignore or reduce to fantasy every reality with which they are concerned: ecological, economic, agricultural and cultural. Their great evil originates in the assumption that all the world may safely be subjected to the desires and controls of a centralizing intelligence.

This is what Secretary of Agriculture Clayton Yeutter means by his phrase, "international harmonization." But there is a world of difference between the harmonies that may be made between people and their neighbors, or between people and their land, and an "international harmonization" that can only be made by the imposition of a tyrannical idea by a few powerful people upon all the rest.

The world, in fact, is made up of an immense diversity of countries, regions, eco-systems, climates, soils, societies and economies so various as to bewilder and frustrate the ambitions of centralizing power—and only this can explain the attempt to force the world's natural and inevitable diversity into a legal uniformity. But anyone who is interested in economic and ecological justice will see immediately that justice requires, not international uniformity, but an international generosity toward local diversity.

Anyone who is interested in solving, rather than profiting from, the problems of food will see that, in the long run, the safest food supply is a local food supply, not a supply that is dependent on international trade. Nations, and regions within nations, must be left free—and should be encouraged—to develop the local food economies that best suit local needs and conditions. It is foolish to jeopardize this most necessary freedom and diversity for the sake of an economic idea.

The (Lexington, Kentucky) Courier-Journal *July 26, 1990*

ANDREW A. REDING
A Brezhnev South of Our Border?

Other negotiations underway in mid-1990 presaged a free trade agreement between the U.S. and Mexico. Noticeably absent from the discussions, wrote World Policy Institute analyst Andrew Reding, was any linkage of economic cooperation to "Mexico's authoritarian government and resistance to democratic change."

At last month's Houston economic summit, French and German leaders criticized President George Bush's "double standard" in favoring aid to China while opposing help for the Soviet Union. They could have extended the comparison to Mexico: Washington, which has arranged debt relief and bridge loans for Mexico, is beginning negotiations for a free trade agreement apparently untroubled by Mexico's authoritarian government and resistance to democratic change.

Like the Soviet Union, Mexico has been ruled by a single party for over half a century. The resulting lack of competition and accountability has had similar corrupting effects on its economic and political life. Yet while Soviet President Mikhail Gorbachev is dismantling the Communist Party's monopoly on power, Mexican President Carlos Salinas de Gortari refuses to relax the iron grip of his Institutional Revolutionary Party (PRI) on Mexican society.

Though portrayed abroad as a reformer for his moves to liberalize the economy, Salinas is perpetuating one-party rule through expanded use of electoral fraud and, as recently documented by Americas Watch, by using the police and the army to intimidate and repress the opposition.

Mexico remains the only Latin nation besides Cuba that lacks independent electoral authorities. The federal electoral commission is chaired by the minister of the interior, and the ruling party holds an assured majority of commissioners. The PRI uses this power to deny opposition parties access to the broadcast media, to inflate registration rolls with phantom voters, to arbitrarily remove known opposition sympathizers from voting lists and—when necessary—to alter actual election returns in its favor.

Professional "alchemists," as they are known in Mexico, rework the numbers during the week between election day and the official announcement of results. This legally-sanctioned stalling period is unique to Mexico.

Mexico also has the world's only constitution with a "governability" clause. The provision guarantees the ruling party a legislative majority even should its electoral manipulation fail to deliver a majority of seats. This ensures that the PRI will not have to share power with the opposition, and reduces the Congress to a rubber stamp for unchecked presidential powers.

Far from seeking democratic reform, Salinas adamantly resists opposition demands for independent electoral authorities and for removal of the governability clause. Instead, the new electoral law approved by the Chamber of Deputies on July 14 enables the president to appoint members of the electoral commission without regard for balance and criminalizes peaceful protests against the commission's determinations. To forestall opposition alliances such as those that triumphed in Chile and Nicaragua, it also prohibits joint candidacies.

Salinas' actions betray his campaign promise of "clean elections." In hindsight, it seems he misjudged Mexican voters by believing he would win the 1988 presidential election fairly. Indeed, Salinas intended to dramatize his commitment to modernize Mexican politics through live broadcast of returns on election night.

Things did not, however, go according to plan. As opposition leader Cuauhtemoc Cardenas surged ahead in the early count, the computers tabulating votes suspiciously went "down." While the opposition produced returns from 55 percent of precincts showing Cardenas maintaining his lead, the government stalled. A week later it announced its victory, but refused to disclose results from remaining precincts. According to a Los Angeles Times poll conducted last summer, less than one in four Mexicans believe Salinas was legitimately elected president of Mexico.

Salinas chose power over electoral integrity, with fateful consequences for political reform. Ever since, his party has resorted to fraud to deny victories in state and local elections to Cardenas' Party of the Democratic Revolution (PRD).

In last year's elections in Cardenas' home state of Michoacan, for instance, the PRD was able to prove wins in at least 14 of 18 legislative districts. Yet the government altered tally sheets and threw out over a hundred thousand PRD ballots to ensure continued PRI control of the state legislature.

In a Mexican manifestation of "people power," citizens protested by occupying town halls throughout the state. The government at first responded with sporadic attacks by police and paramilitary groups, killing dozens of protesters; then, this past April, Salinas sent army tanks into Michoacan to retake the town halls.

The government now faces a formidable challenge in the November 11 elections in the State of Mexico. This state of 12 million inhabitants is Mexico's most populous, and—even by the government's count—favored Cardenas by more than two to one in 1988. With the PRI's own polls showing Salinas even less popular now, the ruling party is already gearing up for massive fraud.

Illustrating the government's growing desperation, the PRI is using a more drastic method perfected in last month's special municipal elections in Uruapan, Michoacan: denying opposition sympathizers the right to vote by either removing them from the registration rolls, or by delivering their ID cards to PRI operatives, who then cast multiple ballots. Should these methods not suffice, the Mexico State legislature recently changed the electoral law to strengthen its "governability" provision.

Until now, unrest over electoral fraud has been confined to more rural, less densely populated states, where cycles of protest and repression have not attracted international attention. Massive fraud in the state of Mexico, which includes much of Mexico City, is a different matter. This is the capital, where the PRI is extremely unpopular, and where opposition parties are capable of mobilizing hundreds of thousands of protesters. A repeat of the type of blatant ballot rigging used in Michoacan could be a recipe for disaster.

The Bush administration, which so forcefully denounced electoral fraud in Panama, is overlooking Mexican fraud as it proceeds with negotiations for free trade agreement. Yet if there is a lesson to be drawn from recent experience, it is that economic and political reform are indivisible; without the later, the former is on unstable ground. Unless we begin to link U.S.-Mexico cooperation to genuine political reform, we will contribute to, and ultimately share in, Mexico's growing political problems.

Newsday *August 8, 1990*

ROBERT H. BORK
At Last, an End to Supreme Court Activitism

On the domestic front, the retirement of Justice William Brennan (and later, Justice Thurgood Marshall) created a Supreme Court with a new agenda. Judge David Souter, George Bush's Supreme Court nominee, was so reticent on the issues as to seem rejection-proof. The less reticent Robert Bork, rejected in 1988, celebrated Souter's probable confirmation, which promised an end to the Court's "liberal policy-making."

It is a measure of just how political the subject of the Supreme Court and the Constitution have become that it took Saddam Hussein to get Judge David Souter off the front pages. Perhaps the only benefit we have reaped from Iraq's aggression is the sudden disappearance of opinion pieces by law professors who think that a man who is a bachelor and lives in a small town cannot have the proper "sensitivities" (read "politically correct positions") on women, minorities and the poor.

Well, the liberal activists are right to be worried. As Peter Finley Dunne's fictional pundit Mr. Dooley put it, the Supreme Court does follow the election returns. The justices do not, of course, change their views when the read the poll results, but the direction of our politics determines the kinds of justices we get. Franklin Roosevelt totally remade the Court, and the Constitution, with seven appointments in four years.

Presidents do miscalculate, of course, and a succession of fairly conservative Presidents—Eisenhower, Nixon and Ford—did not alter the liberal policy-making that has characterized the Court since Roosevelt's time. The Reagan Administration took greater care and so, it appears, will the Bush White House. We are almost certainly at long last about to see a shift in the Court's direction.

Mr. Bush made it plain that he wants a Justice who will "interpret the Constitution and not legislate from the bench." That has, indeed, become the central issue in all judicial appointments, and it is what the political fight over nominees is and has been about. As their ideological differences have deepened, our two political parties have become polarized on the issue of what the role of a justice is. Senate Democrats, who by every measure have moved further to the left in the last 10 to 15 years, want justices who will enact an agenda too liberal to pass the legislature or escape an executive veto, either at the national or state level.

It is not prudent, of course, to make that preference the overt theme of opposition to a nominee. The American people do not want judges, acting without any warrant in the Constitution, setting their social issues for them. That is why we are seeing a new tactic on the left. We are told that, since the Constitution is an "open-ended document," no result the Court chooses to reach is legally unjustifiable, and therefore nominees are to be judged politically. That is the meaning of the assertion that George Bush's distinction between interpreting and legislating does not really exist. That is a cliché, we are told: justices do not legislate, they interpret, all of them, Justice Brennan no less than Justice Scalia.

The distinction may have become a cliché, but, like so many other clichés, it expresses a solid truth that must not be obscured.

The Constitution is law. Like all law it is expressed in language. Language has meaning. Judges who depart from any plausible meaning of the language are not interpreting, they are legislating. Imagine that a judge reads a will that leaves the bulk of the deceased's estate to his nephew but makes specific bequests to a number of charities. If the judge then says that the will discloses a generalized concern for charity and so the nephew's share will go to other charities favored by the judge, nobody would think for a moment that the judge was interpreting. Yet that is what the Supreme Court has often done with the Constitution.

The "right of privacy," upon which Roe v. Wade rests, was invented in Griswold v. Connecticut by just such a technique. In striking down the state's anti-contraception statute, Justice Douglas said that since the Constitution protected a number of aspects of privacy it also protected privacy not mentioned in the Constitution. This new, free-floating, undefined right was nothing more than a warrant for the Court to legislate.

The Court does not and will not protect everything done in private (spouse abuse, the taking of narcotics, etc.). It has protected those activities a majority of the justices approved of, striking down statutes democratically enacted by legislatures that did not approve of the same activities. That is legislation from the bench. By no stretch of the imagination can it be called interpretation of the document. The bequest of the right of self-government is diverted from the American people to beneficiaries never intended by those who wrote our constitutional "will."

This form of "judging" is not unique to liberals. In the last century and the first third of this century, conservative activists did it as well. But whichever side does it, it deforms our form of government. As nominations and confirmations come up, as they will frequently in the near future, it is important that Americans understand that it is our form of government, and not simply liberal or conservative results, that is at stake.

The early signs about Judge David Souter are encouraging. He seems not to confuse judging with his own moral and political sympathies. If that proves to be so, he most certainly should be confirmed. If he is, the third branch of our Government will be well on its way to the function prescribed for it by the Constitution. Both our right to self-government and our liberties that the Constitution removes from majority rule will be fully protected.

Surprised by the President's swift nomination of Judge Souter, the activist groups took a few days to come together. But advertisements rallying the opposition are beginning to appear, and demands are being made that the judge declare his position on abortions, preferential racial policies and much more.

Such efforts are almost certainly futile. Mr. Bush seems determined to return the Court to its proper role as a legal rather than a political institution. That he will do. Whether or not Judge Souter is confirmed, the odds are with the President. Should the Senate reject this nominee, Mr. Bush can send up somebody similar, and another and another if need be. The senators will find it increasingly uncomfortable to turn down one nominee after another at the behest of liberal activist groups; indeed, the groups themselves cannot mount massive campaigns one after the other. Eventually, Justice Brennan will be replaced by someone with a quite different view of the judicial role.

Then the extreme liberals can take their case to the democratic process and the American people, where it belongs.

The New York Times *August 29, 1990*

NAT HENTOFF
A Prosecutor's Judge —From the 19th Century

Columnist Nat Hentoff found nothing to celebrate about David Souter. The future Supreme Court justice, he wrote, was a man with "a prosecutorial turn of mind" and a jurisprudence better suited to a time when "the Bill of Rights was kept under glass."

In the 19th century, most judges in this country were—as Supreme Court Justice Benjamin Cardozo described them—"legal pharmacists." Dry men, usually with very little personal experience outside of law libraries. They dispensed "the correct rule prescribed for the legal problem presented" and guarded against involving their own feelings, their own experiences, or the files of the times in the judgment of a case.

These mechanical judges, said Cardozo, prided themselves on working in "the realm of pure reason," standing "aloof . . . on chill and distant heights," far above the members of the coarse populace who, genuflecting, came before the courts to get a dose of justice, which most often tasted like castor oil.

David Souter, the man who, in all probability, will be the 105th justice of the Supreme Court, comes out of that time of gaslight and horse-drawn carriages. It is not only his way of life—solitary, immersed almost entirely in 19th century books, no more likely to be found in a bar than Mother Teresa. What makes Souter of another era as a jurist is his way of interpreting laws as narrowly as he possibly can. And usually in favor of the state.

For instance, during his 12 years in the New Hampshire court system, he ruled in favor of the prosecutor 90 percent of the time (just as in the 19th century, when the Bill of Rights was kept under glass). So, when the defense claimed that certain evidence had been illegally obtained, Judge Souter refused to suppress the evidence. And the state also prevailed when there was a question before the judge as to whether *Miranda* warnings had been properly given, as well as in other questions on the believability of the police.

It could be that, unlike law enforcement troops in other states, the New Hampshire cops have on their bedside tables the collected Bill of Rights opinions of William Brennan. Or it could be that David Souter simply trusts agents of the state more completely than he does the laity.

Until the end, William Brennan held off, to some extent, the admission of illegally obtained evidence and the denial of habeas corpus relief to defendants. With Souter on the High Court, the Fourth Amendment and access to the courts will sooner rather than later vanish—except in old volumes of constitutional law.

There is also an odd Dickensian twist of character in Souter. Some of Dickens's figures professed great devotion to rectitude and yet, under certain circumstances involving their careers, they somehow managed to engage in situational ethics.

Consider the case of David Souter when he was attorney general of New Hampshire. The then governor, Meldrin Thompson, had a righteous whim. The governor was a great believer in the balm of religion and, accordingly, ordered that flags on all public buildings be flown at half-mast on Good Friday. Thus, every resident of New Hampshire would be spurred to reflect on Jesus that day. For his governor, Souter defended this throwback to the official churches of the colonies before the First Amendment separated church and state. Well, you see, said Attorney General Souter, Jesus was a historical as well as religious figure and should be honored as such.

Okay, then how about ordering the flags on all public buildings to fly at half-mast on Passover in honor of that distinguished historical figure Moses? And on a special day for Muslims? Muhammad should be honored in this manner if Jesus is to be venerated by the state.

It is possible that Souter actually believed that this public homage to Jesus—whose weight as a historical figure is because he is a religious figure—did not bruise the Establishment Clause of the First Amendment. If that is so, Senator Biden or Metzenbaum might ask Souter during the confirmation hearings about this attempted secularization of Jesus. As of now, the Supreme Court is one vote away from demolishing much of the body of separation-of-church-and-state law.

The other possibility is that Souter obeyed Governor Thompson in the latter's public devotion to Jesus because, as Sam Rayburn used to say, you got to go along to get along.

Continually, this loyalist judge reveals a clear prosecutorial turn of mind. In 1983, with Souter now on the Superior Court, New Hampshire state employees were protesting that their labor negotiations were being deliberately and unjustly stalled. Hundreds of them called in sick—SOS (sick of Sununu), the beloved governor and now the President's chief of staff. At the request of Sununu, Souter held a middle-of-the-night hearing and told the workers to get back to their jobs. To drive the message home, according to Aaron Epstein of the Knight-Ridder News Service, Souter ordered "their union to telephone its members individually with the back-to-work order or face a $5000-a-day fine."

Sununu later appointed Souter to the New Hampshire Supreme Court, and when William Brennan resigned from the United States Supreme Court, it was Sununu—along with New Hampshire Senator Warren Rudman—who pressed hard for the ultimate elevation of the dependable judge back home.

There has been much frustration and frenzy about Souter's lack of a paper trail on abortion. But it should be remembered that John Sununu is the most strong-willed man in the Bush administration, is wholly trusted by Bush, and would not—for all the denials that abortion was even whispered to the nominee—have recommended a Supreme Court justice who does not share Sununu's own unwavering pro-life views.

Also relevant is that after Bush was elected, Sununu said that this administration was going to end abortion by means of the judicial selection process.

In the course of publicly congratulating themselves on their choice, Bush and his men have made much of David Souter's judicial experience, including his presence on the First Circuit Court of Appeals. To begin with, Souter was a federal circuit court judge for only three months and spent just one (1) day hearing cases. He delivered no opinions in the First Circuit before the large hand of John Sununu took him up and lifted him to Washington.

Souter was on the New Hampshire Supreme Court for seven years. On a busy, contentious high state court dealing with complicated, diverse issues—such as New York's Court of Appeals—a judge can acquire a lot of valuable experience in seven years. But the New Hampshire Supreme Court—as described by *New York Times* Supreme Court correspondent Linda Greenhouse—is a five-judge court "on which dissent is infrequent, opinions hardly ever contain a footnote, and a day's work is as likely to consist of a zoning appeal or child custody dispute as a case of constitutional dimension."

The drowsy New Hampshire high court is hardly a training ground for a Supreme Court nominee. Yet, Bush and his attorney general, Dick Thornburgh, have been trying to legitimize their pick by saying that William Brennan also came from a state court. But Brennan, in New Jersey, dealt with a wide range of cases—including challenging criminal issues. And on that court, he wrote a number of dissents of such constitutional dimension that they're still worth reading.

On a *Nightline* program concerning the nomination of this judicial pharmacist to the Supreme Court, Thornburgh uncomfortably revealed how little Souter's judicial background had to do with this shamelessly political choice. (None of the pressure groups can get at Souter, though they'll certainly try, because, despite being Sununu's protégé, Souter has nothing substantive in print about his attitude toward *Roe* v. *Wade*).

But on *Nightline*, Thornburgh was talking about Souter's brilliant intellect and how he applies that intellect to the cases he decides. Okay, said Chris Wallace, "Tell us one or two decisions that impressed you and convinced you that this man with a relatively slim record as compared to some of the other possible nominees was the one who should be on the court."

Thornburgh looked like President Dwight Eisenhower did when, toward the end of his first term, a reporter asked him for a list of Vice-President Richard Nixon's accomplishments. Eisenhower paused and said he'd think of some by next week.

Attorney General Thornburgh could not think of a single specific decision by Souter that had impressed him and the other selectors.

"It's kind of difficult," Thornburgh said lamely, "to pinpoint any single decision. What you have to look at is the totality of the character—"

That's what is dismaying. The totality of the character of Souter's judicial opinions is thin of blood, largely obeisant to the authority of the state, and indifferent to the lives people lead outside his courtroom. For Souter, the law is composed of formulas to be applied by Cardozo's pharmacists in a tidy way. Justice is not nearly as important as neatness.

There's an ancient theory that justices can change once they've been on the Court. Some do. Harry Blackmun started as a conservative and then became an ally of William Brennan in many cases. But Souter appears to have an unshakably stingy approach to constitutional law. It is nowhere near William Brennan's warm and generous embrace of the law as enhancing the equality and dignity of everyone touched by it.

As David Margolick put it in *The New York Times*: "On the New Hampshire Supreme Court, where unanimity is commonplace and whose spectrum runs less from liberal to conservative than from humanistic to hyper-logical, lawyers here say Judge Souter is *at the far edge of the latter*." (Emphasis added.)

By contrast, William Brennan used to say: "A judge who operates on the basis of reason . . . and sterile rationality alone risks cutting himself off from the wellspring from which such concepts as decency and fairness flow."

It is all too likely that, in the years ahead, those concepts will be in very short supply at the Supreme Court, particularly with the addition of this reclusive Dickensian judge, the narrowest of men to have been nominated for the Supreme Court in this century.

The Village Voice *August 7, 1990*

JUDY MANN
The Justices vs. the Pregnant Girls

One of the rights that was most at stake under the new Supreme Court was free access to abortion—already restricted in many states since the Court's 1989 Webster *decision. After the Court's June review of Minnesota's parental consent statute, columnist Judy Mann rebelled against the spectacle of "eight men who have never been pregnant . . . governing women's reproductive well-being."*

There is something fundamentally wrong with a situation in which you have eight men who have never been pregnant dictating the fate of pregnant, teenage girls. More than half of our population is female and yet there is only one female on the highest court, which is now wading with both feet into the body of law governing women's reproductive well-being.

The eight male U.S. Supreme Court justices are about as qualified in those matters as are the ostensibly celibate priests who try to force women to have unwanted children from the bully pulpits of the Roman Catholic Church. Do women try to make rules governing the terms and conditions under which men are allowed certain medical procedures? Of course not.

How and why we sit still for allowing men to determine how we handle pregnancies is a mystery. They know nothing of the health and economic consequences of pregnancy other than from secondhand experience. It is not at all unlike the old men who sent the young men off to fight in the Vietnam War.

The Supreme Court's decisions limiting the ability of women to secure safe abortions are couched in the usual high-minded legalese about what is constitutional and what isn't. That, as this court has demonstrated more than any court in history, is being dictated by politics. Twenty-five years of civil rights legislation was shredded by five court decisions last year.

So was 15 years of safe, legalized abortions when the court upheld the right of states to set conditions that made it more difficult for women to obtain them. Only four justices remain firmly in the abortion-rights camp a mere 15 years after the court ruled that a woman had a fundamental right to privacy in reproductive matters.

This week the court has again upheld state laws that will impede abortions. The victims, this time, are teenage girls—as naive, helpless and politically weak a class of people as you could find. The court majority, under the guise of protecting them, subjects them to procedures that suit its goal of limiting abortions.

The court ruled that states could insist that parents be notified before a teenager gets an abortion, as long as teenagers who feel they can't notify their parents can go before a judge and get a waiver of the notification requirement.

Think about this for a moment. A scared, pregnant 15-year-old who for whatever reason feels she can't tell her parents can go before a black-robed judge she's never seen in an intimidating courthouse where she's never been to tell him she's pregnant and wants an abortion.

There is no guarantee that she won't draw an antiabortion judge who will refuse to help her. The Fund for the Feminist Majority, which is producing a video on the impact of parental consent laws, found that only six to eight waivers a year have been granted in Indiana in the four years its law has been in effect.

Fund President Eleanor Smeal tells of a 14-year-old who was a ward of Indiana and in permanent foster care. She became pregnant. The state forces its wards to go before a judge. The foster mother recommended abortion as did the court-appointed referee.

"The court denied it," Smeal says. "The young woman appealed to the Indiana Supreme Court. The Supreme Court ruled that they would not look into the merits of the case as long as the judge followed the right procedure. He's the final word. In Indianapolis, the judge is a known right-to-lifer." In talking to clinics for research for the video, says Smeal, video producers could find only one case in which an Indianapolis teenager had gotten a judicial bypass.

In other states, such as Minnesota and Massachusetts, thousands of bypasses have been granted. In Michigan, however, an 11-year-old was impregnated by her mother's boyfriend. "A right-to-life judge delayed and delayed until she was forced to have the child," says Smeal. "The next year he took the baby away because she was too immature and neglectful."

We live in a society in which girls are taught to be submissive and boys are taught to be aggressive. A teenage girl is highly vulnerable, in part because she is taught so little about reproduction and contraception.

"She's the one who pays and pays a lot," says Smeal. "Nobody asks who the boy is. We don't notify his parents. He can go on and ruin another girl, and does. There is in this such an element of punitiveness.

"The real purpose of this is to make her against her will have a baby at an age that she can neither sustain it emotionally, physically or economically. As one doctor said, it stops them dead in their tracks."

In the case of Becky Bell, the 17-year-old from Indianapolis who did not want to let down her parents and who died of a botched abortion, the notification law simply left her dead.

The Washington Post *June 26, 1990*

AMANDA SMITH
Failure to Ensure Child-Care Leave Harms Employees, Employers

As columnist Amanda Smith observed, those women who did choose to have children often found themselves struggling to maintain both jobs and families, with little security or support. A legislative effort to address this situation was struck down by President Bush's June veto of the 1990 Family and Medical Leave Act.

"We get five days off each month to care for a sick child, but if we don't use it, we can't save it for the next month," a young mother in Prague, Czechoslovakia, complained to me during a trip there.

"Children don't always limit their sickness to five-day periods."

"In the United States," I told her, "most people get no time off at all to care for a sick child."

She stared at me, shocked.

I remembered how my secretary, Connie, a young single mother, had struggled every time her daughter was ill, juggling office responsibilities and frantic calls to doctors and day care. Her whole life would have been different if she'd had some time off with pay.

But surely, I thought, the cost would be exorbitant. This must be an example of why communist economies are crumbling, top heavy with too many benefits and no incentives to work.

When I returned to the United States, I decided to do a little investigating.

According to an International Labor Office survey, it's true that 11 European socialist countries have child-care leave. So do 19 European "Market Economy" countries. So do 97 other countries in Africa, Asia, the Pacific, the Middle East, North and South America. And most have leave with pay.

Japan gives 12 weeks, with 60 percent pay. West Germany gives 14 to 19 weeks with 100 percent. These nations are not crumbling. But even impoverished Ethiopia thinks that leave care for sick children is a priority.

What is the connecting principle between these countries? It's not economics. It's not politics. It seems to be a belief that it's important for people to be able to take care of their families. Odd notion.

Who's not on the list? The United States. Oh, and China.

There's a Family and Medical Leave Act which recently passed the U.S. House of Representatives. Does it catch us up to the rest of the world? Hardly, though it does cover both mothers and fathers, which many other countries don't.

The proposed bill provides 12 weeks leave, with health benefits but no pay. It doesn't apply to businesses with fewer than 50 employees, so it doesn't affect 95 percent of employers and 61 percent of workers in this country, say Congressional sources.

Leave can be taken to care for a newborn or adopted child, or for serious illnesses such as cancer. However, chicken-pox and the flu, the type of illness that most parents need time off for, aren't covered.

Not perfect, but at least it's a start.

That's exactly the objection, according to its opponents.

President Bush has promised to veto this bill. Why? Because business is afraid that this benefit will lead to others. As conservative critic James Kilpatrick puts it, "Parental leave is a light burden, but so was the one that broke the camel's back."

Whoa. Which camel?

The government camel? Then maybe we'd better unload some of the rest of its pack, such as planes that don't fly. Or paying welfare and unemployment benefits to people who only need to have their own jobs waiting for them when the family crisis is over.

The big business camel? Business is carrying the burden now of losing trained workers who have to quit their jobs to care for their families.

Or the individual employee camel? Here's the real point. As things stand now, America's workers are paying the whole price, in anxiety and lost jobs and lost income.

Governments and commerce exist to serve the people, not the other way around. It's time we got that straight.

The Albuquerque Tribune *June 22, 1990*

RUTH ROSEN
It's Not Just a Tragic Part of Life

By 1990, some women's health advocates had begun to focus on breast cancer which was reaching "epidemic proportions," affecting one in ten American women. Underdiagnosed and underresearched, breast cancer was, wrote University of California professor Ruth Rosen, "a women's issue waiting to be recognized as such."

When does a disease become a political issue? When it is contagious, incurable and kills those who are still vigorous enough to mount a campaign to grab public interest and funding. Every year 140,000 women are diagnosed with breast disease; every year 41,000 die of it. I am not the only person who, while watching one more television program on AIDS, has noted that every two years more women die from breast cancer than all the people in the United States who have ever died from AIDS. Yet because breast cancer is not a contagious or predictably incurable disease, and because women have not yet defined it as a "women's issue," what should be seen as a major social and political problem is regarded as a tragic and somehow biologically fated part of women's lot.

This is not to suggest that AIDS should receive any less attention or funding. On the contrary, women have a great deal to learn from groups that have successfully publicized and politicized the horror of the AIDS epidemic.

But it is time for national women's organizations to comprehend that a disease that afflicts so many women is more than a medical problem—it is a social concern entitled to the full force of national activism. What, for example, has caused the incidence of breast cancer to rise from one out of 11 women to one out of 10? Is it the result of better detection, longer life spans or have environmental pollution, oral contraceptives and dietary habits somehow caused a greater proliferation of the disease? Why do so many doctors and insurance companies fail to encourage or cover preventive mammograms?

Because women are at particular risk, breast cancer is a women's issue waiting to be recognized as such. This doesn't mean that other problems, including abortion rights, are any less important. But a single-issue orientation has obscured the reality that breast cancer kills women with terrifying frequency.

In Boston and Oakland, women who have survived cancer have started organizations (the Cambridge Women's Community Cancer Project and the Oakland's Women's Cancer Resource Center) to lobby for better preventive care, increased research funding and improved insurance coverage and to provide information and support groups for breast cancer patients. Other women, however, should not leave this battle to those who are exhausted from treatment or in the process of dying.

The National Women's Health Network, a national organization that promotes and monitors women's health-care delivery in the United States, has testified at congressional hearings that the government must reconsider its current priority of funding research for treatment while ignoring research for prevention. They are lobbying for the resumption of a canceled study on the association between dietary fat and breast cancer and for a new study to explore the connections between breast cancer and oral contraceptives.

There are many obstacles to overcome, including those in medical training. Only 2% of medical students take elective courses in preventive medicine; the academic award system rewards those who engage in basic research and technology development rather than those who devote themselves to prevention.

Attention to women's health care, moreover, is sadly neglected. In 1987 the National Institutes of Health spent less than 14% of its $7.6-billion research budget on women's health issues, although women make up more than half the population. The General Accounting Office has reported that National Institutes of Health has made little progress in including women in research study populations, and, as a result, women's problems are not taken seriously until they reach a critical stage.

Look around you. One-tenth of your sisters, daughters, wives, lovers, mothers and female friends (who manage to survive other life-threatening accidents or diseases) will, in the course of their lives, receive a diagnosis of breast cancer.

It's time for feminists, the public and politicians to grasp that breast cancer is a disease of epidemic proportions that affects enormous numbers of women and, hence, hundreds of thousands of their children, partners and friends.

This is a silent political constituency waiting to be discovered. There is no greater human right than the right to live out one's natural life span.

The Los Angeles Times *September 28, 1990*

STEPHEN B. BRIGHT
Death Sentence Lottery

By 1990, a large majority of the public favored the death penalty, and the Supreme Court had proven unsympathetic to the habeas corpus *rights of death row inmates. But the conduct of capital cases, wrote Southern Prisoners' Defense Committee director Stephen Bright, was awash in discrimination and injustice.*

The system of imposing the death sentence in this country is not working. It completely fails to select for the ultimate punishment those offenders who have committed the most heinous crimes.

A member of the Georgia Board of Pardons and Paroles has said that if you take 100 cases punished by death and 100 punished by life and shuffle them, it is impossible to put them back in the right categories based upon information about the crime and the offender.

One reason is the quality of justice that poor people receive in capital cases.

A black man was sentenced to death in Georgia in a trial that started with jury selection at 9 a.m., and ended 17 hours later at 2 a.m. with a death sentence. In between, the jury was deadlocked as to guilt, but the defense lawyer agreed to replace the one holdout juror with an alternate. Three minutes later a guilty verdict was returned. In Mississippi, a man was sentenced to death at a trial where he was represented by a third-year law student.

Capital cases have been assigned to defense lawyers on a low-bid system in one Georgia circuit. The only qualification to submit a bid was membership in the Georgia bar. The lowest bidder got the case.

In four different capital trials in Georgia, the defense lawyer at some point in the proceedings referred to his client as a "nigger." The death sentence was imposed in all four.

A defense lawyer who has handled a number of capital cases in Georgia testified recently that the only criminal law decisions from any courts with which he is familiar are "*Miranda* and *Dred Scott*." (The latter, decided in 1856, was not a criminal case.)

Last year in Alabama, a capital trial had to be delayed for a day in mid-trial because the defense lawyer was drunk. He was held in contempt and sent to jail to dry out. The next morning he and his client were both produced from the jail, the trial resumed, and the death penalty was imposed a few days later.

One-fourth of those now on death row in Kentucky were represented at their trials by lawyers who have since been disbarred, suspended or imprisoned.

Much of the support for the death penalty is bolstered by the belief that the legal process for imposing a death sentence is elaborate. Reading the Supreme Court's decisions upholding capital punishment in 1976, one would think that a number of procedural protections ensure that death is imposed only for the most aggravated crimes committed by the most depraved killers. The reality of capital punishment is quite different.

Inadequate legal representation is pervasive in the death-belt states of the South for several reasons, but the primary one is money. Alabama limits compensation for out-of-court preparation in capital cases to $20 per hour, up to a limit of $1,000. Mississippi and Arkansas limit the total compensation of defense counsel in a capital case to $1,000.

Perversely, the mistakes these lawyers make are insulated from appellate review. The courts hold that such defense lawyers "waive" the rights of their clients when they fail to recognize and object to violations of the Constitution. Thus, the poorer the level of representation that the defendant receives, the less scrutiny the case will receive on appeal.

Consider the case of two codefendants, Smith and Machetti, who were both sentenced to death by unconstitutionally composed juries in separate trials. Machetti's lawyers challenged the jury composition; Smith's lawyers did not. A new trial was ordered for Machetti at which a life sentence was imposed. The federal courts refused to hear Smith's case, because his lawyer had not raised the issue at trial. Smith was executed.

Nonetheless, a number of proposals have been introduced in Congress to cut back further on review of death sentences by federal courts. Proposals have also been introduced to improve the quality of legal representation, but they do not address the need for adequate compensation to attract qualified lawyers and the need for specialists to handle capital cases.

Throughout history, the death penalty has been inflicted upon the poor and members of racial minorities. Nothing has changed with the new statutes approved in 1976. Too frequently the death penalty is punishment not for committing the worst crime but for being assigned the worst lawyer.

The Washington Post *July 3, 1990*

DANNIE M. MARTIN
A Mount Everest of Time

Life sentences were what many criminals were receiving under new sentencing laws instituted as part of the war on drugs. Dannie Martin, a federal prisoner and frequent op-ed writer, observed that these sentences left convicts with "futures totally devoid of hope, and people without any hope are dangerous."

The big prison story these days is the story of Patrick Grady and Gordon Brownlee and Kevin Sweeney and Curtis Bristow. They all made serious mistakes, and they will all have decades to brood over those mistakes.

Grady 42, had been a close acquaintance of mine over the past two years. He's a Vietnam veteran who wears a mustache because a Viet Cong fragment grenade slightly disfigured his upper lip and part of his cheek.

He was also wounded in the leg by gunfire and decorated repeatedly for valor in combat. Along with his wounds in Vietnam, Grady picked up a drug habit. When he returned to his hometown Seattle, he began selling drugs to support it.

In 1988, he was convicted of numerous counts of conspiracy to possess and sell cocaine. It was his first felony charge. A federal judge in Tacoma, Wash., sentenced him to 36 years in prison. He will have to serve 31 years before he can be released.

Grady has a wife and a 4-year-old daughter and professes shock over the severity of his sentence. "I can't believe that the system of government that I put my life on the line for could do this to me," he says.

"I may be naive, but I've always thought a person could recover from one mistake. I grew up on the old cliche about a 'three-time loser.' Now I've made a mistake, and my wife will be 70 when I get out and my daughter will be 34. That's the end of my family, I can't ask them to wait that long."

Grady doesn't say much about his sentence, but I can see in his eyes a form of terror and despair akin to what was probably there when he saw a fragment grenade land nearby. A few days ago, he asked me a question.

"How is it that I get 36 years in prison for selling cocaine when people who rape a woman, bash her head in with a rusty pipe and leave her for dead only get 10 years? Am I supposed to be four times more evil than them?"

The bitterness and numb disbelief of Patrick Grady are mirrored in the minds of thousands of men and women in the federal prisons, and the numbers are increasing at an alarming rate.

In 1989, there were 44,891 criminal cases filed in federal courts, according to a U.S. judicial report. That was almost triple the 15,135 cases filed in 1980. Those numbers, more than anything, represent the escalation of the drug war in the past decade. More than one-fourth of all criminal cases filed in district courts are drug cases, according to the same report.

But there's a darker side to those statistics because many people sentenced under new federal drug laws aren't ever getting out of prison. Some who will get out may be so old that they won't remember coming in.

Even prisons such as the one here at Phoenix that are designed for medium-security prisoners are experiencing a large influx of men who have been sentenced to nightmarish terms of incarceration.

Since 1987, federal sentences have been nonparolable. The maximum good time that can be earned is 54 days a year. Thus, a person with a 20-year sentence will serve about 17 years if he or she is a model prisoner. It used to be that a 20-year sentence would result in seven to 12 years of "real time."

Many people outside applaud the big numbers and harsh sentences. But those I see in here who are weighed down by the years are not gun-slinging stereotypes; they are real, hurting people and they have families outside whose lives, like their own, are devastated. The people who support those new sentences should at least look at their effect on the people I meet in here.

A former college professor from the Bay Area whom I met here at Phoenix got life without parole for possession of seven kilos of cocaine. A Sacramento man who is 45 years old received 27 years for conspiring to manufacture methamphetamines. They both have wives and children who hope they will get out someday.

Now that most of the power is in the hands of prosecutors, long sentences are no longer oddities—they have become the norm.

Gordon Brownlee, a San Francisco native who lives down the tier from me tells about the pressure a San Francisco prosecutor put on him.

"I was arrested in 1989 with one gram over five kilos of cocaine and charged with possession with intent to sell. Had it been under five kilos, the sentence range would have been five to 40 years. But the extra gram made it 10 years to life," he says.

"The only criminal record I had was a charge in 1982 for trying to buy marijuana from an FBI agent. The prosecutor told me that if I would become an informer I could get off lightly, but if I didn't he would use the "prior" to enhance my sentence to 20 years to life."

Brownlee is 42 years old and has a wife and baby daughter. On July 28, 1989, after a plea of guilty, he was sentenced to 20 years in prison. His release date is 2006.

Few people in here, including those who were apprehended for drug violations, believe they should get a slap on the wrist or be let off lightly. But convicts believe that this country has entered an era of criminal justice when the punishment for drug offenses heavily outweighs the crimes, and the result in human terms is disastrous.

Bob Gomez, an elderly man who helps fellow convicts with legal work, contends that an oversight by Congress created most of the problem.

"A few years ago," he says, "Congress designed some harsh new sentences for drug offenses. Those terms were drafted with the thought in mind that offenders could be paroled in one-third or do the entire sentence in two-thirds of the total amount.

"When the new nonparolable sentences were approved, they simply grafted the big numbers onto the new sentencing code. No politician had the temerity to jump up and say, 'Hey, we're giving these guys too much time.'"

The problem goes beyond the sheer number of years people get under the new drug laws. Enforcement agents outside, spurred on by the public's drug hysteria, at times seem to be coercing crime as much as they are fighting it. . . .

It's easy for a judge to say "20 years" or "30 years." It takes only a few seconds to declare. It's also easy for the person in the street to say: "Well, this criminal has harmed society and should be locked up for a long time."

The public is unable to imagine what the added time does to a convict and what it does to his family.

Two years is a lot of time. Twenty or 30 years is a Mount Everest of time, and very few can climb it. And what happens to them on the way up makes one not want to be around if and when they return.

The first thing a convict feels when he receives an inconceivably long sentence is shock. The shock usually wears off after about two years, when all his appeals have been denied. He then enters a period of self-hatred because of what he's done to himself and his family.

If he survives that emotion—and some don't—he begins to swim the rapids of rage, frustration and alienation. When he passes through the rapids, he finds himself in the calm waters of impotence, futility and resignation. It's not a life one can look forward to living. The future is totally devoid of hope, and people without any hope are dangerous—either to themselves or others.

These long-timers will also have to serve their time in increasingly overcrowded and violent prisons. As I write this, authorities are building a pre-fab unit next door to my cellblock that will hold 300 new convicts. Some two-man cells here already hold three people. There are 1,200 of us in a prison that was designed and built for 500.

A more sinister phenomenon is the growing length of the chemical pill line daily at the prison hospital, the place where convicts go for daily doses of tranquilizers and psychotropic drugs such as Prolixin and Haldol. The need for these medications is a sign of the turmoil inside these long-timers.

Indeed, it is ironic that men who are spending decades incarcerated for illicit drug activities are now doped up by government doctors to help them bear the agony of their sentences.

Two years ago, the chemical pill line was very short. Now it snakes along for a good distance. Society is creating a class of men with nothing else to lose but their minds.

The San Francisco Chronicle *October 7, 1990*

JUDITH MCGOWAN
In the Bronx, A Dubious Victory

Most Americans, it seemed, took little interest in the issues debated by politicians and op-ed writers, neglecting even to take part in the democratic process. This negligence was acutely felt by Judith McGowan, who had just been elected Democratic District Leader in her middle-class Bronx Assembly district—by only 4 percent of its constituents.

On Sept. 11, I won a primary election. I am the new Democratic District Leader in the 80th Assembly District of New York State. In my district, those standing for election that day included candidates for New York City Civil Court judge, New York State Senate, New York State Comptroller and the U.S. Congress.

Approximately 117,000 people live in my district. Of these, 57,000 are registered voters, 37,000 are registered Democrats. We sent letters and pamphlets to the 15,000 Democrats who vote often enough o that sending them an "invitation" to vote and information about the candidates might not be a waste of postage. Yet fewer than 4,000 people voted in my race—just 4 percent of the residents.

I won by a margin of less than 1,400 votes. A shift of 695 votes—one-half of 1 percent of those in my district—would have awarded the power in our area to an insurgent slate.

It's said that in a representative democracy, voters vote not on issues, but on who decides the issues. Thus, 701 people could have determined whether this district leader supports an assemblyman and state senator who are for or against the death penalty, for renewable energy sources or increased dependence on nuclear energy, for retaining or abolishing school decentralization.

And some might care whether or not our City Council representative is for or against commercial rent control. Will the next state comptroller owe more to business, labor or the electorate? Some might even be affected by our choice of Congressmen (will we have declared war?) or even who will be the leader of the Bronx County Democratic Party (our previous leader is in Federal prison).

If you live in my mostly middle-class North Bronx district, chances are about 1 in 8 that you received our "invitation" to vote in the mail. But because our postage and printing funds were limited, I stood on street corners and knocked on doors for more than three months. Many rejected my information with the contempt that courteous people reserve for sellers of pornography or crack.

Knowing that those who do vote are, in disproportionate numbers, over 50, and fearing how much worse things will get if this trend is not reversed, I have a habit of badgering young people if they do not vote or worse, haven't bothered to register.

On primary day I asked a neighbor, a recent college graduate, why he wasn't registered. He said, "I don't know. I guess I'm just not political."

"What would you do if you were drafted for Saudi Arabia tomorrow?"

"I'd go, of course!"

"Without any say over who it is that orders you there?" He promised to register.

We'll see.

The New York Times *October 13, 1990*

PART FOUR

THE CHANGING ORDER

OCTOBER–DECEMBER 1990

THE 1990 BUDGET NEGOTIATIONS WERE AMONG THE most divisive in history, and in October the American government actually shut down for days at a time while the president and the Congress fought it out. The Democrats sought to take advantage of Bush's apparent weakness by proposing increased taxes for the wealthiest Americans. But the president had his own agenda, which included a reduction in capital gains taxes, and threatened to veto anything else. Their thirteenth-hour compromise was a victory for Bush: The Democrats approved the capital gains tax break for the rich, along with higher "sin taxes" on whisky, beer, and cigarettes—sales taxes that come down hardest on the middle and lower income groups. But, importantly, Bush also lost favor with his own right wing, on whom the Republican party is dependent, by failing to exercise leadership and refusing to take a tough ideological stance on taxes. Bush looked to be vacillating through all this—an indecisive president. Increasingly, the Persian Gulf crisis seemed to provide the best opportunity to boost Bush's floundering image.

Meanwhile, there were signs that the nation's attention was fixed on ongoing divisions over race. In the fall elections, the harbinger of the future came in the unlikely, almost comic form of David Duke, a young member of the Louisiana legislature who had a lengthy history as a leader in a revived Ku Klux Klan. As recently as 1988, when he ran for president of the United States, Duke's campaign had been engineered and financed by the far Right: A former lieutenant of American Nazi Party leader George Lincoln Rockwell had been his campaign manager. Now, in the fall of 1990, Duke was running for the U.S. Senate in Louisiana. From the beginning he was written off by the press, but as time wore on, disconcerting polls showed his strength gaining in the old populist districts in the northeastern part of the state, while support for the incumbent, Democrat Bennett Johnston, declined. With Duke suddenly picking up support, the Republicans joined in an effort to stop him. The moderate Republican quit the race and the party threw its support behind Johnston, ensuring him a majority of the vote.

Duke was no populist. He ran as a Reagan conservative, but with a difference. That difference was racialism, and it had surprisingly broad appeal. As leader of the National Association for the Advancement of White People, Duke focused on issues like immigration, welfare, and affirmative action—which, he claimed, was racism itself, helping minorities at the expense of white people. Such ideas made sense to a surprisingly large number of white Americans, who were struggling for a piece of the shrinking economic pie and were willing to see the battle lines drawn along racial lines.

In the election Duke got over 40 percent of the vote—600,000 votes in all—which included two-thirds of the white vote. More significantly, his campaign lifted issues like affirmative action into mainstream politics. A few weeks later Jesse Helms, running for re-election as a Republican in North Carolina, would repeat the strategy in his race against Harvey Gantt, a liberal African American. Helms's successful campaign featured a television ad showing a white hand crumpling a job rejection slip.

In November, George Bush vetoed the 1990 Civil Rights Bill, designed to combat discrimination in the workplace; he said it was because he believed the bill promoted employment quotas. Bush declared that he opposed "discrimination and bigotry of any kind," and took measures to distance himself from figures like David Duke, but others accused him of being soft on racism. "Bush's actions belie his words," wrote columnist Carl Rowan. "This president is a prisoner, not a leader, of a Republican Party that is still anti-black, anti-women's rights, and far behind the tide of racial change."[1]

Just after the fall elections, on November 8, the president announced a major new deployment of U.S. forces to the Persian Gulf. This deployment would double the number of troops in the region, bringing the total to over 400,000. In addition to reserve units traveling overseas for the first time, many of these troops were comprised of forces moved to the Middle East from frontline positions along the now-defunct Iron Curtain. Heavy armored divisions were already making their way by air and sea transport from Europe to Saudi Arabia.

The administration's rhetoric was shifting, too. Early in the crisis, Bush and Secretary of State Baker had spoken of the threat to oil resources as a reason for U.S. involvement in the Gulf. Now their statements focused more on reasons of high principle—the violation of defenseless Kuwait, and the Hitler-like character of their former friend Saddam Hussein—as well as on the perceived Iraqi nuclear threat.

Both his actions and his statements seemed to clearly indicate that the president was preparing for offensive military action in the Gulf. And on November 29, he received the blessing of the United Nations Security Council, which passed a resolution authorizing the use of "all necessary means" against Iraq if it did not withdraw from Kuwait by January 15, 1991.

Meanwhile, Saddam Hussein had begun to release his foreign hostages—but he deployed 250,000 additional troops to Kuwait and southern Iraq to match the increased strength of U.S. forces. The few efforts to secure a negotiated settlement to the conflict were stillborn, and by the year's end, there was a growing sense that a war in the Gulf was inevitable.

Events in the Middle East were but one manifestation of how paramount struggles over control of markets and resources had become in the post–Cold War world. The terms of global trade remained a dominant issue everywhere, in debates over the future shape of the changing world order. The bone of contention in such discussions was trade between the developed world and the Third World, between the northern and southern hemispheres. And the goal in all this, for the U.S. and other industrialized nations, was to gain inexpensive raw materials and at the same time create new markets for their manufactured goods and services.

This kind of trade has little to do with academic notions of the free market, since, as *The Ecologist* pointed out, it is dominated by a small number of transnational corporations, nation-states, and entrepreneurs. While the press talks about shortages, world trade is actually organized principally around an effort to control not shortages but surplus—in the interests of the developed world. It is not a matter of finding enough food, for example, to feed all the hungry people in the world, but of ensuring profits to the corporations and elites who control the flow of food through the world's markets.[2]

The General Agreement on Tariffs and Trade was just one of three international institutions set up by the Western developed nations following World War II to bring the colonies and developing nations into line with the industrialized world. The other two were the International Monetary Fund and the World Bank. The initial job of the IMF was to peg currencies to the dollar or to gold. Then—largely under the control of the U.S.—the World Bank set out to reconstruct war-torn Europe, and later turned to the Third World, building an infrastructure to speed its import of manufactured goods and exports of raw materials.

The GATT is an ongoing agreement, periodically renegotiated, which now covers about a hundred signatory countries and regulates over 80 percent of world trade. It was developed to harmonize and liberalize trade—all the time making sure Third World governments did not make goods they could otherwise buy from the developed nations.

As the 1990s began, the transnational corporations, many of them headquartered in the U.S., already controlled almost all the trade in grains, coffee, tea, oil, cotton, timber, iron ore, and many other crucial commodities. But these companies were anxious to further enlarge their business ventures, so they wanted to include under the GATT such services as advertising, stockbrokerages, and banking, and remove restrictions over investments. In the winter 1990 round of negotiations the industrialized nations, led by the U.S., promoted an expansion of the GATT along these lines.

These proposals met with some resistance from the developing countries. But in the past, Third World efforts to become power players in the international trade game—from Mohammed Mossadeq's nationalization of Iranian oil to Salvador Allende's takeover of the Chilean copper industry—had been met with gunboat diplomacy. U.S. actions against these nations had been justified by ideology and the need to maintain the Cold War balance of power, but in the post–Gorbachev era, such pretexts were becoming impossible. And for a brief time, while the Bush administration scrambled for new rhetoric, the impending war in Iraq would appear in its true guise: as a war over control of the world's energy resources.

CARL ROWAN
George Bush: Protector of the Rich . . . and the Bigoted

Columnist Carl Rowan was not surprised by Bush's Civil Rights Bill "veto outrage." "This president is a prisoner," he wrote, "of a Republican Party that is still anti-black, anti-women's rights, and far behind the tide of racial change."

Many leaders of black, Hispanic, women's and other civil rights groups are livid over President Bush's vow to veto the Civil Rights Act of 1990, a measure to combat discrimination in the work-place.

Ralph G. Meas, executive director of the Leadership Conference on Civil Rights, seems stunned, even to the point of calling Mr. Bush "a Ronald Reagan in sheep's clothing."

The black Republican who was appointed by Bush to chair the U.S. Civil Rights Commission, Arthur A. Fletcher, speaks angrily of White House Chief of Staff John H. Sununu and "the whole conservative element" that advises the president as people who "just don't want civil rights laws to have any enforcement provisions."

Well, why am I not surprised that Bush is willing to become the first modern president to veto a major civil rights bill? Because I saw early on that while Bush talks an enlightened game regarding civil rights and racial justice, his actions reflect the mentalities of aides and associates who still think the way Lester Maddox, George Wallace and Orval Faubus, three adamant segregationists, once did.

On February 9 President Bush said: "I believe in the kind of society that is free from discrimination and bigotry of any kind. I will work to knock down the barriers left by past discrimination, and to build a more tolerant society that will stop such barriers from ever being built again."

Nice talk. But Bush's actions belie his words. This president is a prisoner, not a leader, of a Republican Party that is still anti-black, anti-women's rights and far behind the tide of racial change that has swept over the once violently racist parts of the South.

Look at the vote on this civil rights bill that Bush is vetoing! Every Democrat from Alabama, House and Senate, voted for this antidiscrimination measure. The same for South Carolina . . . and for Democrats from the heart of the Confederacy, Virginia. People who once defended Jim Crow with passion now find wisdom, compassion and benefits to the entire nation in a civil rights act that Yankee Bush can't seem to understand.

Only 15 Democrats in the House and none from the Senate voted against this bill. But under White House pressure, 139 Republicans in the House and 34 in the Senate voted against a measure that would give fundamental justice in job opportunities to women and minorities.

So Bush thinks he can lure minorities and thoughtful women to the GOP?

This veto outrage gives us another appalling example of George Bush's version of leadership. Faced with a choice of siding with the Chamber of Commerce or millions of Americans who desperately need fair shots at a decent job, Bush went with the Chamber and its demogogic rhetoric about how a bill that specifically bars quotas "in hiring or promotion" is somehow "a quota bill."

But what's new? In the current tragic budget and deficit-reduction fiasco, Bush has held the nation hostage to his compulsion to protect the rich, even as his aides pop up on TV shows claiming unctuously but falsely that they are "protecting the working men and women of America."

Some confused Americans are asking for "the real George Bush to stand up." I already know who the real George Bush is, and he isn't going to stand up for much more than the greedy rich and the conscienceless corporate bigots that he professes to deplore.

Spineless creatures have a little trouble standing up.

Chicago Sun-Times *October 21, 1990*

PAUL GREENBERG
Decline and Fall of Civil Rights

Columnist Paul Greenberg, editorial page editor of the Pine Bluff *(Ark.)* Commercial, *who had won a Pulitzer Prize in 1969 for editorials advocating civil rights, supported the president's veto of the 1990 bill, which he believed to be an example of "marketing a shoddy product under an attractive label."*

This year's civil rights bill fell one vote short in the U.S. Senate, and President Bush's reluctant veto was sustained. But it will be back. "Like MacArthur," says Benjamin Hooks of the NAACP, "we shall return. . . ."

The civil rights bill will return, all right, but not like MacArthur. More like a bad penny.

It will be back because civil rights, unlike affirmative action, is still a good term in American politics. Therefore a civil rights bill will be introduced at every session of Congress. There is a market in words and ideas just as there is for goods, and so long as there is a demand for good words and ideas, you can bet somebody will try to fill it by marketing a shoddy product under an attractive label. There are no fair-labeling laws in politics.

In a society like America's, dedicated to individual rights rather than group benefits, people are bound to be for civil rights and against employment quotas. Therefore, when quotas are introduced, it must be in the name of civil rights. But as a great advocate of civil rights once put it, you can't fool all the people all the time. And if quota bills keep getting introduced under the name civil rights, the phrase will lose its magic. It already becomes suspect.

The civil rights label hasn't been ruined yet, despite its advocates' best, or rather worst, efforts. You could tell Mr. Bush hated to veto this bill. He put off that regrettable necessity time and again, hoping to hammer out some compromise that would allow a Republican president to start signing civil rights bills again. In the end, he just couldn't do it. Every time he picked up this civil rights bill, it whispered: *quotas.*

The bill's backers had included a solemn clause saying it had nothing to do with quotas. But saying something doesn't make it so. (Just ask anybody who's ever been discriminated against by an Equal Opportunity Employer.) This bill still used numerical "disparity" in a workforce as presumptive evidence of racial discrimination. Any employer who wanted to avoid legal problems—and who doesn't?—had a tempting out under this bill. Just establish an informal quota.

It's sad to watch this deterioration of good words, which amounts to the impoverishment of the American mind. There was a time when civil rights bills outlawed racial discrimination rather than enshrined it. The time was the 1960s. The civil rights acts of 1964, 1965 and 1968 opened up public accommodations, the voting booth and housing. The civil rights bill of 1990 would have established a numerical standard (never say "quota") for employment.

This a standard Congress would never accept for itself, all its employees were exempted from the proposed act. That's revealing. And it pretty much confirms what many Americans have come to think of Congress. A solid majority of senators favored it. After all, it didn't apply to them. Like so much out of Washington, this civil rights bill was one more exercise in hypocrisy.

It's a sad process, this conversion of civil rights to "civil rights." As for the civil rights movement, it stopped moving some time ago and became another special interest with a Washington office and Washington lawyers. (The one class this bill would have benefited unequivocally was lawyers; it would have invited battalions of them to argue over its legalese.) . . .

Naturally, those senators who pointed out that "civil rights" no longer means civil rights scandalized their colleagues. Candor often does. Nothing seems to more alarm certified liberal opinion than the fear that someone, somewhere might tell a recognizable truth and get large numbers of people nodding in recognition. John Silber, the unsuccessful Democratic candidate for governor in Massachusetts, seemed to frighten the national leadership of his party for much the same reason.

This year's civil rights bill was no great loss, though it would have been nice to keep the sections that simply outlawed discrimination instead of institutionalizing it. The great loss is the very idea of civil rights.

Once upon a time, civil rights were unifying and universal—a way to open society to the claims of individual merit. Now "civil rights" becomes a code word for dividing society into competing, resentful groups. The old idea of civil rights may be on its way to join welfare, liberal and law-and-order in the great graveyard reserved for phrases that have been twisted to death.

The Washington Times *November 8, 1990*

TOM TURNIPSEED
Deserving David Duke

Many tried to dismiss Duke's strong showing in Louisiana as an anomaly, and the Republican Party openly disavowed him. But attorney and anti-racism activist Tom Turnipseed argued that Duke jived well with the Republicans' own "Southern Strategy."

The Republican Party deserves David Duke despite desperate attempts by the Republican hierarchy to disavow the Louisiana bigot. In 1968 a racist Republican "Southern Strategy" was devised to co-opt George Wallace's appeal to white bigotry and has been the building block of Republicanism in the South and beyond for more than 20 years. So the "chickens have come home to roost" (as Wallace would say) when Duke, the former Nazi and Klan leader, received an astounding 44% of the vote in the U.S. Senate race in Louisiana.

The Republican street strategy in the small towns and cities of South Carolina and throughout the South has been to spread the word that the "blacks are taking over the Democratic Party," and good white folks should vote Republican. White flight suburbs of the South have become bastions of "Republicanism" with Republican candidates receiving up to 75% to 80% of the vote. Many whites who identify with Democratic principles and have voted the Democratic ticket are now being "shamed" for being in the same party with blacks and made to feel that they are betraying the "great white race."

South Carolina, the first Confederate state to secede from the Union, was the pivotal point in modern political party realignment on the race issue. Although the national Democratic party had been relatively progressive on the race issue since F.D.R., Southern Democrats fought civil rights in Congress and party platform debates. In 1948, Governor Strom Thurmond led a "Dixiecrat" revolt against the national Democratic civil rights platform as a third party, "States rights" presidential candidate. Later, in the U.S. Senate Thurmond set a national filibuster record by his marathon speech against a civil rights bill. South Carolina again led the South on matters of racism when Thurmond switched to the Republican Party in 1964 to embrace Barry Goldwater's anti-civil rights stance in the Presidential campaign.

Goldwater lost, but in 1968 when Wallace was riding a strong white backlash to the civil rights movement, "ol' Strom" persuaded Richard Nixon to adopt a "Southern Strategy" which let potential Wallace voters know Nixon was for law and order and opposed to busing and quotas. The "Southern Strategy" worked for Nixon and has worked ever since for Republicans as they use racial polarization to succeed in the South.

Reagan and Bush, guided by Lee Atwater, a Thurmond protege from South Carolina, used fear of crime and blacks to polarize white voters toward their national conservative constituency by talking about ending busing, quotas and crime in the streets and running Willie Horton ads. . . .

Perhaps the most frightening use of racist politics is the Republican Justice Department's alleged use of selective prosecution and harassment of black elected officials. The Congressional Black Caucus devoted their annual weekend conference [in 1989] to the harassment of African-American leaders. Since almost all black elected leaders are Democrats, they make tempting targets for a politically oriented Justice Department of a political organization that has positioned itself as the "white folk's party." . . .

The Republicans can try to duck and dodge David Duke, but because of past performance, they really deserve each other. It's sad that the party of Abraham Lincoln has become the party of David Duke. But the greatest challenge for the Democrats is to find leadership proud of their party's diversity and strong enough to bring racial reconciliation to a country facing perilous economic and ecological problems.

The (Columbia, S.C.) Point *October 26, 1990*

HAL CROWTHER
The Mystery of Jesse Helms

Another barely disguised racialist campaign was victoriously fought by Jesse Helms in North Carolina. Running against black opponent Harvey Gantt, the veteran U.S. senator again showed himself to be—according to columnist Hal Crowther—a "living relic of the time when white made right and prejudice was open, raw and dangerous."

"Well, I'm out of step with the homosexuals, yes sir," crowed the United States senator, as 300 $35 Republicans lowed their approval. "They haven't given a nickel to my campaign. Where do you stand, Harvey?"

It wasn't some heavy-handed skit on an unbuttoned TV comedy like *Saturday Night Live* or *In Living Color.* It wasn't a time warp or a movie called *Senator Strangelove.* It was Asheville, Buncombe County, North Carolina, and it was September 1990. The speaker, a one-time segregationist rabble-rouser of the airwaves, is a legally elected member of the United States Senate named Jesse Helms. He has been feeding noisily at the public trough for 18 years, courtesy of the voters of North Carolina. He's still hungry, and shows no inclination to yield his place at the trough to a younger animal, or one more aware of the passage of time. Race-baiting and Red-baiting got him where he is, and he sees no reason why gay-baiting shouldn't keep him there. He's a living relic of a time when white made right and prejudice was open, raw and dangerous. He's a one-man anchor, buried deep in the muck and rubble of the past, who keeps us from spreading some sail and catching a fresh breeze that blows toward something better.

He's our boy. I've never heard anyone defend him (I've heard people who probably vote for Helms speak of him as if he were a bad habit, a regrettable weakness like cigarettes—or dwell on the real but irrelevant shortcomings of his opponents); many of us stumble into embarrassment and incoherence just trying to explain him. My wife and I caught a shrill, defensive note creeping into our voices as we tried to answer a *Los Angeles Times* reporter who wanted to know why the facts about Sen. Helms never seemed to harm him—why educated white moderates would vote for a man who courted the custodians of South African apartheid and served as unofficial lobbyist for a dozen right-wing dictators; why poor whites continued to vote for a senator who let them slide into Third World poverty while he pampered big business.

"They don't care about the facts" sounded disloyal and condescending, in the presence of an incredulous outlander. It's hard to find a generous way to say that there may be a half a million voters here who will violate every principle, even self-interest, in the service of an attitude—and a very bad attitude at that.

When I don't have some Yankee treating me like a guilty South African, I'm a fairly objective student of Jesse Helms. I've had a ringside seat for three of his four campaigns, and I've gone through several theories that attempted to explain him. At first I thought it was fairly simple, that everyone who supported him was either a cynical capitalist with no conscience or a bigot with no apologies—an appalling but effective coalition.

During his campaign for a third term against his strongest opponent, former Gov. Jim Hunt, I discovered that Helms was harvesting votes from what I took to be a perverse and defiant streak of regional pride. I tried to capture it in a paragraph that has been reprinted more often than anything else I've written on the subject of politics:

I think that's the key to Jesse's longevity in North Carolina. He's ours, and there's no one like him anywhere. No one else has one. Try to think of him as a dreadful pet, a mascot, something like a huge pit bull, useless and vicious, that sits in its own mess at the end of a tow-truck chain and snarls at everything that moves.

"Ain't he a pisser, though?" the owner says with pride.

There are folks that like to keep pit bulls, and pythons and piranhas. It's a perverse kind of affection.

I saw the lighter side of this stubborn affection as an exercise in liberal-baiting, like painting a Confederate flag on the door of your pickup. Since a U.S. senator is basically useless anyway, why not use Jesse as a way of warning carpetbagging engineers and pointy-headed professors that North Carolina wasn't about to become a clone of Connecticut or Wisconsin? . . .

Try to put yourself in the place of a native North Carolinian of a certain age. Tobacco and segregation were the two things you could count on—the pillars of your society, in a sense. And suddenly tobacco is a deadly poison and your favorite old Red-baiting, union-busting segregationist, Uncle Jesse, is Attila the Hun. Every day the local liberals and the national media are telling you that the twin constants of your Daddy's and your Granddaddy's lives are evils worse than communism. It's a lot to swallow in one generation, and it's not surprising to see a lot of people get their backs up, to see them digging in against an alien-looking future.

When I thought about the mystery of Jesse Helms I weighed all these things—cynicism, pride, prejudice, stubbornness, xenophobia, humor, future shock, money. The one thing I never considered was *total* ignorance: a large, critical bloc of potential voters who had no idea, after all these years, who Helms was or what he stood for. In my own ignorance, I assumed there could be no undecided voters in a race between Harvey Gantt, a black architect from Charlotte, and Jesse Helms—a lineal descendant, though tastefully emasculated and manicured, of night riders, slave traders and the late Jim Crow.

It would take *Ripley's Believe It Or Not,* I thought, to find a single voter who was honestly undecided. But *Independent* reporter Barry Yeoman heard reports of 100,000; he took his notebook on the road and discovered dozens of citizens who claimed that their votes were still up for grabs. He discovered why, in many cases: Though they knew almost nothing about Harvey Gantt, which is the unfortunate lot of most challengers, they knew almost nothing about the incumbent either. . . .

This is something that Jesse Helms must have known all along, this truth that those of us who work in the media find so hard to comprehend or accept: that a huge bloc of voters in every election are just blank slates, lumps of wet clay waiting for the imprint of a single slogan, an image, a single word if it happens to be the candidate's name.

Armed with this knowledge, he's evolved a brilliant strategy. Why won't he come out and debate, appear, cooperate, comment? his enemies rage. Why should he? The less the voters know about Sen. Helms, the better he looks. His record is a scandal, and he isn't going to pick up many votes on his face, his voice or his personality. . . .

This was the great nightmare of Thomas Jefferson, the failure of public education that would return half the population to the passive, subhuman condition of serfs. Who anticipated television? We could take comfort from the fact that wet-clay voters are in no way unique or indigenous to North Carolina. Or we could despair because they point us to the end of popular democracy as a useful form of government.

The North Carolina Independent *October 10, 1990*

SUSAN SHOWN HARJO
October 12: A Day of Mourning for Native Americans

Susan Shown Harjo, president of the Morning Star Foundation, found implicit racism in the yearly commemoration—and upcoming "quincentenary" celebration—of Columbus Day. The "discovery" of America, she wrote, was a piece of "Eurocentric economic mythology" insulting to Native Americans, who were still struggling to secure equal rights and preserve their culture after five hundred years.

The New World was discovered by Christopher Columbus on Oct. 12, 1492, according to eurocentric economic mythology, usually called "history" in the school systems of Europe and the Americas.

According to common sense, however, this "New World" was "discovered" only in the sense that a second-story-man "finds his fortune" in someone else's home. As Onondaga Chief Billy Lazore is fond of saying, "When my ancestors greeted Columbus on these shores, he wasn't dragging no land behind him."

In two years, the various colonizing nations in Europe and the Western Hemisphere will celebrate the 500th Anniversary of this event, which is known in federalese as the "Quincentenary Jubilee."

There will be an updated, motorized re-enactment of the voyage of Columbus' three ships—one is being rebuilt now after having been torched in dry-dock in Spain—and his 1992 crew will be tall, tanned and healthy, rather than the small, syphilitic, scurvied lot in the original. There will be parades, funny hats worn and new myths born out of this 8 x 10-glossy, colorized-classic celebration of the "history" of the past 500 years.

Underlying the Columbus Jubilee will be the do-or-die spirit of Manifest Destiny—that the white people had the divine right to everyone else's land, and the god-given duty to move or mow down anyone in their way. The 1992 hoopla will reflect the white-supremacist notions perhaps best articulated by Rudyard Kipling (the British poet who lived in India and also left us the "Sambo" legacy): "Oh, little Sioux or Japanese, Oh, don't you wish that you were me?"

"No" is the short answer to that rhetorical question. A longer answer would not be necessary, but usually is for those who think the melting pot is a swell place and everyone would be grateful to swirl around in it while, as the saying goes, the scum floats to the top and everything on the bottom gets burned.

Milk-o-phobia (noun, Mod. Ind., the fear of homogenization into the white world) is a difficult concept to explain to many people, especially those who offer us equality as the greatest expression of liberalism and good will. Simply put, equality is fine for openers, but some of us have something better in mind.

We, the indigenous peoples of this red quarter of Mother Earth, were here when Columbus lurched across the Atlantic Ocean in search of India, washed up on our beaches and called us "Indians." The misnomer stuck, finding its way into the Constitution and other U.S. governance documents (except for the Declaration of Independence,where we are called "the merciless Indian Savages").

When Columbus publicized that he found gold in this "Paradise on Earth," the powerful religious and secular institutions of Europe set about separating us from our property and debating whether or not we were human beings. When it was decided that we probably were human beings with souls—at least for the purpose of signing over land—the priests introduced the "Requiremento," which had to be read to the Indian people before they were killed in the name of God.

This precursor to the Miranda rights went something like this: You have the right to remain on your land while you give us your gold. You have the right to exchange your land for a bible. If you do not understand these rights, too bad. You have the right to go to heaven right now.

Along with the centuries of murder, torture and theft came the more subtle forms of dehumanization—separating families, deculturizing children, imposing foreign languages and religions, changing our national and personal names to pejorative or meaningless ones.

Those who insisted on cultural and territorial distinctiveness were decried as separatists, but did manage to reserve the lands which preserved our existence into the modern era.

Today, from Cape Fox to Xingu and sea to shining sea, we are treated as strangers in our own homes, complete with I.D. cards and numbers. Our children see their parents and traditions mocked and cartooned in the sports world, supermarkets and popular media. When land, water, fishing and other legal rights were asserted and exercised, there is an instant and ugly backlash that reminds us how close to the surface the anti-Indian sentiment is among a rather substantial segment of the dominant society.

Ironically, since we are the poorest people in the U.S. and throughout the hemisphere, we are viewed as greedy when we insist on keeping and controlling what little we have left.

In this time of shifting demographics, when the white people are diminishing in number in contrast to the people of color, the white folks are trying to make friends and make up for lost time. This is the season of reconciliation, kiss-and-make-up, marry-into-the-family, let-bygones-be-bygones.

Churches—the same ones that wiped out whole peoples, fought us for our souls and still think we are pagans—now give us lovely words about a time of grace and healing.

It is a difficult time for us to fully accept this extended hand, when the other is still picking our pocket. It is hardest of all for us to let the dead past bury its past, when our relatives are still being dug up and, along with our sacred objects, desecrated in museums and sold on the open market.

Seasonal platitudes may comfort some, particularly those who are tired of the struggle and believe we have no future. Some will fall for the we're-sorry-we'll-never-do-it-again-have-a-nice-columbus-day routine. Words are important—treaties are a testament to that—but we've had words, and words have had us.

We now need words which are backed up by actions to reconcile generations and centuries of inequities. Only then will we hear words for their own sake and genuine meaning. Until then, we will continue to look for the fine print and to see the fine conciliatory statements as velvet gloves covering iron fists.

Indigenous peoples hemisphere-wide have called for Oct. 12, 1992, to be a Day of Mourning. We invite all people to join us in observance of the missions of our relatives who have been the target of genocidal and dehumanizing practices from 1492 to today.

The Lakota Times *October 16, 1990*

ANTHONY LEWIS
When You Believe in Lies

In October 1990, the perennial budget crisis reached new heights, actually forcing the federal government into temporary shut-downs. The crisis, wrote New York Times *columnist Anthony Lewis, had its roots in the "fairy story" of Reaganomics.*

If you want to know why we have a paralyzing budget crisis, you have to go back to the golden days of Reaganism. That was the early 1980s, when the smiling President was telling us that we could cut taxes and still have it all.

A few right-wing intellectuals told the truth then. The real idea of those massive tax cuts, they said, was to bleed the Treasury white—so there would be no money for domestic spending. Ideologues like The Wall Street Journal's editorial writers said that with gleeful candor. They thought Government was bad, so we would be better off with less of it.

Of course the official Reagan economists were not so candid. They said they had discovered a Philosopher's Stone called supply-side economics: reduce taxes, and we would have higher Government revenues and higher private saving and investment.

Those official explanations were lies. Water did not run uphill. Lower taxes brought lower revenues. The rich, made richer by Reagan policies, saved and invested less, not more.

But the American public loved the fairy story. When Walter Mondale said it was not true, the public put him down as a spoilsport. It voted for Ronald Reagan, and when George Bush stopped complaining about voodoo economics and said you could too spin straw into gold, it voted for him.

The trouble was that most Americans did not agree with the real aim of the right. They did not want a pygmy Government, they wanted the Government to do lots of things that cost money: provide medical care for the elderly, protect the environment, run national parks, control air traffic . . .

So there we are. The reality, as intended, is that the Federal Government does not have the resources it needs. But the voters will not let go of the fairy story. They want the Government to keep spending without raising taxes.

The result is political paralysis. The politicians who have to face the voters in a month — the members of the House of Representatives—do not want to deprive any citizen of a benefit or impose on any citizen a higher tax.

The problem is much harder to solve in the United States than in other democratic societies because of the nature of our political system. It is, first of all, a divided system, in which a President and Congress may—and now do—answer to different parties and ideologies. It is not a parliamentary system, in which the Prime Minister can tell her party members to toe the line or see their Government fall.

Then our system has always allowed interest groups to exercise great influence. It may seem logical to tax private airplanes when levying new taxes on luxuries. But the plane manufacturers in Kansas speak to Senator Bob Dole, and planes are exempted.

The politics of interest groups is frustrating. It tends to legislative interests, because a few highly motivated legislators can block action. But the system, as Justice Brandeis said, was designed not to produce efficiency but to diffuse power.

In the old days there was one mediating influence. That was the political party, which could find a common denominator for legislators—a position on which a majority could stand. But parties have lost much of their meaning.

Republican members of Congress today do not have to look to President Bush. A Newt Gingrich, determined to protect the rich from even disproportionately modest tax increases, can vote against the President although he is a Republican whip. He looks for support to political action committees, and he will get it.

Does it matter? The sums involved are not very large in an economy as big as ours. But the demonstration of political will—or rather the lack of it—does matter. Europeans and Asians, the rising economic powers, are already finding confirmation of their suspicion that the United States is in decline.

Those who warn about American decline, like Prof. Paul Kennedy of Yale, are met with the indignant response that this is still the world's most powerful country militarily: Look at the Persian Gulf. But that misses Professor Kennedy's point, which is that we are not keeping our economic performance up to our commitments abroad.

One of Mr. Kennedy's critics, Prof. Joseph S. Nye Jr. of Harvard, wrote the other day that the United States need not fear decline if it simply addresses "such domestic issues as the budget deficit, savings rate, educational system and condition of our cities." Exactly.

The New York Times *October 9, 1990*

ROBERT S. MCINTYRE
A Soaking (in Gravy) for the Rich

The thirteenth-hour budget agreement, wrote Robert S. McIntyre of Citizens for Tax Justice, failed to solve the problems that had brought on the crisis—irresponsibility and injustice.

As you no doubt have heard by now, the budget agreement just reached is the same soak-the-poor-and-the-middle-class approach that was the hallmark of the 1980's.

Most of the new revenues will come from $87 billion in increased excise taxes—on gasoline, beer, cigarettes, etc. These added levies will take about 11 times as high a share of the income of poor families as they take from the rich. Families earning $40,000 will pay almost six times as high a share of their income as will the wealthy.

Yes, a few of the tax increases in the package are designed to hit the well-off, but there is a long list of new tax shelters. When you add it all up, the very wealthy probably will end up paying lower taxes—while the rest of us definitely will pay more.

But cheer up, say many analysts. Overall, American taxes are among the world's lowest. Still not satisfied? Well, you may have a point.

Taxes are indeed low in the U.S. by international standards. But so are government services. Our Federal, state and local spending on social programs totals less then 21 percent of our gross national product—lower than any major industrialized country except Japan. In contrast, social spending in France, Germany, Italy, Sweden and the Netherlands averages 30 percent of their G.N.P.—almost half again as much as here.

In Europe, taxes typically pay for health care and for extensive retirement benefits. In the U.S., these costs are largely paid for privately, while a quarter of our Federal spending goes for defense (including defense of Europe) and a sixth goes to pay interest on the national debt.

And that's not all. Our Government spends more than it takes in, and takes more than it should from people with the least.

George Will theorizes that Republican popularity has been due in part to the willingness of the Reagan and Bush Administrations to borrow heavily against the future, thereby giving people $1 in services for every 75 cents they pay in taxes. It's an interesting hypothesis, but it doesn't square with reality.

Congressional Budget Office data show that a typical middle income family will pay about 7 percent more than if the tax code had remained as progressive as it was in 1977. For poor families, the tax hike is 14 percent. But the richest 1 percent of the population will pay 36 percent less this year than under the 1977 level of progressivity—an average tax cut for this elite group of $82,000 each.

Meanwhile, on the domestic spending side, only Social Security and a handful of other programs have kept up with the growth in the economy. In fact, from 1980 to 1989, Federal spending on everything but Social Security, defense and interest fell from 9.7 percent of the G.N.P. to only 7.3 percent—a drop of more than one-quarter. And in the new budget agreement, elderly people will pay more for Medicare (through higher insurance premiums) and get less (through increased deductibles.)

You'd think that Democratic politicians might find it politically attractive to try to reverse these regressive trends. But recent Democratic Presidential candidates have been strangely reluctant to raise the issue of fair—not just higher taxes.

This year, to their credit, Democratic leaders in Congress made a real effort to improve tax fairness. But while they averted the egregious capital gains break proposed by the Administration, they failed in their overall goal.

Of course, the Democrats have a lot of excuses for the unfortunate summit outcome. It would have been even worse to allow Gramm-Rudman to shut down the Government. The Administration's intransigence about not taxing the rich made real negotiating almost impossible. Somebody had to be "responsible."

But the bottom line is that the summit agreement sends the bill for the deficit to the wrong people, while giving the wealthy yet another free ride. If that means most Americans still think they're paying too much for what they get from government, it's not hard to sympathize.

The New York Times *October 3, 1990*

PETER BAHOUTH
World is on Brink of War to Protect Our "Way of Life"

By October, American troops were massed on the Kuwaiti border, but many Americans were still wondering what it was all about. Peter Bahouth, executive director of Greenpeace USA, saw the U.S. preparing to fight for nothing more admirable than "Americans' right to waste."

Everyone is interpreting the complicated and abstract Persian Gulf picture in a different way. Is it about law and order? Is is about sovereignty? A mad dictator? Oil?

The only common thread of opinion is that we are all confused by the contradictions that we see. Not too long ago we sold arms to Iraq with the approval of the same administration that now calls Iraq's leader the new Hitler. The Bush administration says that the conflict is about protecting the price of oil, but that price has gone from $21 before the conflict to as high as $40. The oil companies themselves are reaping huge profits as the government spends a billion dollars monthly to underwrite U.S. military presence.

We are left to rely on what we instinctually feel about the conflict. Certainly the most "real" image we get is the one we see on TV every day of soldiers sending their love to families back home. We can relate to this image because it is sincere and it involves very real human emotions. Contrast that with President Bush's statements about protecting the American way of life.

When the president refers to our way of life, he's not talking about protecting those loved ones back home, but about preserving a way of life founded on a myth of unlimited resources. We go to the store, we pump the gas, we plunk down the cash, and we get what we want.

But everyone knows (although we don't often think about it) that what we consume must come from somewhere, that someone or some group is making decisions about the choices we are given, and that someone is getting rich in the process. On top of that, we are also increasingly aware that our current "way of life" ruins the atmosphere, fouls the water, poisons our children and buries us in garbage.

Am I against consumers? No. But I am against being fed things we don't need or things that we don't want. I am against continuing a way of life today that destroys any possibility of life tomorrow. For centuries, people went to war for what they needed. Then they went to war for what they wanted. Now we are going to war for something we waste.

Americans' "right" to waste is as well protected as if it were enshrined in the Constitution. We have become the most energy-wasteful nation on the face of the earth. Our oil addiction needs to be addressed not only in our personal consumption habits, but on a national level. Since the early '80s, the federal government has seemed determined to assert our destructive "right":

• Both the administration and Congress have fought increases in fuel economy. Easily achievable goals for increasing gas mileage have been all but abandoned, while a modest national increase of 2.8 miles per gallon could save an amount of oil to equal what we imported from Iraq and Kuwait combined.

• President Reagan decimated federal alternative energy research, and then even abolished the credits for solar home construction—crippling much of the promising solar energy industry, and darkening the future for escaping our national oil addiction.

• Some of the loudest congressional voices calling for military action in the Middle East are just as eager to surrender territory back home: The oil industry is once again coveting the Arctic National Wildlife Refuge and oil fields off the shores of California, Florida and Alaska. Despite a legacy of oil spills and tanker accidents, Congress may bow to industry pressure.

The national disgrace of all this is that both the war and the waste are easily avoidable. The technology exists today, on the shelf, to make homes so heat-tight that they would stay comfortable all year in any climate with little or no energy input. We can also make comfortable cars that get more than 80 miles per gallon, triple the efficiency of our industrial motors, and build urban mass transit for a fraction of the cost of building highways. The truth is that even a simple set of actions on energy could go a long way toward making the perilous concentration of oil in the Persian Gulf irrelevant to world affairs.

Where would the funding for safer energy come from? We could start with the $1 billion a month our Middle East "presence" is costing us. Add on the $100 billion a year we spend on obsolete nuclear weapons. (Have you thought about how little value our massive nuclear arsenal has had in the current crisis?)

So when President Bush says that we are preserving the "American way of life," listen to your gut. Is he really saying the United States is the land of artificially cheap petroleum? The land of buying things that we don't need? One doesn't have to be an environmentalist to see the stupidity of the line we are being fed.

Birmingham News *October 22, 1990*

GEORGE WILL
Thatcher, de Gaulle, and Nationalism

Columnist George Will applauded British Prime Minister Margaret Thatcher as the ideological heir to the "prophetic nationalist" Charles De Gaulle. "Thatcher recoils" he wrote, "from the drip-by-drip dilution of national sovereignty through the incremental transfer of power" to the European community. But by the end of the year, Thatcher's resistance to movements toward European unity would be instrumental in her ouster from office.

Fifty summers ago, an austere French soldier in his 50th year sat before a microphone in BBC studio 2B and told France that she had lost only a battle, not the war. It was June 18, 1940, the day of Churchill's "finest hour" speech. And the 125th anniversary of the battle of Waterloo.

History has recently been histrionic. The 200th anniversary of the French Revolution coincided last year with the collapse of the husks of Europe's supposedly "revolutionary" tyrannies. This year, while Europe experiences the rebirth of nations, and while Britain's prime minister is punished politically for resisting the dilution of national sovereignty in the name of the abstraction "Europe," France commemorates the 100th anniversary of a prophetic nationalist, Charles de Gaulle.

Other than in their implacability, Margaret Thatcher and de Gaulle are radically dissimilar.

She rose through Parliament, he through "treason." His noble broadcast was a call for disobedience against France's government, which condemned his to death in absentia.

Thatcher revels in party skirmishes. De Gaulle disdained "the ballet of parties," practicing a Caesarism of plebiscitary democracy, claiming "the individual authority of the state," personally. (Being Caesar is hazardous: He was the target of at least 30 assassination plots.)

Thatcher has the brusque, hectoring manner of a national nanny. De Gaulle had what a biographer calls a baroque style of leadership suited, de Gaulle thought, to a nation "made by 40 kings over 1,000 years." De Gaulle, who kept spiritual company with those kings (and Joan of Arc), was forever in flight from banality. Thatcher's goal is to bang elementary arithmetic into British heads—the costs of life, the calculations of capitalism.

De Gaulle was both Washington and Lincoln—founder and preserver—of the Fifth Republic, which three times (1958, 1960, 1962) was threatened with civil war. Thatcher's more mundane aim has been to make Britain efficient.

Thatcher wants the British to be better shopkeepers. De Gaulle used the myth of French grandeur therapeutically, to purge disgrace —the collapse in 1940 that was followed by collaboration.

He would "make use of dreams to lead the French," to seduce them away from the passions of private interests, to national glory. Intoxication by myth was his answer to a perennial dilemma of democracy: How do you exercise the art of leadership amid the brokering of interests that is the basic business of government by consent?

De Gaulle, wrote Henry Kissinger in his memoirs, was "the son of a continent covered with ruins testifying to the fallibility of human foresight." But because he understood the political primacy of nations (he spoke of "the so-called United Nations"), he had foresight. He saw, over the horizon, Germany reunited and the Soviet Union again being Russia.

Because de Gaulle's mind had a retrospective cast and his rhetoric had a mystical tinge, detractors dismissed him as an anachronism oblivious to the wave of the future. Spotters of such waves were sure the next one would wash away much of the sovereignty and distinctiveness of nations, producing a fuzzy federalism of homogenized peoples.

Thatcher is similarly condescended to by advanced thinkers who stigmatize her as a "reluctant European." But her reluctance partakes of de Gaulle's farsightedness about the increasing, rather than decreasing, saliency and utility of nationalism.

And in one particular, she is de Gaulle's superior. She knows that the nub of the matter is parliamentary sovereignty, meaning that great good by which mankind's political progress is measured; representative government.

De Gaulle understood that among all of Marx's failed prophecies, the most failed was the most fundamental. It was the notion that industrialism made man a merely economic creature and that all non-economic forces—religion, race, culture, ethnicity and especially nationalism—had lost their history-making saliency. Today's rebirth of Europe's captive nations, including those imparting centrifugal force to the overdue disintegration of the Soviet Union, is refutation of Marx and confirmation of de Gaulle.

Today, socialism's old aspiration, the thin gruel of proletarian internationalism, has been supplanted by liberalism's still more watery soup of "Europeanness." Thatcher recoils from the drip-by-drip dilution of national sovereignty through the incremental transfer of power from national parliaments to the supranational bureaucracy in Brussels. There is a steady attenuation of control of lawmakers by elections, a weakening of the crucial criterion of legitimacy; consent of the governed.

As de Gaulle's nationalism was, so Thatcher's is the face of the better future. And what has this to do with Americans' lives today? Today, the threads connecting public consent with the gravest governmental decisions touching life and death—war and peace—are being tangled, frayed, perhaps even severed.

U.S. officials are seeking Ethiopia's, the Ivory Coast's, Zaire's forbearance—permission?—for Americans to sacrifice blood and treasure in an enterprise supposedly swathed in special legitimacy because of 10 resolutions from the United Nations ("the so-called United Nations"), all to advance an abstraction: "the new international order."

America needs a more Gaullist foreign policy, more stabilizing contact with concreteness: U.S. national sovereignty, U.S. national interests, U.S. national decisions.

The Washington Post *November 11, 1990*

ROBIN BROAD, JOHN CAVANAGH, AND WALDEN BELLO
U.S. Plan for Latin Debt Relief is a Non-Starter

Not to be left behind the European Community, President Bush promoted the idea of free trade throughout the Western Hemisphere, but linked it to plans for Latin American debt repayment and U.S.–monitored economic development. Economic analysts Robin Broad, John Cavanagh, and Walden Bello warned that the strategy might be good for American banks, but it would not benefit the people of Latin America.

Air Force One today will ferry George Bush and his advisers on a rare trip to the south—a week-long tour of the five crisis-ridden Latin American nations. Pushing an "Enterprise for the Americas Initiative," Bush hopes to extend the all-encompassing "motherhood-and-apple pie" concept of free trade to the entire Western Hemisphere, from Canada to Argentina.

In short, Bush will offer his Latin counterparts the carrot of increased access to North American markets if they continue repaying their debts and agree to a development strategy that emphasizes private enterprise and opening of economies to U.S. investment.

Bush's model suggests that developing countries can export their way to South Korea or Taiwan status through the purgatory of what is known as "structural adjustment." But the strategy is deeply flawed. It will reap short-term benefits for large U.S. banks at enormous cost to the people of Latin America and to the longer-term stability of the hemisphere.

The debt repayment component of the package has led to a perverse capital outflow from Latin America to U.S. banks. Since 1983, Latin American nations have repaid creditor banks and institutions more than $100 billion *more* in debt service than they have received in new loans and aid. This leaves precious little either for social programs or development projects.

Furthermore, the model that Bush is peddling has already proved a failure in the dozens of countries across Africa, Asia and Latin America where "adjustment" has been applied for more than a decade. Supervised by the World Bank and the International Monetary Fund, these adjustment packages mandate severe cutbacks in government spending to balance budgets, elimination of trade barriers and social subsidies, encouragement of exports, devaluation of currencies and dismantling of nationalist barriers to foreign investment.

In practice, structural adjustment has damaged environments, worsened structural inequities, bypassed popular participation and failed even in the very narrow goal of pulling economies forward. Ecological sustainability has been undermined in country after country. In the frenzy to increase exports, countries often resort to the easiest short-term approach: unsustainable exploitation of their natural-resource base.

The stories of ecological disasters lurking behind export successes have become common: Timber exports have denuded mountains, causing soil erosion and drying critical watersheds. Cotton, soybeans and other cash crop exports have typically depended on polluting pesticides and fertilizers. Large fishing boats have often destroyed the coral reefs where fish breed and live. Tailings from mines have polluted rivers and bays.

Structural adjustment hurts the poor as well. As government spending is reduced, social programs are decimated. Once 1989 World Bank working paper concluded that a byproduct of the "sharply deteriorating social indicators" that accompany contractionary adjustment packages is that "people below the poverty line will probably suffer irreparable damage in health, nutrition and education."

Signs of failure are even emerging in South Korea and Taiwan, the miracle models of high-speed, export-oriented capitalist development. After decades of systematic exploitation, the South Korean labor force erupted in thousands of strikes during the late 1980s, undermining the basis of that country's export success. Meanwhile, decades of uncontrolled industrial development have left large parts of Taiwan's landscape with poisoned soil and toxic water.

This is not meant to deny that developing countries need substantial reforms, that some governments consistently overspend or that markets have a role to play. Rather, the lesson of the 1980s teaches that there are no shortcuts to development. Development strategies will not succeed and endure unless they incorporate ecological sustainability, equity and participation, as well as effectiveness in raising living standards.

Out of the generalized failure of development over the 1980s, there is a different kind of consensus emerging among people the Western development Establishment rarely contacts and whose voices are seldom heard. A new wave of democratic movements across Latin America, Asia and Africa is demanding another kind of development. In citizens' organizations, millions of workers, farmers, women and environmentalists are saying they want to define and control their own futures.

Alan Durning of the Worldwatch Institute estimates that across the developing world, more than 100 million people belong to as many as several hundreds of thousands of these organizations. Many are informal economic institutions that have sprung up to fill the economic void left by cuts in government spending. There are examples of successful worker-owned businesses, transportation collectives, peasant leagues, micro-enterprise credit associations and other citizens' initiatives across Latin America that are touching larger and larger numbers of people.

These movements reject the heavy emphasis of free-market development on exports based on cheap Latin American resources and labor. For the southern half of our hemisphere, the only possibility of creating a market of consumers possessing effective demand is to eliminate the severe inequalities that depress the purchasing power of workers and peasants. The "how-to" lists here all require government action — through such steps as land reform, progressive taxation and advancement of worker rights. . . .

As he travels through Latin America, Bush would do well to look beyond the failed development models of the past few decades. Instead of a free-trade initiative, Latin America desperately needs substantial debt relief that would provide the resources for sustainable development.

But debt relief is not enough. If there is ever to be a more unified and sound Western Hemispheric market, the marginalized millions of the hemisphere must be made effective consumers and, more important, central participants in planning their future. Indeed, these are the people with whom George Bush should discuss future initiatives for the hemisphere.

The Los Angeles Times *December 2, 1990*

ROBERT WEISSMAN
Prelude to a New Colonialism

The latest round of negotiations in the sweeping international trade agreement, the General Agreement on Tariffs and Trade (GATT), bogged down in December, but potential settlements promised to have a seminal impact on the world's future. Critics such as Multinational Monitor *editor Robert Weissman argued that the U.S.'s proposed changes to the GATT, if instituted, would pave the way for a "recolonization" of the Third World.*

For two months this winter, the General Agreement on Tariffs and Trade (GATT) negotiations were broken off after a U.S.-European dispute over farm subsidies. Amid the confusion, U.S. observers agreed on one thing: The Third World was the clear loser. Government and media commentators alike assert that a new version of GATT, an international agreement that regulates more than 80 percent of world trade, among approximately 1200 signatory countries, would spur development in Third World countries by giving them access to the markets of the industrialized countries.

The real objectives of the current round of GATT negotiations, however, are antithetical to development, and they have gone unmentioned. Led by the United Sates, which has consistently introduced the most far-reaching and radical proposals into the talks, the industrialized countries have attempted to lock in and further promote the deregulation of international trade that occurred in the 1980s. More specifically, they have sought to encourage the Third World's growing export dependency and to tighten multinational corporations' control over Third World markets and resources.

At the prompting of internationally oriented companies and business groups such as American Express, Cargill Inc. and the Multilateral Trade Negotiations Coalition (the leading business lobby on GATT), the United States and other industrial countries have attempted to bring three new areas under the GATT rubric: intellectual property, services (in fields ranging from finance to telecommunications to construction) and investments.

The proposed expansion of GATT, which has historically dealt only with trade in manufactured goods, threatens to undermine the ability of Third World countries to manage their economies and foster domestic industry. Appropriately, the Malaysia-based Third World Network, a nongovernmental organization, labels the industrialized countries' GATT proposals a means of "recolonization."

The industrialized countries are trying to gain Third World support for GATT by offering the South improved access to Northern markets in agricultural products and textiles. But even these purported concessions from the North are double-edged. "Benefits" will accrue only to developing countries that orient their economies to produce goods to meet foreign demand rather than domestic needs. In agriculture, this is likely to be associated with the creation of large plantations, intensified use of pesticides, displacement of peasants who produce for local consumption and clearing of rain forests.

The dubious benefits of improved access to Northern markets are far outweighed by what the developing countries will be forced to give up. In the past, GATT has acknowledged the special circumstances of developing countries and granted them exceptions from its rules. The "development principle," which exempts Third World countries from some tariff and other regulations to enable them to protect nascent industries, is now threatened by the aggressive initiatives from the industrialized countries.

Proposals from the industrialized countries in the area of intellectual property alone could foster a massive transfer of resources from the South to the North. The U.S. proposal calls for all countries to adopt and strictly enforce U.S.-style patent, copyright and trademark laws. It attempts to address claims by multinational corporations that they lose $40 billion to $60 billion each year to Third World "pirates" who counterfeit their goods and infringe on their patents. From the Third World perspective, however, the recovery of the multinationals' "losses" implies a huge transfer of income from the poor countries to the rich, even if the figure (estimated by the U.S. International Trade Commission on the basis of a survey of American business) is significantly inflated.

The U.S. proposal reflects the concerns of business groups like the Pharmaceutical Manufacturers Association and the Intellectual Property Committee (I.P.C.), a coalition of thirteen major companies, including I.B.M., Du Pont, General Electric, Merck and Company, and Pfizer. According to the I.P.C., this overlap of the U.S. government and private-sector positions is not a coincidence. The group claims that its "close relationship with the U.S. Trade Representative and [the Department of] Commerce has permitted the I.P.C. to shape the U.S. proposals and negotiating positions during the course of the negotiations."

One of the important objectives of the proposal is to extend patents to "all products and processes, which are new, useful and unobvious." This would allow the multinational food, chemical and pharmaceutical companies to gain control over much of the world's genetic resources, most of which are embedded in seeds and herbs in tropical Third World countries.

Multinationals hope to gather information from the genetically rich Third World, manipulate it with rapidly evolving biotechnology expertise and then patent the new seeds, pharmaceuticals or other products. The Third World will receive nothing in the bargain, because under the proposed regulations naturally occurring organisms would not be patentable, though genetically altered ones would be. The genetic resources that are the components of the "new" products are not considered the province of the nation in which they occur (unlike minerals, for example) because Northern scientists have classified them as a universal common heritage.

The multinationals want more than just genetic resources from Third World countries. When corporations send botanists to the Third World to gather samples of plants, says Pat Mooney of the Rural Advancement Foundation International (RAFI), "they do not just collect plants, they collect the knowledge of local people; the botanists don't have the slightest idea" which plants are valuable until they are told. The botanists gather the plants that local farmers and herbalists have cultivated and bred and that the natives unsuspectingly report as useful to the multinationals' representatives. . . .

The consequences for the Third World of the other new areas of GATT will be no less severe. Responding to lobbying efforts by American Express and other service multinationals, the industrialized countries are pushing for free trade in services. Because services are not discrete items like manufactured goods, free trade in services means that service companies must be free to operate in foreign countries.

Martin Khor Kok Peng, vice president of the Third World Network, says that if the Northern service proposals are adopted, "many of the service industries in the Third World will come under the direct control of the transnational service corporations within a few years. This would mean the eradication of almost the last sectors in the Third World which are still controlled by national companies."

The industrialized countries' service proposals even threaten Third World countries' cultural autonomy. "National treatment" clauses would require that foreign corporations receive the same treatment as national companies. Khor says that with a national treatment clause, "media companies . . . in the United States or Australia may be given the freedom to set up media companies or to buy out media companies in the Third World, including television and the print media, and therefore control the cultures of Third World countries."

The Northern counties' proposals on investments would preclude Third World countries from limiting foreign investment or requiring foreign investors to abide by special regulations. Measures designed to promote economic development and technology transfer, such as those prohibiting foreign investment in certain sectors, requiring investors to use local materials in the production process and mandating that foreign investors work in joint ventures with local companies, would be prohibited. This would seriously impair Third World development efforts.

Even a total breakdown of the GATT talks would have given Third World countries only a temporary reprieve, for the United States is pushing its GATT agenda in other forums. Under the "Special 301" section of the 1988 Trade Act, the Office of the U.S. Trade Representative is required to impose sanctions on countries that do not provide strong intellectual-property protection. The U.S. T.R. imposed sanctions against Brazil under Special 301 in 1988. In April 1990, it identified twenty-three countries with which it plans to negotiate over intellectual property standards. If those countries do not show signs of "improvement," they will face the same type of sanctions as those imposed on Brazil.

Even more ominous, the Bush Administration is preparing to enter into free-trade negotiations with Mexico. It has also proposed a free-trade agreement for the entire Western Hemisphere. These agreements would go beyond even GATT in usurping Third World sovereignty and opening the economies of developing countries to multinational corporations.

The industrialized countries' free-trade initiative comes at a time of economic crisis for the South. Hoping that improved access to industrialized countries' markets will jump-start their ailing economies, many developing countries are acquiescing in Northern demands. The tragedy is that, in so doing, the Third World is participating in its own recolonization.

The Nation *March 18, 1991*

HARRY M. CAUDILL
Corporations Should Provide for Adequate Public Library

Harry Caudill's last articles were published in the Mountain Eagle *of Letcher County, Kentucky, just days before his death. Caudill, as a writer, teacher, and state legislator, had consistently devoted himself to the people and the land of eastern Kentucky. His groundbreaking 1963 book,* Night Comes to the Cumberlands, *was an impassioned exposé of their poverty and the exploitation that caused it, and helped to inspire the social welfare programs of the 1960s. Caudill's final pieces typified his unadorned and uncompromising vision of social justice.*

The time has come for the people of Letcher County to provide themselves with an adequate public library building and ample books for study and research. Mrs. Mary Bingham's generous gifts to the new college and to the expansion of the land holdings at the Bad Branch Preserve have tempted some of us to believe that similar accomplishments are possible with grants from the people who own eastern Kentucky's gas, oil and coal deposits.

In 1980 Corporate Data Exchange Inc. made a study of eastern Kentucky's mineral companies. It has published the names of major eastern Kentucky oil, gas and coal enterprises. The companies that extract the minerals are themselves owned by much larger corporations.

The work of Corporate Data Exchange Inc. reveals the names of the corporations that mine the coal, and in turn the names of the companies that own those corporate entities. There is little reason to suppose that ownership patterns have changed much since 1980. Some of those companies and their respective holdings are as follows:

COMPANIES/SHAREHOLDERS	SHARES	HOLDINGS
National Steel Company		41,000 acres
1. Lord Abbett & Company	703,500	
2. J.P. Morgan & Company	174,000	
3. Wells Fargo & Company	72,099	
4. American Express Company	40,000	
5. Mellon National Corporation	314,538	
6. U.S. Steel Corporation	41,900	
Duke Power Company		13,000 acres
(Eastover Mining Company)		
1. Lord Abbett & Company	603,800	
2. Wells Fargo & Company	213,800	

COMPANIES/SHAREHOLDERS	SHARES	HOLDINGS
(Eastover Mining Company, cont.)		
3. Manufacturers Hanover Corporation	466,738	
4. Wachovia Corporation	2,597,655	
5. Kirby Financial Group	275,000	
6. U.S. Steel Corporation	432,000	
Bethlehem Steel Company		104,000 acres
(Beth-Elkhorn Corporation)		
1. Lord Abbett & Company	1,549,900	
2. J.P. Morgan & Company	2,065,563	
3. Wells Fargo & Company	140,834	
4. American Express Company	125,000	
5. Manufacturers Hanover Trust Co.	649,926	
6. Princeton University Endowment Tr.	130,000	
7. Wachovia Trust Company	199,689	
8. Stanford University Endowment Trust	93,380	
9. Robeco Inc. (Holland)	300,000	
E.I. Dupont and Company		26,000 acres
(Conoco—Consolidated Coal Corp.)		
1. Lord Abbett & Company	703,500	
2. J.P. Morgan & Company	392,000	
3. Wells Fargo & Company	189,721	
4. Manufacturers Hanover Corporation	657,766	
5. Citicorp	720,130	
6. Chase Manhattan Bank	218,424	
7. Kirby Financial Group	243,729	
8. Dupont Family Interests	13,129,243	
9. U.S. Steel Corporation	208,302	
Diamond Shamrock Corporation		60,000 acres
(Falcon Coal Company)		
1. J.P. Morgan & Company	103,000	
2. Wells Fargo & Company	124,616	
3. American Express Company	99,000	
4. Citicorp	192,648	
5. Sears, Roebuck & Co.	150,800	
6. Princeton University Endowment Tr.	100,000	
7. Wachovia Corporation	160,762	
8. Kirby Financial Group	213,300	
9. Dupont Family Interests	422,000	
10. Mellon National Corporation	340,511	
U.S. Steel Corporation		41,000 acres
(U.S. Coal & Coke Corporation)		
1. J.P. Morgan & Company	2,190,000	
2. Dupont Family Interests	1,142,668	
3. Manufacturers Hanover Trust Co.	1,067,680	
4. Lord Abbett & Company	952,100	
5. Mellon National Corporation	448,106	
6. Robeco (Holland)	402,000	
7. Wells Fargo & Company	266,784	

COMPANIES/SHAREHOLDERS	SHARES	HOLDINGS
American National Resources Corporation		100,000 acres
(Virginia Iron, Coal and Coke Corporation—VIC)		
1. National Life Insurance Company	138,000	
2. Wells Fargo & Company	85,398	
3. American Express Company	118,797	
4. Citicorp	600,000	
5. Stanford University Endowment Trust	164,439	
6. Royal Insurance Company (England)	116,200	
MAPCO		40,000 acres
(Martin County Coal Co. OO Martiki)		
1. Citicorp	85,830	
2. Sears, Roebuck & Co.	190,800	
3. Chase Manhattan Bank	874,263	
4. Royal Insurance Company (England)	117,000	
5. Robeco Inc. (Holland)	100,000	
6. Dupont Family Interests	165,165	
Total acreage of all eight companies		885,000 acres
Columbia Gas Company		
(Kentucky-West Virginia Gas Co.)		
Fee simple and leasehold gas rights		
1. National Life Insurance Co.	125,000	
2. Wells Fargo & Company	246,920	
3. Manufacturers Hanover Trust Co.	2,578,469	

The foregoing corporations and their predecessors have owned the east Kentucky mineral fields for nearly a hundred years. It will be noted that most of the corporate land owners are great banks and super-rich American families. The title to the great resource companies tend to descend from generation to generation.

These companies and the families who own them are not without generosity. Collectively they give away vast sums to county, state and foreign benefits. In addition to these corporate gifts, individuals in such families as Duke, Rockefeller and Mellon pass out tens of millions of dollars to favored charities here in America and in foreign countries.

The Bible tells us that if we ask we shall receive. We have never asked anything of Lord Abbett and Company, J.P. Morgan and Company, Wells Fargo and Mellon National Corporation, and accordingly, we have received nothing. There is much truth in the old adage "ask and you shall receive."

For example, John D. Rockefeller Sr. spent about $75,000 in a campaign that eradicated hookworm from Kentucky early in this century. A mere $750,000 would relieve the entire South of this awful scourge. After Mr. Rockefeller had achieved this signed benefit for the state he was never asked for anything else, in so far as I have been able to discover.

Let us ask the Fiscal Court and the Library Board to get busy and give this county an expanded, amply staffed and equipped library. The vacant Hobbs building on Main Street in Whitesburg could be bought, renovated, stocked with needed books, shelves and other equipment for about $500,000.

A really good library would have tremendous impact on child development, and we might even make great readers out of many.

It is noted that Stanford University, Princeton University and Harvard University own huge blocks of stock in Diamond Shamrock Corporation, American Natural Resources Corporation and Bethlehem Steel. Their annual bequests come to these universities from all over the United States and it is difficult to believe that they would fail to promote and finance a Letcher County Public Library.

J.P. Morgan Jr. and his father were America's most successful bankers and put together many of the great financial institutions that still shape America.

Let us urge all school teachers and public officials to get behind this much needed library project. I have never had a doubt that the money will come flowing in. After all requests to the Binghams have brought Letcher County $85,000 for Lilley's Woods, $50,000 for the community college, and a half million to the Nature Conservancy of which a large portion will be used to add greatly to the Preserve around the Bad Branch.

If asked would Lord Abbett and Company be less generous? Could Princeton and Stanford say "No"? And what of the Great Dutch corporation, Robeco Inc., and the immense Royal Insurance Company of England?

We should not remain too lazy and shortsighted to ask them.

* * * *

Last week my article dealt with the land corporations that control the coal, oil and gas production in the central Appalachians. I pointed out that these venerable corporations are, in turn, owned by a broad consortium of great American universities, large steel and manufacturing companies, immense U.S. and European banks, and such bonding companies as Lord Abbett and Company.

In this article I will carry that procedure farther, listing the corporations that operate in the Appalachian mineral fields as a whole.

Eastern Kentucky is a part of the immense Appalachian fuel fields. Other kindred regions include western Maryland, West Virginia, eastern Tennessee, northern Alabama and western Virginia.

I am indebted to Dr. John C. Wells Jr. for the ownership information used herein. He is the author of an unpublished but excellent doctoral thesis called *Poverty Amidst Riches: Why People Are Poor in Appalachia*. He estimated that Appalachia as a whole originally contained 320,000,000,000 tons of coal.

Looking beyond the local and regional mining corporations he found the following list of corporations that sell Appalachia's minerals. And behind them stand Lord Abbett and Company, the Morgan Banks and those other corporate giants we read about last week.

PARENT COMPANIES	PRIMARY INTEREST	STATES IN WHICH LAND IS OWNED	ACREAGE
Norfolk and Western Railroad Co.	Railroads	Va., W. Va.	448,871
Continental Oil Co.	Energy	W. Va., Ky., Tenn., Va.	372,040
Chessie Systems, Inc.	Railroads	W. Va., Ky.	271,163
Pittston Company	Coal	Va., W. Va.	275,173
Occidental Petroleum Co.	Energy	Va., Ky., W. Va.	253,605
Georgia Pacific Corp.	Paper, Lumber	W. Va., Ky., Va.	229,699
Bethlehem Steel Corp.	Metals	Ky., W. Va.	204,580
Ky. River Coal Co.	Land holding	Ky.	190,000
Penn-Va. Corporation	Land holding	W. Va., Va., Ky.	158,002
Berwind Corporation	Manufacturing	W. Va., Va., Ky.	154,200
Ethyl Corporation	Chemicals	Ky., W. Va.	134,211
National Steel Corp.	Metals	Ky.	130,000
Eastern Associated Coal Co.	Energy	W. Va.	103,775
Bates Manufacturing Co.	Manufacturing	Va., Ky.	85,109
Charleston National Bank & Trust Company	Banking	W. Va.	82,068
United States Steel Corp.	Metals	W. Va., Ky.	70,187
Coal Creek Mining and Manufacturing Co.	Land holding	Tenn.	64,199
Union Carbide Corp.	Manufacturing	W. Va.	59,617
Beatrice-Yukon Mining Co.	Coal	Va.	51,843
Ford Motor Co.	Automobiles	Ky.	51,126
Tennessee Land & Mining	Land holding	Tenn.	50,940
Koppers Corporations	Manufacturing	Tenn.	50,771
The American Association	Land holding	Tenn., Ky.	50,661
Tennessee Valley Authority	Federal Agency	Ky.	40,220
Big Sandy Company	Land holding	Ky., Va.	39,224
Payne-Baker Family Trust	Land holding	Tenn.	37,206
Ford, Fanst & Cheely	Land holding	Tenn.	37,097
Youngtown Sheet & Tube Co.	Metals	Va.	35,189
Kennecott Copper Co.	Metals	Va., Ky.	33,267
National Shawmut Bank of Boston	Banking	Va.	25,285
Blue Diamond Coal Co.	Coal and steel	Tenn.	20,181
Blackwood Land Co.	Land holding	Va., Ky.	19,446
LeVisa Fuel Co.	Coal	Va.	12,263

PARENT COMPANIES	PRIMARY INTEREST	STATES IN WHICH LAND IS OWNED	ACREAGE
Francis Brothers Inc.	Family Trust	Tenn.	23,676
Plateau Properties, Inc.	Family Trust	Tenn.	12,040
Swords Creek Mining Co.	Coal	Va.	10,243
Aluminium Co. of America	Metals	Ky.	10,700
Republic Steel Co.	Metals	Ky.	5,134
		TOTAL ACREAGE	3,814,193

Three quarters of these companies have their principal offices in New York, Boston, Detroit, Cleveland, Philadelphia, Pittsburgh and London.

Holdings of similar "exploiting" corporations in Pennsylvania, Maryland and Alabama bring the total to at least 5,000,000 acres.

These companies have already "harvested" the timber from their lands, cutting the trees repeatedly for lumber, railroad ties, whisky barrel staves and mining props. Since the purchase price for the land ranged from ten cents to ten dollars per acre the wood alone has repaid the investments many times over.

The minerals, though, are the real money makers. As long ago as 1965, *Dun's Review* reported that Penn-Virginia Corporation and Kentucky River Coal Corporation were the most profitable investor-owned companies in the United States, clearing some 61 cents out of each dollar received, after taxes.

In 1976 *Forbes* magazine revealed that Blue Diamond Coal Company increased its liquid assets by 56.4 million dollars in the year ending on June 30, 1975, and have notice of its intent to buy McLouth Steel.

As Wells points out, state and county levies on these properties are absurdly low. Until the levying of severance taxes in the last few years they ran from eleven to 25 cents per acre. Most of the severance levies are used to repair haul roads worn out by coal trucks.

A dozen years ago comparisons revealed that a million dollars worth of mining property owned by Inspiration Consolidated Copper Company in Arizona paid nine times as much money to that state as a million dollars worth of mining property owned by United States Steel Company paid to Kentucky!

Many of these corporations have deplorable safety records. For examples, in 1972 an explosion on Ford's property on Hurricane Creek in Leslie County, Kentucky, killed 38 men. Four years earlier at Farmington, West Virginia an explosion in Continental Oil Company's mine killed 78. In 1972 a culm heap owned by Pittston Coal collapsed after a heavy rain, wiped out 15 small communities and killed 125.

Ashland Oil has thousands of acres under lease.

Howell Corporation, a Houston firm, mined 11,000 acres owned by Kentucky River Coal Corporation.

Falcon Seaboard Corporation, largely the property of Texan Wayne Chrisman, removed Kentucky mountain tops to "recover" $225,000,000 worth of coal for the Tennessee Valley Authority.

W.R. Grace and Company operates through a huge and growing subsidiary called New Era Resources, Incorporated.

Medusa Corporation quarries road aggregates and other stone products.

Columbia Gas Company supplies much of the eastern market with natural gas from more than a million Appalachian acres.

International Harvester mines coal for its plants and those of its subsidiary, Wisconsin Steel Company.

A consortium of domestic oil companies has leased the "deep horizons"—strata some 12,500 feet below the surface—in at least a million and a quarter acres which the companies expect to drill for oil and gas within a few years.

Duke Power Company mines coal for its power plants. One of its mines digs coal today on Rockhouse Creek in Letcher County. Doris Duke, reportedly America's richest woman, is the biggest stock owner of this company. Surely her social conscience would prompt her to help Letcher Countians set up a modern, comprehensive public library. Unless the request is made we will never know.

American Electric Power Company digs about 7,000,000 tons of steam coal annually.

General Motors Corporation and Exxon were formerly the owners of Ethyl Corporation, a chemical giant. This company owns Elk Horn Coal Corporation and its extensive operations in high quality coking coal. Elk Horn Coal is the largest shareholder in Kentucky River Coal.

In *The Rich and the Super-rich* (Lyle Stuart, 1968) Ferdinand Lundberg demonstrated a probability that the descendants of John D. Rockefeller own large (and perhaps controlling) interest in several of these Appalachian corporate titans. The companies include Bethlehem Steel, Continental Oil, Norfolk and Western Railroad, Exxon, U.S. Steel, Chessie Systems, Standard Oil Company of Ohio (which mines through its subsidiary, Old Ben Coal Company), and International Harvester Corporation. If these estimates are correct, West Virginia's U.S. Senator John D. Rockefeller IV should examine the corporate operations in Appalachia that have endowed him with much wealth and power. If he is at all sympathetic to suffering humanity he must feel some urge to correct the glaring abuses that have enriched him.

And what of Armand Hammer, founder and chief official of Occidental Petroleum whose Island Creek Coal Company has sunk

$36,000,000 of Rumanian money into a colossal mining network in Buchanan County, Virginia? Should his company be allowed to spread devastation across the Virginia landscape and social chaos among its people in order to provide cheap coke to the Balkans?

A natural leader in the search for constructive change should be former U.S. Senator Howard Baker of Tennessee, a beneficiary of the 37,206-acre Payne-Baker Family Trust.

Warren Delano, an uncle of President Franklin D. Roosevelt, organized the Kentennia Corporation, a large coal firm in Harlan County, Kentucky. His descendants and heirs may still own stock in it.

The Appalachian states ought to join at once in a new effort to modernize and cleanse the hill country and, in doing so, should demand aid of the region's corporate owners. If pressured the exploiters are scarcely in a position to withhold their cooperation and their money.

Do our county officials have the courage to ask these money-making giants to contribute funds to build Letcher County a first-rate public library? They have contributed heavily to such projects in the counties where the children of the "Big Bosses" go to school. They should do no less for the children of Letcher County and their parents.

Just for a starter I would be astonished if Mr. Floyd Gottwald of Ethyl Corporation were to fail to welcome a request from the Letcher County Library Board and to see that a generous grant to the board was approved.

The Mountain Eagle *November 21/28, 1990*

ELLEN GOODMAN
The Long Death of Nancy Cruzan

As the year ended, so did the life of Nancy Cruzan, a young woman whose tragic case had exemplified right-to-die issues in the 1980s. For columnist Ellen Goodman, her family's long struggle provoked thoughts about "the quality of life, the quality of mercy" and "death in the technological age."

Death did not come gently to Nancy Cruzan.

It took almost eight years from the car accident that left her unconscious to the death certificate. It took almost three years from the time her parents asked to end treatment to the time a Missouri court agreed. It took 12 days from the moment the feeding tube was removed to the moment she stopped breathing.

The last week in the life of the young woman whose body was locked in a fetal position and whose mind was permanently obliterated was not easy either. Pickets appeared on the hospital lawn. Protesters forced their way onto her floor. Reporters stood death watch, sending out updates on the deteriorating condition.

Joe and Joyce Cruzan, for their part, spent days in their daughter's room and nights in the mobile home set up on the hospital lawn. But in the end, they wrested from the state and from modern medicine the terrible right to bury their child.

Her death did not come gently to any of the Cruzans. I will spare the family another message about the larger good in their loss. They have been through enough. I can only imagine how this ordeal prolonged and distorted their mourning. There is no upbeat, sunny side for the family.

But for those of us who knew not Nancy Cruzan but the inanimate *Cruzan* case, there is an extraordinary legacy. The *Cruzan* case, like that of Karen Ann Quinlan, became a story that made America talk publicly and at length about death in the technological age.

In the press, the case was often cast as the right to die versus the right to life. In the courtroom, especially the Supreme Court, it was about the right of families versus the right of the state.

But in the everyday language of Americans talking to each other, Nancy Cruzan's terrible fate made spouses as well as lawyers, friends as well as legislators, talk about the quality of life and the quality of mercy. We were forced to confront the paradox that the same technology that can save us can also doom us to what Nancy's own doctor called "a living hell."

As Daniel Callahan, the director of the Hastings Center said in a sort of eulogy, "There is the balance of Greek tragedy here. We want the very advances that have given us this problem."

For much of human history, the medicine man or woman was also the caretaker. Medical mercy meant helping people, and helping people often meant helping them to die peacefully.

But in our lifetime, medicine improved in its ability to save life, and doctors redefined kindness as a cure. Death became a technological failure. As Callahan says, "The National Heart and Lung Institute is not set up to allow us to die more peaceably from heart disease but to cure it."

Our gratitude to science, our own passionate pursuit of medical salvation, now comes with increasing unease about this same technology. We fear that there may be too much of a good thing. That we can't stop it.

This is what Nancy Cruzan came to represent as she lay twisted, bloated and unconscious in her hospital bed. As people came to feed her what the hospital ludicrously called "supper." As the doctors described her condition as a "persistent vegetative state." As others argued—is this better?—that they had seen tears in her eyes.

She came to represent the unintended consequences of technology, the side effects of our best intentions, the cruelty of our modern medical mercy. She came to represent something worse than death.

In time, people may wonder why Americans spent so much time arguing about sustaining one unconscious woman while so many others in our society died for lack of medical care. But every family that has been prompted to talk aloud about life and death, every hospital that has been forced to think about aggressive treatment, every medical school that has been prodded to teach young doctors about dying, has a piece of Nancy Cruzan's legacy.

May she, at long last, rest in peace.

The Boston Globe *December 29, 1990*

PART FIVE

WAR

JANUARY–MARCH 1991

ON JANUARY 16, 1991, PRESIDENT BUSH, WITH THE approval of the United Nations and the U.S. Congress, sent out the first American bombing raids over Iraq and occupied Kuwait. For the next month, the allied forces pounded their enemies with thousands of bombing sorties—destroying Scud missile-launching sites, "softening up" troop concentrations in southern Iraq and Kuwait, and knocking out much of Iraq's economic infrastructure. After four weeks of allied air attacks, Saddam Hussein, with help from the Soviets, made what appeared to be an effort toward negotiations to withdraw—but President Bush brushed these overtures aside as having too many conditions, and launched phase two: a ground war. Within the week, Kuwait was liberated and the Iraqi forces were in ruined retreat. Bush called for a ceasefire, and declared an allied victory.

But this swift victory for the allies took an enormous toll in human life and in various forms of "collateral" damage. An unprecedented level of military censorship prevented documentation of much of the damage wrought by Operation Desert Storm from reaching the mainstream U.S. press, but by the spring of 1991, varied estimates had begun to filter out of Iraq. According to a report published by Greenpeace in May 1991, "During the embargo period, the war, and its aftermath, the lives of over six million people were directly affected, either by being killed or wounded, made refugees, or losing their homes."

Estimates showed between 151,000 and 183,000 Iraqis, Kuwaitis, and allied soldiers killed between the time the conflict began in August 1990 and early May 1991. In addition, over two million foreign workers employed in Iraq and Kuwait were forced to return to their countries of origin, indefinitely deprived of their livelihoods.[1]

While the use of "smart bombs" and other celebrated high-tech weaponry may have ensured a shorter war, it hardly led to a more humane war. Laser-guided bombs were used to efficiently knock out key installations of Iraq's civilian infrastructure, and the very success of the new weapons assured unprecedented levels of civilian disruption and presaged mass starvation and epidemics.

Before the war began, international sanctions had already hurt Iraq's agricultural economy by cutting off imports of pesticides, fertilizers, and feed for livestock. Coalition bombing then destroyed much of the infrastructure essential to food production, including the water supplies and pumps that fueled the irrigation system. The country was rendered dependent on imported foods, the prices of which were rising, but at the same time, most people could not go to work. The banking system was disrupted, so no one had the currency they needed to buy the food anyway. And while the June harvest loomed, the country's agricultural future remained imperiled.

The U.N. embargo had slowed the supply not only of food, but of medical supplies as well. The allied bombings hastened the outbreak of disease by knocking out hospitals, transportation systems, electricity, heat, communications, and water purification facilities. As of April, the water system in Baghdad was still operating at only 10 percent of its capacity, and Basra, in the south, had not had any pumped water since the war's outbreak. Visiting health officials and human rights workers reported exponential increases in the cases of diarrhea, vibrio cholera, typhoid, and malnutrition.

Famine and epidemic disease were only some of the catastrophic problems facing postwar Iraq, a country that shows every sign of being the newest Ethiopia. A nation of around 17 million, it had seen at least 300,000 men killed in the eight year Iran-Iraq war, and quite possibly another 100,000 during the Gulf fighting. It seems likely that as much as 20 percent of the men between eighteen and thirty have been killed in warfare. Half of the population of Iraq is under fifteen, and anywhere from one third to two thirds of that number are children under five years old. Not only are these children likely to be the hardest hit by the epidemics, but many are now orphaned, without any means of support.

The environmental fallout from combat and sabotage transformed the war zone into an ecological disaster area. The 3 million barrels of oil dumped into the Persian Gulf caused long-term damage to marine life, desalinization plants, and the fishing industry. And the toxic smoke from 580 burning oilwells in Kuwait has poisoned the atmosphere, posing a dire threat to human health, wildlife, agriculture, and water supplies, in the Gulf region and beyond.

For Iraq, the war was an unmitigated disaster: It's army was destroyed, its environment and infrastructure devastated, and its population subjected to massive suffering—but its brutal dictator remained in power. For the U.S., its effects were more complex.

Like the Opium Wars in eighteenth-century China or the coup in Salvador Allende's Chile, the war in the Gulf was an example of Western gunboat diplomacy that set limits on indigenous control of regional resources. Its purpose was to let Saddam Hussein know he could not unilaterally interfere with the production and distribution of oil. The war's end result—the reduction of Iraq to a devastated Third World nation with Saddam still in charge—served U.S. interests well. Saddam stood as a sort of hostage in reverse: As long as he remained in power, Iraq, since it had not reformed itself, could not pump any oil without permission of the United States.

In the new world order, the power of nations would be measured less by the size of their nuclear arsenals than by their ability to wield control over world trade—and, in particular, over access to raw materials and markets in the developing countries. The Gulf war served to provide a stern reminder to Third World nations who sought to control their own resources or balked at new trade alliances: a reminder that the world's remaining superpower stood ready to enforce the rules of trade, by force if need be. And in the postwar environment, President Bush's other plans to enhance America's position in this new world order gained momentum. In May he persuaded Congress to permit him to proceed unimpeded on "fast track" negotiations toward a new trade pact with Mexico, which would create a U.S.–dominated free trade zone on the North American continent and, in turn, give America added authority in hammering out deals under the General Agreement on Tariffs and Trade (GATT).

For those who did not share the president's vision of the new world order, of course, such developments were no cause for celebration. But even supporters of the administration's position could not deny that the war yielded unwelcome results. To begin with, one of the war's primary goals had been to protect the supply of Kuwaiti oil; yet months after its end, an estimated 9 percent of the world's petroleum consumption was going up in flames. The war had also seriously injured the economies of America's two important allies, Kuwait and Saudi Arabia. Once rich sheikdoms, both ended the war facing serious economic problems, crippling environmental problems, and an uncertain future. Human rights abuses in "liberated" Kuwait had only increased, with thousands of people—including a large number of Palestinian residents—summarily tried and punished as collaborators. And while the U.S. had hoped the war would make possible new security arrangements in the region, opening the way for a lasting peace between the Arab states and Israel, the postwar Middle East remained as volatile as ever. Finally, the long-term effects of the environmental damage on the region and the world were yet to be measured, but sure to be devastating. There was already evidence that the toxic chemicals released by the oil fires had caused health damage not only to regional civilians, but to American troops as well.

In the United States, the effects of the war on domestic issues were just beginning to be felt months after its conclusion. In the wake of a war over the trade in oil, the president was well-positioned to pursue not only his hemispheric trade plans, but also his new National Energy Strategy, which called for increased domestic oil drilling and a return to nuclear energy. In the guise of victorious commander-in-chief, he generally gained new clout with Congress—where members who had opposed the war were now accused of being unpatriotic—and new momentum for his nascent 1992 presidential campaign.

Another of Bush's uncelebrated victories in the Gulf war was his administration's all-too-successful management of war news. From the time of the first troop deployments, the Pentagon restricted the media's access to the war, imposing requirements for obtaining credentials, subjecting arriving reporters to a fitness test, and holding journalists to a pool system. By the time the war started, the pools allowed only 132 journalists, some of them technicians, to cover 500,000 troops.[2] Robert Fisk of the London *Independent* wrote that "in theory the 'pool' means that the reports of journalists travelling with military units are available to all television networks and newspapers. In practice, it means that the only reporters officially allowed to witness events at 'the front' . . . have their reports read and often amended by military censors." Fisk reported that journalists who attempted to work outside the pool system often lost their accreditation, had their tapes and papers destroyed, or were deported from Saudi Arabia. "This is supposed to be a war about freedom," he wrote, "but the Western armies in Saudi Arabia—under the guise of preserving 'security'—want to control the flow of information."[3] This unprecedented level of news censorship set a dangerous precedent that would almost surely be imitated in the future not only by the military, but by the rest of the government as well.

The U.S. war machine rolled over not only the Iraqi troops and the mainstream media, but American public opinion as well. Most polls reported the approval rating for the U.S. war effort at about 80 percent, and the president's ratings were also high. Dissenting voices were ignored or sharply criticized—a phenomenon which, like the success of news censorship, set disturbing precedents for the future.

The war also had a lulling effect on the domestic population, distracting attention from the growing fiscal problems of cities and states and the growing social strains presaged by America's changing demography. The war briefly covered up a wide range of domestic issues—and even when these issues returned to the forefront, in the late spring and summer, they remained somewhat obscured by the hundreds of Gulf war victory parades, and the facade of national unity these celebrations brought. On the home front, the U.S. Persian Gulf win seemed a flashy, but hollow, victory.

RICHARD NIXON
Why U.S. Policy is Right in the Gulf

As the new year began with the nation on the brink of war, former president Richard Nixon offered some "straight talk" on how a use of military force against Iraq would serve U.S. interests, and represent a "highly moral enterprise."

It is time for some straight talk about why 400,000 young Americans spent Christmas in the deserts of Saudi Arabia and why in less than two weeks the U.S. may be once again at war.

We must first be clear about what the conflict is not about.

If we must resort to military force to drive Saddam Hussein from Kuwait, it will not be a war about democracy. While our goal is to restore Kuwait's legitimate Government, it is hypocritical to suggest that we hope to bring democracy to Kuwait. Except for Israel, there are no democracies in the Mideast, and there will be none in the foreseeable future. The Emir of Kuwait is among the world's more benevolent dictators, but once he is back in his palace in Kuwait City, he will still be a dictator.

Nor is intervention justified because Saddam Hussein is a cruel leader. President Bush has been criticized for equating him with Hitler. Whether he is that bad is irrelevant. He is bad enough. His soldiers are murdering, torturing and raping defenseless Kuwaitis and pillaging their country. He violated international law by using chemical weapons against Iran and the Kurds.

But if our policy were to punish cruel leaders, we would not be allied with Syria's President Hafez al-Assad. Heordered the massacre of 20,000 innocent people in the city of Hama in his own country, has supported international terrorism and presided over an army that has committed brutal atrocities in Lebanon. Both Syria and Iraq threaten our interests, but today Iraq poses a profoundly greater threat.

Those who fault President Bush for enlisting President Assad's support should remember Winston Churchill's classic rejoinder to those who criticized him for supporting Stalin after Hitler invaded the Soviet Union during World War II: "If Hitler invaded Hell, I think I would find a kind word to say about the Devil in the House of Commons."

We are in the Persian Gulf for two major reasons.

First, Saddam Hussein has unlimited ambitions to dominate one of the most important strategic areas in the world. When Senator Bob Dole said we were in the Gulf for oil and Secretary of State James Baker said we were there for jobs, they were criticized for justifying our actions on purely selfish grounds. We should not apologize for defending our vital economic interests.

Had we not intervened, an international outlaw would today control more than 40 percent of the world's oil. While, by stringent energy conservation, the U.S. might be able to get along without oil from the Gulf, Western Europe and Japan could not. What happens to the economies of other great industrial nations directly affects the economy of the U.S. We cannot allow Mr. Hussein to blackmail us and our allies into accepting his aggressive goals by giving him a choke hold on our oil lifeline.

Because he has oil, he has the means to acquire the weapons he needs for aggression against his neighbors, eventually including nuclear weapons. If he succeeds in Kuwait, he will attack others, and he will use whatever weapons he has to achieve his goals. If we do not stop him now, we will have to stop him later, when the cost in young American lives will be infinitely greater.

There is an even more important long-term reason for rolling back Iraq's aggression. We cannot be sure, as many believe and hope, that we are entering into a new, post-Cold War era where armed aggression will no longer be an instrument of national policy. But we can be sure that if Saddam Hussein profits from aggression, other potential aggressors in the world will be tempted to wage war against their neighbors.

If we succeed in getting Mr. Hussein out of Kuwait in accordance with the U.N. resolution and in eliminating his capacity to wage war in the future—which must be our goal if he refuses to get out peacefully and forces us to act militarily—we will have the credibility to deter aggression elsewhere without sending American forces. The world will take seriously U.S. warning against aggression.

Some critics argue that we should continue sanctions for as long as 18 months before resorting to force. They contend that even if sanctions do not work, Mr. Hussein will be so weakened that he will suffer fewer casualties if war does come.

They are wrong on three counts. First, while the Iraqi people suffer the effects of sanctions, President Hussein will direct his resources so that the Iraqi military will not. Second, while the sanctions will weaken Iraq, they will weaken us even more, because of the political difficulty of holding our alliance together abroad and maintaining support for our troop commitment at home. Finally, the most the critics can claim is that it is possible that sanctions might work. It is certain that military force will work. The stakes are too high to risk failure.

Other critics believe diplomacy will eventually convince Saddam Hussein that he should get out of Kuwait. But neither diplomacy nor sanctions has a chance unless he knows that if he does not get out of Kuwait peacefully, the American people and our allies will be united in support of driving him out militarily.

Should Secretary Baker's meeting with the Iraqi Foreign Minister, Tariq Aziz, fail to produce an agreement that complies unconditionally with the U.N. resolution, we must remember that when dealing with an insatiable aggressor a bad peace is worse than war because it will inevitably lead to a bigger war.

If we must go to war, it will not be just a war about oil. It will not be a war about a tyrant's cruelty. It will not be a war about democracy. It will be a war about peace—not just peace in our time, but peace for our children and grandchildren in the years ahead.

If Saddam Hussein gains in any way from his aggression, despite our unprecedented commitment of economic, diplomatic and military power, other aggressors will be encouraged to wage war against their neighbors and peace will be in jeopardy everywhere in the world. That is why our commitment in the Gulf is a highly moral enterprise.

The New York Times *January 6, 1991*

ROGER ANGELL
Notes and Comment (A Country at War)

Less than two weeks after the U.S. flew its first bombing raids over Iraq and occupied Kuwait, writer Roger Angell—a veteran of World War II and the father of a draft-age son—sadly reflected on how rapidly America could become, once again, a nation at war.

The news about the Gulf war came to my house in a telephone call from my son, who was visiting friends in California. He said he'd just been watching a CNN news program that included the voices of three reporters in a Baghdad hotel describing the sights and sounds of the bomber attacks and the anti-aircraft fire that were suddenly going on around them: the sights and sounds of war. While we talked, I turned on a television set, and my son and I exchanged what other news we had just then, and said glum, reassuring things to each other, coast to coast. My son sounded scared, and who can blame him? He is twenty years old. This call, I should explain, was long distance in more ways than one, for I am seventy. The space of years between my son and me has felt odd at times—difficult for both of us on occasion, and often funny—but mostly it's been everyday and insignificant. If anything, it has been a bond, a family quirk we have in common. Last week, it took on a new meaning, because his generation doesn't know what it is like to live in a country at war, while mine, although it had almost forgotten, has been intimate with war in hundreds of ways. Counting the Second World War and Korea and Vietnam, and measuring (as I do in my head) from September of 1939, rather than December of 1941, and leaving out several of our military actions that were skirmishes, and distant wars involving other nations, I find that there have been more than twenty years of mornings when I awakened with the knowledge of being at war. Living in this country, I have been extraordinarily protected from the unremitting violence of this century, yet, along with many Americans my age, I can quickly remember a dozen or more friends who died in war, and twice that number who were wounded or otherwise terribly damaged. I also served three and a half years in the Army Air Forces, almost two of them in the Central Pacific. All this is old hat, of course—a commonplace to millions of us still—but what matters, I think, is that this dull, faded, enormous experience seemed about to go out of date for good. With any luck, with a little more (or a lot more) intelligence and courage and patience and imagination all around, my generation and the ones just after it might have taken the knowledge of war with us when we left, and good riddance. Now it's back, and what my son wanted from me on the telephone that night, I realized, was news from a country he had never planned to visit.

I was very close to my son's age when Pearl Harbor came along, and I think I am more frightened for him now than I was for myself back then. War is deadlier than it used to be but, let us hope (let us pray), quicker. Maybe it will miss him altogether. Meanwhile, the other experience of war—the news of it, every morning and night; the awful attraction of it; the technical and sporting jargon; the maps and the weapons diagrams; the rumors and the jokes (those three CNN men, in the much replayed report, couldn't entirely hide their thrill at being in that hotel: there was a courtside, big-basketball-game tone to it); the cheerfulness of officers and experts; the euphemism ("collateral damage" is brand new: it means civilian casualties); the zesty little lift to our stride (*We're in a war now: chin up!*) that accompanies us everywhere now that we have one easy thing to think about instead of a thousand difficult or insoluble ones; the reflexive belief in good luck (a quick war, a war won, and nobody's sons in it), and then waking up in the night and thinking about what is really going on, which is the willed imposition of death and destruction on many thousands of men, women, and children, far away—well, all this is experience that my son will pick up very easily indeed. He's already started. He's back from California now, and back in college. He's excited about a new seminar he's taking on the Impressionist painters, but what he, like the rest of us, is mostly studying is war. My own refresher course has begun. In the morning, with my coffee, I watch the bright screen and the maps and expert with the pointer; I try to remember the new names (Uum Qasr, Khafji, Tornado IDS), and I pay more attention to what's going on than I did a few weeks ago. It's more interesting—let's face it. The old stuff is coming back, too. This morning in my office, I overheard a young colleague of mine talking on the phone—talking about the war. "They said it was more than seven hundred missions," she said, and walking past her, I murmured, "Sorties, sorties." She'll learn.

The New Yorker *January 28, 1991*

JONATHAN SCHELL
Modern Might, Ancient Arrogance

After four weeks of devastating U.S. air attacks, author and Newsday *columnist Jonathan Schell suggested that the fighting in the Persian Gulf war violated even the "rough justice" of wartime.*

A number of senators, among others, have recently voiced the fear that if the United States launches a ground war against Iraq, there may be heavy American casualties, and that, if this happens, public support for the war may erode. It's a fear that raises the question of what the public's "support," if it did not include the expectation of casualties, consisted of in the first place. Did we really support *war*, or only some illusion of what war is? . . .

Our apparent feeling of invulnerability is a singular feature of this conflict. A good deal has been said about whether the American war effort is just. The debate has hinged on the question of whether the end we are pursuing can justify the means we employ. But justice, it seems to me, also enters into our thoughts and feelings about war in ways that have little to do with any calculus of means and ends. It has never been obvious why, in most times and places, killing in war has been found acceptable whereas killing in peacetime is condemned as murder. One reason, I suspect, has been that, in war, those going out to kill had to risk death. Soldiers killed only those who were ready and able to kill them, and in this seemingly irreducible reality there was a certain justice. The soldier won his right to kill, you might say, with his willingness to sacrifice his own life.

This rough justice, rooted in the nature of war itself, had little to do with peacetime justice, whether conceived in terms of Roman law or Hebrew commandments, and still less to do with Christian compassion. It was decreed by no human power, but by human powerlessness in the face of swords or bullets or bombs. If it can be associated with any civilization, it is probably with that of the ancient Greeks, who named human beings "the mortals" and found a basis for our common humanity in our ultimate subjection to our fate, whose greatest fact is death.

To everyone's surprise, the war in the Persian Gulf lacks this simple equality in the face of death of the opposing armies. We Americans, with our complete mastery of the air, wage war in three dimensions against a foe trapped, like the creatures in certain geometrical games, in two dimensions. The result is that the killing and the dying have come apart. In this war so far and for the most part, we kill and they die, as if a race of gods were making war against a race of human beings.

Now we face a new round of decisions: whether to launch a ground war, whether to kill Saddam Hussein, and even whether, in certain circumstances, to use nuclear weapons. The danger is that, intoxicated by our thoroughly modern technical superiority, we will be tempted into a thoroughly ancient arrogance. Do we imagine that we belong to a different species from our foes? Has it escaped us that the things we do to others may one day be done to us? Have we forgotten, as we send our lethal machines over a foreign land, that we, too, can die?

Newsday *February 12, 1991*

COL. WILLIAM DARRYL HENDERSON
How Army is Marketing the Gulf War to "Soft" Public

As the ground war approached, public support for the U.S. actions in the Gulf remained high. According to retired Army Colonel William Darryl Henderson, this support demonstrated the American military's successful employment of marketing techniques in "packaging its agenda for public consumption."

Eight years ago the U.S. Army began sending key officers to classes on ways of marketing commercial products. They brought this knowledge back and used it on Congress, the White House, the public. Now they are using it in their tightly controlled press briefings in Saudi Arabia and at the Pentagon to maintain public support for the Gulf war.

The military knows, as a hard lesson learned from the Vietnam War, that continuous public support is essential to seeing its strategy through to completion. Many top-ranking U.S. officers believe that the American public is soft and does not have the stomach for the dark side of war. They believe pictures of killed and maimed soldiers and descriptions of the tragedies of the battlefield—as well as the many snafus that occur—will erode support.

This can be avoided if the press is harnessed and sold the Army view of the war—and selling the press has become standard procedure in the Army.

The Army's interest in commercial marketing techniques dates to the early 1980s and the creation of the all-volunteer army through major advertising campaigns and other marketing techniques.

The military, especially the Army, has come to rely heavily on such techniques in packaging its agenda for public consumption.

High-level staffs attend seminars on how to market programs and objectives. Staff officers are sent to civilian marketing courses. Failures of Army programs are often described as marketing failures. Repeatedly, officers are urged to be upbeat, to characterize a situation as the glass that is half full, not half empty. The result has been a marvelous public relations success over the past several years.

Good news is heavily marketed. Bad news is buried; it doesn't sell well.

Bad news is managed in three basic ways:

- By restricting access to it.
- By presenting it as an isolated incident to be expected in the fog of war.

• By allowing it to dribble out in a controlled seepage over a number of days or weeks in order to avoid one big story with major negative impact.

Bad news can't always be restricted and controlled—especially if low-ranking soldiers become aware of it. They will almost always tell, especially if the press has access to their units. But current press pool rules in the Gulf cut off the press and public from these soldiers.

The recent U.S. casualties resulting from "friendly fire" provide an example of managing bad news.

The deaths of the Marines were presented as "inevitable" in the confusion of war. We were cautioned not to overreact because little could be done to control such incidents.

This is nonsense. Most casualties from friendly fire result from sloppy work, especially when our troops are bombed by U.S. aircraft. Invariably in Vietnam such accidents were traced to human error, often resulting from strangers working together without adequate training. They didn't have to happen.

Sometimes, when the marketing effort makes unsupportable claims or it is realized that bad news will become apparent and contradict prior marketing efforts, the bad news is allowed to leak out over time. Usually the public doesn't realize what is happening. The favorable first impression is made by the good, but false, news—and it tends to stick.

Recent reports on the "continuing successful air war" cited the great precision and effectiveness of the air strikes by enthusiastically stating that one typical mission dropped 24 bombs and left the target area with 25 Iraqi tanks burning. Two days later it was briefly mentioned that the Iraqis were deceiving U.S. pilots by lighting oil pot fires next to their tanks.

During the first two days of war, when the marketing effort was in high gear, briefings from the Gulf and the Pentagon depicted high-tech war at its most benign. Gee-whiz videos showed smart bombs surgically on target. The dangerous Republican Guards were largely destroyed, according to information passed to the most visible Pentagon reporter, Wolf Blitzer of CNN.

There was no bad news. U.S. public reaction was as expected. Support for the war rose almost overnight, from 47 to 80 percent.

A few days later the bad news that couldn't be restricted and forgotten started to dribble out. The Pentagon mentioned that the Iraqis were using decoys. Israel was hit by Scud missiles from launchers that had reportedly been destroyed.

It was briefly acknowledged that allied air forces spent a large part of the first two days bombing plywood missile launchers. By this time, however, the Patriot missile was being marketed and the previous good, but false news that turned into bad news was displaced.

Similar news management was used to diffuse bad news about the Republican Guards. After initial Pentagon claims to Blitzer that the guards had been "decimated," the bad news began to leak out. First, there was only a comment that the Iraqis were using decoys. Then it was announced that the Republican Guard was being targeted for air strikes, with no retraction of prior reports that it had been decimated.

Finally, in preparation for the ground war, the bad news was released that again the Air Force had spent days bombing plywood tanks.

Three weeks into the war, public support remains strong, at about 78 percent. Much of the credit for this must go to Army and Pentagon good-news marketing efforts.

The San Francisco Examiner *February 10, 1991*

DAVID ALBRIGHT AND MARK HIBBS
Hyping the Iraqi Bomb

One means of "marketing" U.S. policy in the Gulf was to emphasize the danger posed by Iraq's purported nuclear capability. But early in the conflict, analysts David Albright and Mark Hibbs wrote that the Bush administration, experts, and the media had "escalated Iraq's nuclear threat." Their evidence would remain relevant when the issue resurfaced months after the war's end.

Credible estimates of the amount of time Iraq needs to produce weapon-grade uranium range between five and ten years—just about where they were when Saddam Hussein invaded Kuwait on August 2. But that message was distorted for a few weeks in late 1990, while the United States prepared for war.

On November 22, President George Bush told U.S. troops in Saudi Arabia that Iraq was a lot closer to possession of nuclear weapons. "Those who would measure the timetable for Saddam's atomic program in years may be seriously underestimating the reality of that situation and the gravity of the threat," Bush said.

By the New Year, Iraq's nuclear threat had receded. "How soon will Saddam get the bomb?" the title of a *Time* article asked in mid-December. "Not nearly so soon as the Bush Administration claims," it prudently concluded.

The administration was not the only source of the exaggerated claims, however. As the United States prepared to go to war with Iraq, the interests of the administration, some nonproliferation experts, and media feature editors coalesced. Together they escalated Iraq's nuclear threat on the basis of sketchy and sometimes bad or incomplete information.

During the late 1980s Iraq's ongoing effort to make nuclear weapons made only sporadic headlines. On the eve of a visit to the United States by Israeli Premier Yitzhak Shamir in April 1988, the *Washington Post* asserted that Iraq had a secret two-year crash program to develop a nuclear weapon, financed by Saudi Arabia. Two years later, an internationally coordinated sting operation exposed an Iraqi attempt to acquire detonator components usable in nuclear weapons [see the preceding article]. Neither event prompted a significant reassessment of the timetable for an Iraqi nuclear weapon. "Too much important know-how and technology was missing," according to an official at the U.S. Arms Control and Disarmament Agency.

Another strain of the story focused on Iraq's effort to develop centrifuges to enrich uranium for use in weapons. Before the invasion, *Der Spiegel*, followed by U.S. nonproliferation and export control experts, asserted that machine tools acquired by Iraq from Germany could be used to make centrifuges. But no one who made these claims pointed out the difference between making centrifuges and making some centrifuge components. That distinction "could make a difference of about five years" in Iraq's enrichment timetable, according to an official at Urenco, the European trilateral centrifuge manufacturer and operator whose plans were diverted to Iraq.

It was also said that Iraq had working centrifuges. Based on unspecified sources, William Safire asserted in a series of five articles in the *New York Times* between August and November that Iraq was enriching uranium with 26 centrifuges on hand and was producing a lot more centrifuges. "With the first few thousand off the line, a 'cascade' can be set up to separate U-235 from uranium in a gaseous state. Each cascade can turn out 50 pounds of weapons-grade uranium—enough for a city-destroying atom bomb—every three months."

U.S. officials who watch Iraq's nuclear program say they have never seen any intelligence documents indicating that Iraq has 26 working centrifuges, or any at all. They assume the story was launched by Israeli officials and backed by officials at the U.S. Defense Intelligence Agency who have an interest in motivating the United States to strike Iraqi targets.

If reports that Iraq has working centrifuges are true, the credibility of assertions that Iraq had indeed been making fast progress would be enhanced. But statements from Bruno Stemmler, a German centrifuge engineer who saw the results of Iraq's centrifuge development program in 1988, indicate they are far off the mark. U.S. officials say the Stemmler report is consistent with technical intelligence on Iraq's centrifuge program. The report is also consistent with recent statements by South African centrifuge engineers about the development timetable for their own indigenous and, until now, clandestine centrifuge effort. . . .

By mid-November, U.S. troops were languishing in Saudi Arabia, diplomatic initiatives were getting nowhere, and domestic support for Operation Desert Shield was slipping. A November 20 CBS/*New York Times* poll concluded that a majority of Americans would not go to war in the Gulf to protect access to Middle East oil, but would support a military effort to prevent Iraq from getting the bomb. A few days later President Bush asserted that Iraq might be months away from nuclear weapons.

On November 24, 1990, just two days after Bush sounded the alarm, National Security Advisor Brent Scowcroft and Defense Secretary Dick Cheney clarified that there was, in fact, no new evidence prompting an escalation of the Iraqi nuclear threat. Statements by Bush were instead based on a "worst-case assessment" which assumed that Saddam would try to build a bomb in a hurry using the small quantity of highly enriched uranium Iraq had pledged to use for peaceful purposes under the Nuclear Non-Proliferation Treaty (NPT). The uranium had recently been reinspected the International Atomic Energy Agency (IAEA).

It didn't matter. For two reasons the message took weeks to sink in.

The first is what one U.S. government nuclear official called an "emerging war psychology" which took hold in some administration circles as the Gulf crisis unfolded. "As long as significant interests are backing a war effort here," he said, "nagging questions about Iraq's real nuclear capabilities just won't be heard."

In testimony before the Senate Armed Services Committee on November 30, William R. Graham, a defense consultant, turned the tables on those who would challenge Gulf hawks to show evidence that Iraq was close to possessing nuclear weapons. "Instead of asking for proof beyond a shadow of a doubt that Iraq has completed all the design, engineering, and non-nuclear testing work required to create a weapon," Graham said, "we would ask ourselves this question: Why wouldn't Iraq, under Saddam Hussein, have done these things?"

Few were asking if Iraq *could* do them, and those who did found the burden of proof on their shoulders. Safire insinuated that those who wanted to see evidence were part of a "burgeoning appeasement movement" which was threatening the president's showdown in the Gulf.

The second reason it took so long to put Iraq's potential nuclear threat into perspective was the surfeit of half-truths, unsourced assertions reported as facts, rumors, and just plain errors which already filled press clipping files. Bush's November warning was front-page news, and a flurry of articles, drawing these files, followed into mid-December.

One *Newsweek* reporter was put onto the story "when our senior editors made the connection between the White House and the media poll which shows America will buy the message." A skeptical reporter at a major U.S. daily said in late November he had "serious doubts" about the administration's case. But because editorial writers had made the "Saddam bomb" a personal crusade, the reporter said, "I'm not about to get involved until I find out from upstairs what our story line is."

Bulletin of the Atomic Scientists *March 1991*

YAHYA SADOWSKI
Power, Poverty, and Petrodollars

As critics debated the legacy of the Gulf war for America, its legacy for the countries of the Middle East seemed increasingly bleak. Brookings Institution analyst and Middle East Report *editor Yahya Sadowski offered a comprehensive analysis of the war's ominous consequences for the economy and stability of the region.*

The diversion of oil profits into the Gulf war and reconstruction (and away from development projects) is going to have a major impact on the economies of the Middle East for years to come. It is too soon to make hard predictions, but certain broad effects are already apparent.

Within the Gulf states themselves, the war has dealt a body blow to the one economic sector—apart from oil—which had shown potential: finance. In March 1990 Offshore Banking Units (OBUs) in Bahrain held $73.3 billion in deposits and seemed to be on the verge of recovering from the problems which had afflicted them in the 1980s. When Iraq invaded Kuwait, thousands of their depositors withdrew $13.7 billion in assets (21 percent) and sent them abroad. Local commercial banks lost 15 percent of their deposits. A similar run consumed 11 percent of Saudi bank deposits, and in the UAE withdrawals rose to 25 percent of liabilities. Kuwaiti banks ceased operations entirely. Iraq looted KD 365 million in securities and $800 million in gold which had been deposited with the central bank of Kuwait.

Rapid government intervention prevented any of these banks from going bankrupt, but this cannot brighten the prospects for the region's financial system. The rapid rise of military spending by Gulf governments makes it clear there will be no "excess funds." Indeed, local regimes began to pare back their normal menu of investment projects, leaving an even smaller scope for banking operations. Japanese and Western financiers are reluctant to deal with Gulf banks, arguing that political uncertainties and shrunken assets make them unreliable partners. No one expects a collapse of Gulf financial institutions, but bankers themselves foresee a period of retrenchment in which larger and more solvent firms will swallow their competitors—and the survivors adopt more conservative and modest lending policies.

The Gulf banks had been one of the major channels through which petrodollars had percolated from the Gulf into the rest of the Arab world. Aid from the oil-rich countries to their poorer neighbors had been declining throughout the 1980s. As the Gulf states divert their revenues to meeting war and reconstruction costs, aid will probably become even less available. Aid to states which appeared sympathetic to Iraq was suspended almost immediately. Saudi Arabia and Kuwait completely halted their contributions to the Palestine Liberation Organization, which had been running over $100 million per year. Jordan, too, quickly lost the $300 million in aid it had been receiving annually from Iraq and Kuwait, and now Riyadh also has cut its support, suspending concessionary oil shipments to Amman (worth $1 million per day and representing half of Jordan's consumption). It also suspended economic aid to Amman, which had totalled $200 million annually and supplied 15 percent of the state budget.

Restricting aid to the Palestinians and Jordan freed up monies which the Saudis could then reallocate to countries which supported the kingdom in the Gulf conflict—chiefly Egypt, Syria, and Morocco. A similar change, benefitting Saudi allies while punishing "unfriendly" states, was evident in the most important single mechanism for redistributing petrodollars: labor migration. Before the crisis, all of the oil-rich Gulf states had employed large numbers of expatriate—largely Arab—workers who provided professional services (teachers, doctors, lawyers, engineers) performed manual labor (construction, agriculture) which local citizens either could not or would not. Remittances formed a major source of hard currency for their home countries. The invasion of Kuwait massively disrupted this system. Half of the Palestinians and most of the Jordanians who were working in Kuwait fled the country after August 2, and those who remained could not get money out. The Palestinians of the West Bank lost access to $100 million a year. In Jordan, half of the $800 million Amman derived from remittances each year came from workers in Kuwait.

These disruptions were compounded when Qatar and other Gulf states began to restrict the entry of Palestinian workers, widely suspected of pro-Iraqi sympathies. In September, Saudi Arabia punished Yemen for its neutral policy on the war by requiring Yemeni workers in the kingdom to find Saudi sponsors or face expulsion. By November 700,000 had already returned to Yemen and another 30,000 were leaving Saudi Arabia every day. This put an end to $1-2 billion a year in remittances, a loss of 20 percent of the country's foreign currency receipts. (Saudi,Iraqi and Kuwaiti economic aid to Yemen also ended.)

The interruption of workers' remittances also hit Egypt hard. At the beginning of 1990, some 150,000 Egyptians had been working in Kuwait and another million in Iraq. After Iraq invaded Kuwait, over 400,000 Egyptians fled these countries, costing Egypt an estimated $1.1 billion in annual hard currency revenues. Saudi Arabia supplied

Cairo with aid to assist in relocating refugees and issued some 684,000 work visas to Egyptians by early 1991.

The substitution of Egyptian workers for Jordanians, Palestinians in Saudi Arabia and Kuwait will reinforce the same pattern evident in the reallocation of aid from those two states. Egypt and Syria may enjoy some relief from the economic constraints which had plagued them in the 1980s. Jordan,Yemen and Sudan, which the Saudis felt had shown too much sympathy for Baghdad, will find their economic problems enormously aggravated.

This does not bode well for any "new economic order" in the Middle East. The Gulf war has made the region as a whole much poorer than it was in 1989, and the inequalities between the "have and have-not" states are likely to become even more pronounced. The growth of poverty and income disparities will translate into popular resentment and sooner or later will fuel political conflict. Instead of a "new order," the future probably holds a return to "the Arab cold war."

Middle East Report *May/June 1991*

WILLIAM M. ARKIN
The Gulf "Hyperwar" —An Interim Tally

As Greenpeace's William Arkin reported, the war's "human toll" on the region was both "shocking" and largely invisible. Months after the war ended, statistics were just beginning to filter out of Iraq—and while the body count for allied forces was mercifully low, Iraqi casualties numbered in the hundreds of thousands.

Will America ever face up to the true impact of the Gulf war? For the last three months, we've conveniently avoided considering the war's effects on the people of Iraq, as well as on the environment.

A war that took 268 American lives and has earned a reputation for being clean, smart and humane, was perhaps the most efficient killing campaign in military history, one in which, according to U.S. and international military and relief specialists, some 200,000 Iraqi citizens have already died. A Harvard study team predicts that those figures will double before the end of the year because of disease and malnutrition.

Though a cease-fire was declared on Feb. 28, the environmental devastation continues. At least 450 oil well fires are burning out of control, and even the most optimistic predictions are that they will rage for at least two more years. Lakes of crude oil, gushing from uncapped wells, are oozing out over the desert. Oil from spills is washing up onto hundreds of miles of Kuwaiti and Saudi shoreline.

But it is the human toll that is the most shocking, particularly the military coalition's low casualties. The most accurate estimates are that 100,000 to 120,000 Iraqi military personnel were killed in the war. From 74,000 to 101,000 Iraqi civilians have died since August —from disease, malnutrition, civil war and, of course, the conflict. Five thousand to 15,000 civilians died in the air war. Significantly, it is estimated that 80 percent to 90 percent of the civilian deaths occurred *after* the cease fire.

Today, there are still more than two million Kurdish and Shiite refugees in the region. The war's effects outside the gulf are significant, too. At least 2.5 million foreign workers residing in Iraq and Kuwait returned to such financially strapped countries as Egypt, Jordan and Bangladesh.

Some in the U.S. military dubbed the Gulf war "hyperwar" because of its unprecedented intensity. Lest we forget, more Iraqi soldiers died in the conflict's 43 days than in the entire eight-year Iran-Iraq war.

Iraq's million-member military was immobilized. The largest allied air force brought together since the Second World War flew more attack missions in a single day than Iranian aircraft flew against Iraq in the entire Iran-Iraq war.

The situation in the region is horrific. But worse still is its growing invisibility. Saddam Hussein, in power and claiming victory, has little interest in letting the rest of the world know the extent of the disaster he precipitated.

The U.S. has particularly gone out of its way not to document war's human cost and has censored information about the environmental damage. Just two weeks ago, William Reilly, the director of the Environmental Protection Agency, returned from Kuwait concluding that conditions were not so bad as "first predicted." He said this despite a May 23 letter from the Kuwaiti Government to the United Nations Secretary General, Javier Pérez de Cuéllar, stating that the environmental damage "has seriously been affecting human health, and the flora and fauna."

The Gulf war may have been the most efficient military campaign in modern history. But it also left a human catastrophe and unprecedented environmental destruction. This is the legacy of "hyperwar." Now that Washington and New York have had their parades, perhaps we should redirect our attention toward the Gulf and remind ourselves of the unavoidable tragedy that accompanies any war.

The New York Times *June 22, 1991*

REND FRANCKE
How to Help Iraq's Innocents

Iraqi American Rend Francke mourned the war's horrible legacy of disease and starvation among innocent Iraqi civilians—more than half of whom were children under fifteen—and challenged the U.S. government to take steps to end their suffering.

We Iraqi Americans have reached the point of despair. It was bad enough to watch in distress as the bombs dropped on the cities day after day. It was worse to find that, after the destruction, the Iraqi regime was allowed to hang on and mow down the insurgents across the country. But the greatest anguish is being endured now, as Iraqi Americans watch the governments of the United States and the allies listen to multiplying reports of hunger and disease with seeming passivity and indifference.

The shortages of food and medicine in Iraq are at catastrophic levels. Children are dying daily from malnutrition, malnourishment and the absence of basic medical care and such common drugs as antibiotics. In addition to cholera, typhoid and gastroenteritis, previously unknown diseases in Iraq such as kwashiorkor and marasmus are killing children.

The reports of the Harvard Medical Group and of the team from the Arab American Medical Association, and the recent report by a U.N. commission, attest to the appalling health conditions in Iraq. A report just released by John O. Field and Robert M. Russell of Tufts University states that children in the south suffer from "chronic malnutrition" caused by the "government's long history of indifference to the Shiites in the south."

It is the irony of the Gulf war that the Iraqi governing elite who brought on this calamity have been hurt least by the aftermath of the war, while the people of Iraq, with whom the U.S. administration "has no quarrel," the ones suffering and dying of the consequences.

The Iraqi people are being severely punished for the sins of a despotic regime. Yet the Iraqi government is not the only one responsible for their misery. The United States and the allies bear a measure of responsibility: Having inflicted severe damage to the economy of Iraq, they then failed to do the one thing capable of helping the people—dismantling the regime that has involved Iraq in senseless warfare for the last 10 years.

It is time for the allies to help Iraqis. The population needs humanitarian relief on a massive scale. Not the small amounts of a few million dollars here and there through relief organizations, but an internationally concerted effort worth hundreds of millions of dollars.

Where should the money come from?

The Iraqi government and its supporters have repeatedly asked for an easing of sanctions. This week the United Nations is due to debate a request from Iraq to export $1.5 billion worth of oil for the purchase by the government of food and medicine. The U.S. administration is also considering such a proposal. Given the recommendations of Prince Sadruddin and the urging of other advocates, the United Nations may approve the partial easing of sanctions. In spite of the repeatedly declared determination of the United States and Britain not to ease sanctions, the weather vane may be shifting.

But it would be a further crime against the people of Iraq to remove sanctions while this regime is still in power. Should the Iraqi government get its hands on $1.5 billion, the beneficiaries would not be the sick and dying children of Iraq, or those that suffer from chronic malnourishment through government neglect. A government that is even now relying on lies and deceit in its relations with the world community, and on brutal suppression and executions for its domestic control, is unlikely to spend its hard-won cash on humanitarian relief. Instead the funds would be used principally to replenish the military arsenals of the regime, to satisfy the rapacity of sycophants in the inner clique and to bestow favors on the loyal Republican Guard.

Meanwhile, Iraq has an estimated $8 billion in frozen assets in U.S. and other Western banks. This money belongs to the people and should be used to alleviate the suffering of the people. It is now incumbent on the United States and its allies to use these frozen assets to help the real victims and losers of the war.

The Washington Post *July 24, 1991*

KENNETH ROTH
Mass Graves in Kuwait

The conflict's legacy for human rights in the Gulf states was terrible as well. According to Human Rights Watch deputy director Kenneth Roth, the aftermath of the war in "liberated" Kuwait brought a "cycle of violence and recrimination" in which unknown numbers of residents were being tortured or killed.

On the southern outskirts of Kuwait City, al-Riqqa cemetery guards the dark underside of Kuwait's liberation. In a corner is a section marked "collective graves." Here lie many victims of Kuwait's ordeal —not only those felled by Iraq's secret police but also those who have died at Kuwaiti hands since liberation.

Twenty-four of the graves appear to date from the Iraqi occupation, judging from the height of the weeds and the dates posted on several makeshift markers. The remaining 20 mass graves, their earth freshly turned, appear to have been dug more recently. Terrified grave diggers whispered to me that many of the bodies showed signs of unspeakable torture.

The registry book in a room in the grave diggers' compound provides clues about the newer graves. Some are filled with Iraqi victims: bodies held for burial until after liberation. But the book also records the burial of 54 "unidentified bodies" of people who appear to have died since March 6—a week after liberation. When the registry shows a cause of death, the victims are described as "killed," in contrast to "natural causes" cited elsewhere. As required, most of the bodies were first received at hospital morgues; this resulted in a paper trail. I was able to obtain documentation for two unidentified bodies received from Farwaniyya Hospital and buried March 19. A March 18 hospital memo reveals that the bodies of people who died March 12 and 13 were received from the Ardhiyya police station.

In one unusual entry in the grave diggers' registry book, an unidentified male buried May 30 was received not from a hospital but directly from the Sabah al-Salem police station. When I asked at the station about him, I was told variously that he was a drug addict and a car accident victim, but there was no plausible explanation of why the body was not first brought to a hospital morgue.

Interviews with three Palestinians and one Iraqi provided a glimpse of what might have happened. Arrested in mid-May and brought to the Sabah al-Salem police station, they were put through a routine so well orchestrated the officers had names for the torture chambers.

The youths said that after questioning—"How many Kuwaiti girls did you rape? How many Kuwaiti officers did you turn in to the Iraqis?"—they were led through what the police called the party room, barbecue room and drinking juice room. In each, they said, at least a dozen uniformed troops tortured them: beatings with sticks and poles; electric shocks and burns with cigarettes and heated rods, and forced drinking of what smelled like sewage water.

Who is responsible for the deaths of the 54 in al-Riqqa cemetery? That the killings appear to have occurred since March 6, after the first wave of private vengeance killings following liberation had largely subsided, suggests that organized forces are to blame. So might the large number of unidentified dead in a country where, since liberation, the proliferation of checkpoints makes leaving home without identity papers unthinkable.

A series of documented post-liberation killings of people in police and military custody substantiates this view. One Palestinian man arrested in early March and held in the military detention facility for one month told me of 11 prisoners killed by torture. I was able to confirm at least three other cases of Palestinians murdered in police or military custody.

In an important speech on May 26, Crown Prince Sheik Saad al-Abdallah acknowledged for the first time that prisoners were being mistreated, and vowed to prosecute those responsible. To fulfill this pledge, he should begin by ordering an investigation into the bodies at al-Riqqa cemetery.

Independent forensic scientists, accompanied by expert international observers, should exhume the graves to determine the cause of death. Hospital records should be examined to ascertain which bodies came from police stations or other detention facilities. Security officers found responsible for abuses should be arrested and vigorously prosecuted.

The mass graves at al-Riqqa cemetery clearly do not reflect the full extent of the killing in liberated Kuwait; some victims have been identified and given individual burials, while others may be buried elsewhere.

But the cemetery is a critical starting point for confronting the official violence that has left many non-Kuwaiti residents, particularly the Palestinian community, terrified.

As Kuwait rebuilds, a top priority should be the establishment of a system of accountability that would bring to justice those responsible for these abuses, allow victims' families to confirm the fate of their loved ones, and begin to stem the cycle of violence and recrimination that threatens to tear the nation apart.

The New York Times *June 11, 1991*

MICHAEL G. RENNER
Military Victory, Ecological Defeat

Among the most devastating legacies of the war was widespread environmental damage—much of it, according to the Worldwatch Institute's Michael Renner, predictable and preventable. The war's ecological impact received surprisingly little attention in the mainstream press, but Renner's comprehensive analysis assembled the latest information on the damage and its dire long-term consequences.

Military historians are likely to remember the recent Gulf War as a modern-day *blitzkrieg*, a triumph of "smart bombs" and other high-tech wizardry. However, while the fighting was brought to a swift conclusion, the onslaught against the environment continues with undiminished ferocity. The Gulf War now ranks among the most ecologically destructive conflicts ever. . . .

The disparity in response to the military and environmental aspects of the conflict could hardly be more pronounced. To force Iraq out of Kuwait, no expense or effort was spared. An alliance of more than two dozen countries was carefully crafted, the United Nations machinery for collective security was thrown into high gear, and hundreds of thousands of soldiers and huge amounts of equipment were ferried halfway around the globe.

By contrast, assessing and tackling the ecological consequences of the conflict has been a much lower priority. For example, the effort to contain and clean up the massive oil spill in the Gulf in February was hampered by lack of money and poor coordination among various Saudi government agencies. Attempts to monitor the impacts of oil fires and to put them out also seem woefully inadequate. An air-quality testing lab in Kuwait has not been repaired, and fire-fighting equipment has been slow in coming.,

The Gulf War demonstrates the need for the international community to set up a mechanism to cope with the ecological damage arising from armed conflicts. In a broader sense, though, it shows that wars and environmental protection are incompatible. Although international environmental-protection agreements are necessary, the most important step that can be taken is to work for peaceful means of resolving conflicts.

Kuwaiti officials estimate that as many as 6 million barrels of oil are going up in flames every day—almost four times the country's oil production per day prior to the Iraqi invasion, or 9 percent of the world's petroleum consumption. Some scientists, including Paul Mason of the British government's Meteorological Office, believe the volume of burning oil is smaller. Beyond dispute, however, is the fact that immense clouds of smoke block the sunlight and turn day into night. In April, daytime temperatures in affected areas were as much as 27 degrees Fahrenheit below normal. . . .

Experts estimate that it will take at least two years to extinguish all of the blazes. By that time, Kuwait may have lost as much as 10 percent of its 92 billion barrels of proven oil reserves—either through combustion or structural damage to its oil reservoirs.

The atmospheric pollution resulting from these fires is almost unprecedented, comparable only to large-scale forest fires and volcanic eruptions. Assuming a burn rate of 6 million barrels per day, as much 2.5 million tons of soot may be produced in a month—more than four times the average monthly emissions in the entire United States in 1989 (the last year for which data are available). In addition, more than 1 million tons of sulfur dioxide and approximately 100,000 tons of nitrogen oxides may be released each month.

The clouds of oil smoke also contain large amounts of toxic and potentially carcinogenic substances such as hydrogen sulfide, benzene, and other hydrocarbons. Overall, according to a U.S. Environmental Protection Agency (EPA) estimate in March, roughly 10 times as much air pollution was being emitted in Kuwait as by all U.S. industrial and power-generating plants combined.

The stew of contaminants makes breathing a hazardous undertaking. Rare is the news story about postwar Kuwait that does not mention the sore throat from which virtually everyone seems to suffer. Kuwaiti hospitals are filled with people fallen ill from exposure to the air pollution, and doctors advise those with chronic respiratory problems not to return to Kuwait. Although considerable uncertainty persists concerning the long-term toll on human health, many air pollutants are thought to cause or aggravate a wide range of conditions, including blood disorders, respiratory problems such as asthma and bronchitis, coronary ailments, cancer, and possibly genetic damage. Scientists now acknowledge that prolonged exposure to even low levels of smog—the product of reactions between nitrogen oxides and hydrocarbons in the presence of sunlight—may cause irreparable lung damage. Young children and the elderly are particularly at risk.

Because Kuwaiti oil has a high sulfur content, acid rain—of which sulfur dioxide is a principal component—is expected to afflict the Gulf region and adjacent areas. Acid deposition (which does not always require rain) is known to destroy forests and reduce crop yields. It can also activate several dangerous metals normally found in soil—including aluminum, cadmium, and mercury—making them more soluble and therefore more of a threat to water supplies and edible fish. "Black rain"—soot that is washed out of the skies or eventually falls back to the ground—is coating people, animals, buildings, and crops with an oily, black film. . . .

The densest smoke is found over Kuwait, eastern Iraq, and western and southern Iran. In Kuwait, scientists with the British Meteorological Office recorded 30,000 soot particles per cubic meter of air, 1,000 parts per billion of sulfur dioxide and 50 parts per billion of nitrogen oxides at an altitude of 6,000 feet—about 30, 20, and 10 times, respectively, the levels in a typical city plagued by air pollution.

As far as 1,000 miles away—in parts of Bulgaria, Romania, Turkey, and the Soviet Union that border on the Black Sea—smog levels caused by the oil fires are as serious as the smog found anywhere in Europe under normal conditions, according to Paul Mason. A much larger area—from the waters of the Nile to the snows of the Himalayas—is susceptible to acid rain and soot fallout, according to the Max Planck Institute for Meteorology in Hamburg, Germany.

The burning of such large amounts of oil over long periods could generate enough soot and smoke to diminish solar radiation, thereby lowering daytime temperatures and reducing the amount of rainfall. One ounce of soot can block about two-thirds of the light falling over an area of 280 to 340 square yards. In Kuwait, the amount of solar energy reaching the ground is at times reduced by more than 90 percent. Reduced photosynthesis combined with the deposition of soot and other toxic materials could imperil crops.

Whether such an effect would extend beyond the Gulf region depends on how high the soot climbs and how long it remains there. . . . By early May, the U.S. National Oceanic and Atmospheric Administration (NOAA) reported that soot levels at about 20 times above normal readings were recorded at the Mauna Loa observatory in Hawaii. Presumably, the Kuwaiti oil fires, some 8,000 miles away, are the source of the soot. Despite the elevated soot levels, NOAA does not expect any "significant" environmental impact in North America.

At the same time that it is potentially causing a short-term cooling, the Kuwaiti oil conflagration is also contributing to the long-term phenomenon of global warming. It may add as much as 240 million tons of carbon to the atmosphere in the course of a year—about 4 percent of the current global annual carbon release. This is comparable to the amount produced by Japan, the world's second-largest economy and fourth-largest emitter of carbon dioxide from fossil fuels. Since carbon emissions need to be slashed by at least 20 percent by the year 2005 just to slow climate change, the Kuwaiti oil fires send us another step in the wrong direction.

Nothing in human experience could help model and predict the precise consequences of the Kuwaiti oil blaze. The Gulf region thus has become a huge air pollution laboratory. Unfortunately, the subjects of these dangerous pollution experiments are people,plants, and animals.

The oil spilled into the Gulf waters is posing a severe test for marine ecosystems. Estimated at more than 3 million barrels by the Saudi Meteorology and Environmental Protection Administration, the Persian Gulf oil spill roughly equals the largest in history—the Ixtoc well blowout in the Gulf of Mexico in 1979—and is 10 times the size of the Exxon Valdez accident.

Following spills during the eight-year Iran-Iraq war, the Persian Gulf was already a highly stressed environment in poor condition to withstand additional ecological assaults. A relatively shallow sea, it is essentially a closed ecosystem with only a narrow outlet to the Arabian Sea through the Strait of Hormuz. . . .

Considerable harm to Gulf fish and other wildlife—including the porpoises, turtles, and seabirds—seems inevitable since many nesting and spawning grounds have been saoked in oil. At least 14,000 birds were killed along the Saudi shore. Some areas are so contaminated that they had to be declared off-limits to fishing, threatening the livelihoods of commercial and subsistence fishers. The Saudi shrimp industry, for example, has been wiped out and is considered unlikely to recover before the end of the decade. Extensive damage to coral reefs and sea grasses also has occurred, according to the EPA. If large quantities of plankton are killed, the entire ecosystem may be threatened.

The presence of more than 1 million soldiers with their immense arsenals has placed severe strains on the already fragile desert ecology of Kuwait, Saudi Arabia, and Iraq. Normally inhabited only by Bedouins, the desert of the Arabian peninsula cannot bear such a massive burden. Desert vegetation is sparse, but it helps to stabilize and protect the soil. Tanks and other vehicles have disrupted and compacted the soil and destroyed plants whose root systems are often close to the surface. As a result, the ground in many areas has been rendered susceptible to accelerated erosion. Seeds that lie dormant for large parts of the year, but which spark to life during spring rains, were likely affected.

If a significant portion of the desert vegetation is destroyed, dry spells might be lengthened and the ecological balance could be tipped into long-term decline. It may take hundreds of years for the desert to recover from the massive pre-war maneuvers and the tank battles, according to John Cloudsley-Thompson, an expert on desert ecology at the University of London. The Libyan desert, for example, still bears heavy scars from World War II combat, as do portions of the Negev in Israel from fighting in 1967 and 1973, and parts of the Mojave in southern California from maneuvers in the early 1940s.

The military presence has additional consequences. The armed forces routinely handle massive amounts of highly toxic materials to maintain and operate their tanks, jet fighters, and other pieces of equipment. Experience on U.S. military bases suggests that these substances could severely contaminate underground water supplies if they're not properly handled. The inhospitable Saudi environment, with its blistering heat and gritty sand, forced the allied troops to use special lubricants of a more toxic nature, according to the U.S. Congressional Research Service, and generally larger amounts of hazardous materials than in more moderate climates. Exposure to even trace amounts of these chemicals through drinking, skin absorption, or inhalation can cause cancer, birth defects, and chromosome damage, and may seriously impair the function of the liver, kidneys, and central nervous system.

The veil of military secrecy and post-war chaos in Iraq have precluded a full assessment of the effects of allied air attacks on Iraq's chemical, biological, and nuclear facilities and its refineries and petrochemical plants. Many of these facilities are located close to civilian population centers along the Tigris and Euphrates rivers. The incineration of materials produced and stored at these installations may well have generated a variety of deadly toxins, including cyanide, dioxin, and PCBs. . . .

Sadly, the environmental disaster in the Gulf was preventable. In the months leading up to the outbreak of armed conflict, the alternatives of resorting to military force or relying on economic sanctions were debated, but the latter option was given too little time to work. Sanctions may have been less swift and certain than force, but would likely have spared many lives and avoided the tragic environmental effects.

That Saddam Hussein would set the torch to Kuwait's oil wells was no secret; he repeatedly threatened to do so if attacked by the U.S.-lead coalition. The U.S. and British governments even commissioned studies about the potential impact of such an act, but proceeded with their military plans anyway. The responsibility for the environmental destruction lies with Saddam Hussein's regime, but the devastation was either underestimated by the allied governments or considered an acceptable price of victory.

With such results, it is difficult to distinguish between victor and vanquished. Indeed, the war's ecological impact extends far beyond the battlefield, blurring the distinction between the combatants and countries that were not party to the conflict and had no say over its course.

In light of the Gulf War's ecological devastation, the time has come for the world community to consider creating a stronger convention for the protection of the environment in war. . . .

But even a strengthened international code is of limited value. The conduct of war and the protection of the natural environment are fundamentally incompatible objectives. War on the environment is, unfortunately, nothing new. From the Punic Wars in the third century B.C. on, armies have poisoned wells, salted soils, and destroyed crops to foil the enemy. However, over time, the environmental impact of warfare has grown as sophisticated technology has boosted the firepower, range, and speed of weapons. In addition, modern industries present many high-profile targets whose destruction can wreak environmental devastation on a vast scale.

It was after the dawn of the atomic age that nations gradually came to realize that nuclear arsenals, if used, would destroy what they were supposed to defend. Now, in the wake of the Gulf War and its immense environmental toll, conventional warfare, too, may come to be seen as a less-acceptable means of settling conflicts.

World Watch *July/August 1991*

SYDNEY H. SCHANBERG
Censoring for Political Security

Newsday *columnist Sydney Schanberg, who had covered the war in Southeast Asia two decades earlier, denounced the Pentagon's unprecedented power to "control and manipulate press coverage" in the Persian Gulf. Schanberg believed that the government's "handcuffing of the press," was more a political ploy than a military precaution.*

"This will not be another Vietnam." That oft-repeated pledge by President Bush is his maxim for the war in the Persian Gulf. He and his men leave no doubt as to what it means, for they quickly explain that this time our troops will not have "their hands tied behind their backs." But there's an addendum to that promise which, though clear from the administration's acts, has not been spoken: "This time, the hands of the press will be tied."

So far, it would appear from polls and general reaction that a lot of Americans are not displeased by the government's handcuffing of the press. We journalists are not a very popular bunch. Some people see us as whiny and self-important, and some even see us as unpatriotic because we take it upon ourselves to challenge and question the government in difficult times like these. I can't say we haven't invited some of this disapproval through occasional lapses from professionalism. But I don't think this suggests we should hunker down timidly now and wait for our ratings to rise. We are required to be responsible, not popular.

Let's look at what the administration has done to control and manipulate press coverage of this war and why it has done it.

First, the why. This is easy. The answer is Vietnam. Many politicians and senior military men cling tenaciously to the myth that the press, through pessimistic reporting, tipped public opinion and cost us the war in Vietnam. There's no factual support for this theory, but scapegoats are useful when the historical evidence is painful. And that evidence suggests that a misguided and ill-conceived policy got America bogged down in a foreign war where the national interest was not fundamentally at stake. Eventually the public grew disheartened over the gap between the promises of success the White House kept making and the actuality of failure. Our losses, human and material, were what tipped public opinion.

This time around the White House isn't taking any chances. All reporters in the American portion of the Gulf war zone have to operate under a system of controls that goes far beyond anything imposed in any other modern war—unless you include Grenada and Panama, where reporters were essentially kept away from the action. Those were the dress rehearsals for the press muzzling in the Gulf—test runs, so to speak, to see if either the public or major news organizations would raise much of an outcry (they didn't).

The new controls go like this. To begin with, there is a list of security guidelines laying down the categories of sensitive military information (details of future operations, specifics on troop units, etc.) that the press cannot report because it might jeopardize American or allied lives. No reporter has any objection to these restrictions. They are essentially the same ground rules the press abided by in World War II, Korea and Vietnam.

It's what has been added to these traditional ground rules, however, that constitutes the muzzle. First, the only way a reporter can visit a front-line unit is by qualifying for the "pool" system, whereby a handful of reporters represents the entire press corps and shares the story with everybody. Only a fraction of the reporters, mostly those from the largest news organizations, can qualify for the pools. . . .

It gets worse. Though the pool reporters are allowed at the front, their visits are anything but spontaneous. The pools get taken only where the military decides to take them. They are accompanied at all times by an escort officer, even when interviewing troops, which means that truth and candor on the part of the interviewees often become instant casualties. When a pool gets back from its guided visit, all stories and footage must be submitted to a "security review" —a euphemism for censorship.

Of the two controls—the pool system and the review of stories for possible security violations—it is the former that is the more odious, for this is tantamount to prior restraint. If reporters can go only where their babysitters decide to take them and can stay only a short time, they have already been subjected to the ultimate censorship. . . .

The "security review" at the end of the pool process merely applies the final, harassing, delaying, cosmeticizing touches on the information and completes the subjugation of the press corps and, by extension, the public. In a typical incident, one of the censors had a problem with the word "giddy," the use of which he decided was a breach of military security. Fred Bruni of the *Detroit Free Press* had used the word to describe some young Stealth bomber pilots who were buoyant as they returned from their first combat mission. Without consulting Bruni, the censor changed "giddy" to "proud." No reality, please, not even when it's innocuous. When Bruni noticed the change, he protested and got the censor to accept "pumped up." Then the military, giving no reason, held the story for two days before sending it to the Detroit paper. . . .

With very rare exceptions, the press has never breached any of the security rules—not in World War II, not in Korea and not in Vietnam. Barry Zorthian, who was the official spokesman for the United States Mission in Saigon from 1964 to 1968, said recently that though roughly 2,000 correspondents were accredited to cover Vietnam in those years and hundreds of thousands of stories were filed, only five or six violations of the security guidelines occurred. He recalled most of these as accidental or based on misunderstanding. To his knowledge, he said, none of them actually jeopardized any military operations or the lives of personnel. . . .

So it's all too clear that the current restrictions have nothing to do with military security and everything to do with political security. Political security requires that the government do as complete a job as possible at blacking out stories that might lead to embarrassment or criticism of the government or to questions from ordinary Americans about the war policy. The press controls in the Gulf are preemptive strikes against the possibility of such stories coming from the front.

But the control and manipulation of information has done something else, too. It has debased the press. . . .

Privately, some government officials have tried to justify the restraints as a necessary counter-tactic against Saddam Hussein's strategy—i.e., his presumed belief that a prolonged war with steady casualties will erode public support of the president. But a president who is seen to be withholding information is also likely to lose public support over time. It may sound corny, but our democracy relies on openness for its strength. It's a messy system, often inefficient and clumsy, but it functions because the public is included, not kept in the dark. It's worth reminding ourselves that the most supremely efficient systems in the world are dictatorships where the press is completely controlled. . . .

As I write, more than 800 journalists have been accredited by the military in Saudi Arabia, roughly 80 percent of them Americans or working for American news organizations. Only about 125 have been allowed into the pools. The rest can do other reporting but are officially banned from the front lines. . . . Contrast this with World War II, when General Dwight Eisenhower issued a quite different order, directing all unit commanders of the Allied Expeditionary Force to give correspondents "the greatest possible latitude in the gathering of legitimate news." The order went on: "They should be allowed to talk freely with officers and enlisted personnel and to see the machinery of war in operation in order to visualize and transmit to the public the conditions under which the men from their countries are waging war against the enemy." Eisenhower's order went out on May 11, 1944, just before D-day. . . .

Also unlike World War II (and Korea and Vietnam), reporters are not being assigned to units and permitted to stay with them for extended periods. They're not even being allowed to fly on bombing missions in those planes where there is room. One such plane is the eight-engine B-52 Stratofortress. It flies in formations of three, each carrying roughly 30 tons of bombs. Such bombloads inflict a tremendous pounding over a wide area, and are usually directed at troop concentrations rather than buildings and installations. Military briefers in Vietnam called it carpet bombing, but the briefers in this war have bridled when reporters have used the phrase. Apparently carpet bombing has a harsh sound and must be deodorized.

In fact, there's a concerted attempt to try to edit out all reminders of Vietnam. It's hard to believe, but the Pentagon has gone so far as prohibiting the filming, or any news coverage at all, of the arrival of war dead at Dover Air Force Base, the main military mortuary. So much for the contention that the press restrictions are necessary for security reasons. . . .

This doesn't mean our politicians and generals are telling us a pack of lies. Not at all. They're just not telling us anything approaching a complete story. That's not their job as they perceive it. But it is the job of an independent press.

Which brings us, finally, to the issue of what the press has been doing for itself to try to reverse the new restraints. Darned little, sadly.

The break with this country's tradition of relatively open access to military operations began in Grenada in October 1983, when the Reagan White House kept the press out until the fighting was over. The major news organizations complained. To quiet us, the White House and Pentagon threw us a bone—the odious pool system. Oddly, we took it with barely a whimper. Then, on the first test of the system—the 1989 Panama invasion—pool reporters were barred from observing the military engagement all through the first and decisive day of fighting. The rest of the press corps, 500 strong, was virtually interned on a military base, even during the aftermath of the combat. As a result, we still have only the sketchiest picture of what took place and how many civilians and soldiers were killed.

And now we have our sanitized coverage of the war with Iraq. When the consequences of the press controls became obvious during the troop buildup prior to the war, a lawsuit was filed on January 10 in federal court in New York to overturn the restrictions on constitutional grounds. It was prepared by the Center for Constitutional Rights, an established civil liberties group, on behalf of 11 news organizations and five writers. The news organizations are for the most part small, liberal, alternative publications—*The Nation, In These*

Times, Mother Jones, L.A. Weekly, The Progressive,Texas Observer, The Guardian and *The Village Voice*—plus *Harper's,* Pacifica Radio, Pacific News Service and writers E.L. Doctorow, William Styron, Michael Klare, Scott Armstrong and myself. Agence France-Presse, the French news agency, having been excluded from the press pool, has filed a companion suit.

All the major media organizations were aware of the lawsuit before it was filed, yet as I write, not one has joined it. . . .

How to explain their inaction now? It's my belief that the press is still living with its own scars from Vietnam. And Watergate. We were accused, mostly by ideologues, of being less than patriotic, of bringing down a presidency, of therefore not being on the American team. And as a professional community we grew timid, worried about offending the political establishment. And that establishment, sensing we had gone under the blankets, moved in to tame us in a big and permanent way. These new press controls are, for me, a reflection of that move.

In late January CBS asked me to appear on "America Tonight" for a program on the press controls. Pete Williams, the Pentagon spokesman, agreed to appear opposite me, which created the potential for a good debate. Then the program's producer called. He said they had to disinvite me because Williams had called back to say the Pentagon's chief counsel had ruled that no Pentagon official could appear with anyone associated with the lawsuit. . . .

I see [the lawsuit] as a necessary instrument of leverage which seeks to persuade the government that the suppression of information, for reasons other than national security or protecting the safety of our troops, is a departure from our traditions that will in the end corrode and weaken the public trust that presidents crucially need to govern.

This is no time for the press to cover a desert war by putting its head in the sand.

The Washington Journalism Review *March 1991*

CHRIS HEDGES
The Unilaterals

Chris Hedges, a New York Times *correspondent in the Gulf, refused to play according to the Pentagon's rules. After the war was over, he described how he worked outside the system to avoid military censorship.*

On January 18, the day I arrived in Saudi Arabia, I was informed that the U.S. Armed Forces Joint Information Bureau had only one pool slot for *The New York Times.* This meant that I and three other *Times* reporters would have to sit through briefings in Riyadh, work the military for information, and rewrite pool reports that filtered in from the field.

This hardly seemed an auspicious way to cover a war, so the next morning, after receiving permission from R.W. Apple, Jr., who ran our coverage from Dhahran, I climbed into a jeep with several British reporters and headed for the border city of Khafji.

I would never return to work within the system. For two months several colleagues and I bluffed our way through roadblocks, slept in Arab homes, and cajoled ourselves into units. Eventually, following armored battalions in our jeeps through breached minefields to the outskirts of Kuwait City, we raced across the last stretch of open desert and into the capital before it was liberated. Our success was due in part to an understanding by many soldiers and officers of what the role of a free press is in a democracy. These men and women violated orders to allow us to do our job. . . .

I was able to spend several days, with the permission of officers, with units preparing for war. Troops in the field usually received the press warmly. Many had spent months in the desert and welcomed the chance to tell their stories. Most had little affection for the public relations officers.

I spent some time with one infantry battalion and got to know many of its officers and soldiers well. I brought them daily papers when I visited, and later I phoned messages to some of their families. When the battalion was ordered to move up to the Kuwaiti border, the commander painstakingly drew me a map so I could find the new position.

When I showed up one February morning, I was taken to the commander's foxhole.

"The order has come down that there is to be no unescorted press here," he began. My heart sank. "I won't tell you how I personally feel about this," he went on, then paused for a few moments and continued: "As far as I go, you are not here. You must park your car away from the camp. If other officers come in you must keep away, and if you get caught you were here because you were lost and were looking for directions." It was agreed that I would never quote him by name or identify his battalion.

By February the order had gone out that M.P.s were to detain all members of the press found north of Dhahran and to confiscate their credentials. So while at first we had been able to run roadblocks so long as we wore khaki dress, now more and more cars were being stopped. One soldier gave me a helmet, which helped immensely.

By working outside the pool, we could speak with soldiers without the presence of an escort. This did not always mean that we wrote stories that criticized the military, although people were more likely to speak openly if they thought their conversations were not being monitored. . . .

I stopped to talk to some officers who ran a field hospital, in the hope that I might be able to write a story about how nurses and doctors whiled away their time waiting for the ground war to begin. But by this time, although I didn't know it, reporters were not just to be turned away from units when they showed up, but arrested. The hospital officials assigned an armed escort to me and I was driven to the headquarters of the Seventh Corps, some ten miles away.

I was taken to the trailers that made up the press center and turned over to a Captain Miller. A few pool reporters were seated at a picnic table. The captain said I was under detention. When I protested, one of pool reporters told me to be quiet.

"You can't talk to him like that," he said. "They'll take away your credentials for good."

A captain, armed with an M-16, was placed in the front seat of my car and a lieutenant in a truck in front of me, and I was escorted to King Khaled Military City. At the end of the two-hour trip, I was turned over to a Captain Archie Davis, who confiscated my Saudi press card. He told me that the rules were for my own good, that he and the other officers were just trying to protect me from the hazards of war. "There are a lot of soldiers out there with pretty itchy trigger fingers," he said.

I was sent back to the Joint Information Bureau in Dhahran, an eight-hour drive, to retrieve the press card from a Major William Fellows. "You have an attitude problem," he told me. But he returned the card.

More than a dozen of us, labeled "the unilaterals" by the military press office, had now been detained by military police. We had to decide whether to risk expulsion or abide by the rules. The next day I left without an escort, violating the rules again. . . .

The ground war was now only days away, and the military police were frequently stopping cars along the road that ran east to west along the Kuwaiti and Iraqi border. By this time, I had my hair cut to military regulations, my jeep marked with the inverted "V" that was on all military vehicles, and a large orange cloth tied to the roof to identify it as part of the allied force. I carried canteens and even a knife, the gift of some marines. I was waved through check points.

By the time the attack was launched, the JIB had issued new regulation: no reporters were allowed to wear military dress, to use cellular phones to file stories, or to mark their vehicles. The new rules came a little late.

The Columbia Journalism Review *May/June 1991*

DOV S. ZAKHEIM
The Vietnam Syndrome is Buried in the Gulf

On the home front, the U.S. actions in the Gulf won high and lasting approval ratings from the public. If sales of American flags and yellow ribbons were any measure, Dov S. Zakheim, an undersecretary of defense under Reagan, spoke for the majority of Americans when he celebrated the end of the anti-interventionist legacy of Vietnam.

Not everyone is happy with the outcome of the war. One need not impugn their patriotism or suggest they were rooting for Iraq to say that many unreconstructed liberals regret the disappearance of the Vietnam syndrome—a reluctance to engage in any overseas military operations and to provide the wherewithal to do so.

Those who espouse "political correctness" must feel beleaguered when reading poll results that reflect President Bush's soaring popularity as well as hearty support for Operation Desert Storm. These liberals have overlooked a decade of increasing conservatism in the electorate's attitude toward the management of national security affairs—conservatism that presaged the exorcism of the Vietnam syndrome.

One of the most noteworthy features of the Reagan revolution was its appeal to young voters. They included members of the Woodstock generation, some of whom had never strongly opposed the Vietnam War, and others who abandoned ideological blinders on defense matters as they put college days behind them.

The Reagan Administration was hospitable to numerous officials who had not reached the age of 40 when they held senior national security policy positions. For them, the Vietnam syndrome already was anachronistic.

During the Reagan years, students began developing far more practical, less jaundiced views of national security issues than those held by many of their thirtysomething professors. Like all students at all times, they displayed a healthy skepticism about the wisdom of certain programs and policies. But unlike the preceding college generation, theirs balanced skepticism with a general sense of support for strong national defense.

Then, as now, many academics bore an old grudge against the Pentagon, no doubt largely nurtured by memories of their salad days in the antiwar movement. Their automatic conjuring of old scores and scars in response to new issues eerily reflected the authoritarian mind set they so vociferously said they opposed.

It is not surprising that they and others of a similar bent have had difficulty coming to terms with the Bush Administration's successful policies in the Gulf and the public's approval of those policies.

Overwhelming support for the Administration's management of the war effort has not merely been a matter of reflexive jingoism. The gulf war differed from the Vietnam War in fundamental ways.

First, for Africans, Saddam Hussein is a clear-cut "bad guy." While many applauded Ho Chi Minh as a nationalist leader who, even before the Americans arrived, had fought to liberate his homeland, no responsible American considers Mr. Hussein anything other than a thug.

Second, the troops in the gulf volunteered to serve; even reservists, whatever their additional motives, recognized their duty to fight when they signed up. In addition, there was no specter of a draft and of involuntary service in a hostile far-off land to haunt young Americans.

Third, casualties were remarkably low, as a direct result of the Reagan and Bush Administrations' trust in their military planners and in the performance of high-tech weapons.

If liberals, who mistrust the military, had their way wholly, they would have killed most of the programs that developed weapons that were so successful on the battlefield, including the Patriot missile, Stealth fighter and the Apache helicopter.

Fortunately, the Vietnam syndrome lies buried in the Persian Gulf. And with increased public awareness that the expression of our national values can take military form, it is unlikely to rise from its grave in the foreseeable future.

The New York Times *March 4, 1991*

BRETT CAMPBELL
The Feel-Good War

Texas Observer *editor Brett Campbell believed that the enthusiasm for Gulf victory parades revealed "a perfervid need on the part of the American public to celebrate* something*" amidst the oppressive realities of myriad domestic problems.*

"We carried you in our arms, on Independence Day. And now you throw us all aside, and turn us all away. . . . "—Bob Dylan, *Tears of Rage.*

As this issue of the *Observer* went to press, cities across Texas and the nation were caught up in militaristic Independence Day parades, many glorifying the Persian Gulf war machines. We too give thanks for the safe return of American troops, while mourning the 100,000 dead Iraqis who seem to have been overlooked, and the more than 200,000 Iraqi children projected to die as a result of allied action.

We also understand why those who attended the festivities were so desperately eager to celebrate American derring-do abroad, because the picture on the home front is quite different. According to the National Jobs with Peace campaign, during the six weeks of the Gulf war, 2,875 Americans were murdered; 3,750 died of AIDS; 225,000 were robbed, raped, or assaulted; 400,000 lost their jobs (bringing unemployment to over 8 million); 20 million suffered from hunger; 34 million went without health insurance.

Children fared especially badly: 1,250 died from poverty; 4,000 more died due to low birthweight (many preventable if their parents had had access to pre- and perinatal health programs); 1,825 were killed or injured by guns; 68,750 dropped out of school; 83,200 were abused or neglected.

While the media vilified Saddam Hussein as an "environmental terrorist," accusing him of torching Kuwaiti oil wells (many of which were set on fire by U.S. bombs), in this country: 65 million acres of farmland were damaged by salinization due to irrigation; 142 million tons of carbon from fossil fuels polluted the atmosphere (accelerating global warming); 4,000 lakes remained victims of acid rain; 310,000 miles of waterways stayed polluted. And two million acres of rainforest were destroyed worldwide.

Anyone who hoped the war would recharge the economy was disappointed. Nine billion dollars was added to our world's-highest trade deficit; the "official" national debt grew by $40 billion, to over $3.3 trillion; $90 billion (mostly from the S&L bailout and Gulf war) was added to the United States' additional $2.7 trillion off-budget debt; and 27 states (including Texas) began the new year with serious budget deficits—a record number. These figures have been lost in the rockets' red glare.

This is not to say that all the nation's problems would have been solved had we never fought Mr. Bush's war. What is depressing (along with the bellicose tone) is the display of jingoism exhibited by some of those who attend these ceremonies—which have now gone on longer than the war itself. The forced intensity of much of the exultation makes me wonder whether it stems from a perfervid need on the part of the American public to celebrate *something.* Like the summer "feel-good" movies, the parades, and the war itself, provided an escape from gritty reality. If World War II was, as Studs Terkel dubbed it, "The Good War," then judging by subsequent festivities, the Persian Gulf action has become "The Feel-Good War. . . . "

The Gulf war provided an easy jubilation because it supplied a clear-cut, seemingly morally unambiguous problem, a Snidely Whiplash-style, stereotypical bad guy (as portrayed by the U.S. media), and a brutally simple solution: bombs and missiles. The messier, institutional scourges that plague our cities, our environment, our children don't admit such convenient villains. And our leaders would have us believe that the solutions aren't as readily attainable as Patriot missiles and F-16 fighters. . . .

The philosopher William James once called on anti-militarists to push society to treat social problems as "the moral equivalent of war" in order to prevent the real thing. Today, not only do we lack a beneficent moral equivalent of war, we have had a war that now seems the moral equivalent of television, with a cynical President as game-show host and the frustrated American people as audience. Mr. Bush may be enjoying high Nielsen ratings, as expressed in the polls, but those numbers listed above, the ones you don't see on TV, tell us more about the national character than any flag-waving spectacle.

The Texas Observer *July 12, 1991*

BARBARA EHRENREICH
Tale of a Whale

For writer Barbara Ehrenreich, an incident halfway across the world from Operation Desert Storm elicited insight into the nature of brutality and mercy.

I went to Key West to escape the persistent delusion that the L.A.P.D. tape was in fact a bit of censored footage from the ground war in Iraq. Four days into my recovery, and much cheered by Anthony Lewis's admission that he had perhaps mistakenly encouraged the dreadful carnage of Operation Desert Storm, I awoke to a commotion on the beach adjacent to our rented compound. A half-dozen young people were crouching in the water around what appeared to be a huge black fish. Eager to participate in the marine biology lesson, I waded out but was shooed off by a hulking fellow with a button featuring a ferocious eagle affixed to his bandanna—another Desert Storm reference, I could not help but note. It was a beached pilot whale, he told me impatiently, and no one was allowed in the water or even on the beach.

Hours passed while the officious but otherwise admirable rescue team busied itself spraying, shading and propping up the suicidal whale. I settled in a deck chair to meditate on the psychology that could approve the slaughter of hundreds of thousands of humans and yet rally so nobly to save the life of one poor, stranded mammal. Perhaps I had even misjudged my flag-waving neighbors up north, to whom the entire Persian Gulf venture must have seemed one vast and thoroughly decent rescue mission. The sun was warm, the water turquoise and the whale's benefactors were pleasingly integrated as to race and sex.

Toward noon, as we all awaited the truck or helicopter that was to fetch the whale to some veterinary haven up the Keys, one of the rescuers screamed, "Shark attack!" This was a bizarre and truly alarming turn of events, considering that the whale and its human companions were in no more than three feet of water, a few yards from dry sand belonging to a luxury hotel. Some of the civilian onlookers later claimed to have seen a black object, and perhaps a fin, moving in the water, but there is no doubt about what happened next. The same muscular fellow who had warned me away earlier took up a stick and began to beat the water furiously. A blood-red stain appeared. When the dead "shark" was hauled out, it was revealed to be a baby pilot whale, which the larger one, perhaps encouraged by so much nurturing attention, had trustingly produced.

While the bereft mother was hoisted into a truck with the sinister label "Seafood," I huddled with my friends to discuss the day's impact on the 6-year-old in our company, a lovely child with no prior experience of infanticide. The rescuers' story, it soon emerged, was that the baby whale was premature, stillborn and, anyway, unbruised. I hope, for the sake of our biped species, that an investigation being conducted by the National Marine Fisheries Service bears that out. In the meantime, I take some comfort from the un-Desert Storm-like finale to the frantic scene in the water: Upon seeing the dead baby whale, the man who had beaten the water with a stick, who wore the eagle emblem on his bandanna, ran onto the beach, threw down his stick, collapsed on the sand, pulled his shirt up over his head, and sobbed.

The Nation *April 29, 1991*

PART SIX

WINNERS AND LOSERS

APRIL–JUNE 1991

THE GULF WAR CONSUMED THE ATTENTION OF THE nation for the first part of the year, pushing domestic issues aside. A majority of the American public seemed to welcome the war abroad as respite from the complex problems of social discord and economic decline at home. And for President Bush—who before the crisis had been coming under increasing attack for a wishy-washy political style in dealing with the deficit, the savings and loan scandal, and the civil rights debate—the war was a political boon. In fact, the president had never seemed especially interested in domestic politics, preferring the terrain of foreign affairs, and he was far more comfortable discussing the new world order than the plight of the big banks or the problems of racial disharmony. In addition to refocusing attention on foreign policy, the war promoted a new image of Bush as a strong national leader and commander-in-chief, and the scores of ensuing victory parades that followed amounted to a launching pad for his 1992 reelection campaign.

As the war fever waned, the nation's economic difficulties looked worse than ever. Federal spending cutbacks, combined with homegrown problems, set off financial crises in dozens of cities and states across the country. Cities faced budget cuts that would harm not only the poor, who would lose essential social services, but also the middle classes, who would feel the results of massive layoffs and of slashed funding for infrastructure, police, firefighters, and cultural institutions.

The savings and loan mess had also gotten worse, and there was no end in sight. With two thousand institutions already shut down, and the cost to taxpayers reaching $500 billion, the administration was predicting more failures. And it was not just the savings and loan industry that was in trouble. There were signs that taxpayers might well have to bail out commercial banks as well. By mid-1991, the press was reporting that funds held by the Federal Deposit Insurance Corporation, which insures banks, were nearly depleted, and F.D.I.C. analysts were predicting that over four hundred banks—including some of the nation's largest financial institutions—could fail in the coming year. In May the Treasury asked Congress for authority to borrow $70 billion to cope with future bank failures. As it was, the government could not figure out what to do with the failed banks and S&Ls it had taken over—along with $160 billion in bad loans and repossessed real estate—and regulators were increasingly reluctant to close more institutions when they could not sell what they had. Instead, they continued working on plans to keep tottering institutions alive, pumping more money into them to keep them afloat—at least through the 1992 presidential election. These actions duplicated the pattern of early response to the S&L crisis, when the federal government shored up financial institutions to keep the scandal from erupting during the 1988 election.

Even though the presidential election was more than a year away, by mid-summer 1991, its implicit presence was felt in the exercise of national politics. While Bush rested on his Persian Gulf laurels, the Democratic party remained fractured, with no clear contenders in the offing. The Republicans had also positioned themselves well for future elections by successfully painting the Democrats in Congress as corrupt, holding onto power because of crooked campaign financing laws. Because they had been able to keep the limelight on Democratic members of Congress, from Jim Wright to Barney Frank, Republicans had largely escaped the sting of corruption charges which began to creep into the news about Bush himself.

The Reagan administration had survived misconduct by top advisers and a series of resignations, dismissals, and indictments. Bush had insisted he would not tolerate any ethical misconduct, but, as California congressman George Miller pointed out in the *New York Times,* there was a "sleaze factor" in the Bush administration. It had first come into view during the earlier days of the S&L scandal, when the president's son, Neil Bush, was accused of conflict of interest dealings in the Denver savings and loan institution where he was a director. During the spring of 1991, President Bush also had to answer to the disclosures of personal use of military aircraft by his chief of staff,

John Sununu. Then there were revelations that Attorney General Richard Thornburgh, under whose guidance the administration had negotiated a settlement with Exxon on the Valdez oil spill, had made personal investments in companies that were part of the consortium that carried the oil. In addition, there were questions about members of the commission that decided which military bases to close: Several members had investments in defense contractors and toxic waste disposal companies, and former New Jersey Republican Congresman Jim Coulter had been employed as a lobbyist for Grumman while a member of the commission.[1]

On top of all this, the Bush presidency was plagued by a brewing scandal that threatened to dwarf all others. Since the days of the Iran-contra affair, there had been whispers in Washington about the so-called October Surprise. As the story went, Ronald Reagan had made a deal with the Ayatollah Khomeni in 1980 to withhold the release of American hostages until after the presidential election, in return for a promise that, once elected, he would arrange sales of arms to Iran. This scenario, if true, implied that Reagan had virtually bought the election—won by a narrow margin over Jimmy Carter, whose image had suffered from his handling of the hostage crisis—at the price of extended detainment of Americans in Iran. It also implied that, while candidates, Reagan and Bush, or their representatives, initiated foreign policy and blocked the competing foreign policy initiatives of the elected government. These allegations drew little attention except from the alternative press, and were given little credibility. In the spring of 1991, however, Gary Sick—a Mideast scholar and member of Carter's National Security Council who had dealt with Iran during the hostage crisis—ressurected the allegations, adding evidence from his own research and implicating George Bush as an integral player. Sick's argument—made public for the first time on the op-ed page of *The New York Times*—set off a flurry of investigations by other newspapers, and raised demands for a congressional inquiry.

But George Bush, the heir to the Teflon presidency, appeared to be little hindered by such implications as he vigorously pursued his vision of the new world order. This new order was to replace the old superpower struggle with the Soviet Union as the core of international relations, and at its base lay a reorganization of the trading relations among world nations. The centerpiece of the debate should have been the General Agreement on Tariffs and Trade, but the latest round of negotiations had come to an impasse over agriculture. The U.S. instead turned its attention toward a continuing effort to build up a series of bilateral trading blocs, that in the end would give it more power inside the GATT arena. The Reagan/Bush administation had made progress toward this goal by incorporating Canada into a free trade zone in 1988. As part of the United States economic strategy for the North American continent, Canada was expected to provide a growing share of energy resources for the next century. During the spring of 1991, the Bush administration moved to repeat the Canadian process and extend the U.S. trading block throughout the North American continent by reaching a free trade agreement with Mexico. Such an agreement could formalize growing American employment of cheap Mexican labor (at a high cost to American workers), and, as with Canada, could lead to exploitation of Mexico's substantial oil and gas deposits. Once its neighbors in the north and south were tied into a hemispheric trade pact, the U.S. would be insured of energy supplies in the foreseeable future, eliminating reliance on other foreign sources, including the Persian Gulf.

The administration had already used its high postwar popularity ratings to overrun critics of its plan for future domestic energy production. The sudden cutoff of Iraqi and Kuwaiti oil helped to galvanize the president's pursuit of an aggressive new National Energy Strategy. Bush's plans for the NES, announced while the war was still in progress, ignored proposed initiatives toward energy conservation, and introduced a program that called for more—not less—oil, to be acquired by drilling in the Arctic and along the coasts, as well as a renewal of nuclear energy.

Back on the home front, another issue that returned with a vengeance to the postwar scene was the battle over "political correctness," waged primarily on the field of college campuses. The larger issues involved in the so-called p.c. controversy—to decide who would prescribe the social contract in a culturally diversifying America—surfaced in what were really two separate debates. One concerned the imposition, on an increasing number of campuses, of codes outlawing speech that was deemed offensive to certain members of the community—women, lesbians and gay men, or racial, ethnic, or religious minorities. These universities considered speech codes a necessary and justifiable response to the disturbing rise in verbal attacks and racist and sexist behavior on campuses. Some opponents of the speech codes had offensive beliefs of their own; but civil libertarians resisted the codes on First Amendment grounds, and many members of the college community agreed that suppressing free expression was not an effective means of combatting racism, sexism, or homophobia.

The more resonant debate—often wrongfully equated with arguments over whether fraternity members should be expelled for shouting nasty epithets—involved the content of college curricula. On many campuses, those who lobbied to expand curricula to include the literature and history of women, gays, and people of color were accused of promoting everything from special interests to Marxist orthodoxy to inferior academic standards to a "New McCarthyism." Proponents of a diversified curriculum argued that they did not seek to stifle the canon of Western civilization, but merely to extend its parameters beyond the narrow viewpoint of white, European, upper-class, heterosexual men—to broaden, not limit, the range of expression. But their challenge to the status quo faced a widespread backlash. In a May commencement address at the University of Michigan, President Bush got into the act, criticizing multiculturalism in his attack on "the notion of political correctness." Bush denounced the "political extremists [who] roam the land, abusing the privilege of free speech, setting citizens against one another on the basis of their class and race."

In fact, the president himself promised to foment racial divisiveness in national politics with his savage attack on the 1991 Civil Rights Bill. Bush, who had always publicly argued in favor of civil rights, denounced the bill for what he saw as its promotion of "quotas." While the measure was expected to pass both houses of Congress, its prospects for surviving a promised veto by President Bush were dubious. The president had vetoed similar legislation in 1990, and Congress's attempt to override the veto had failed by one vote.

The 1991 legislation would compensate for the effects of six Supreme Court rulings that restricted job discrimination lawsuits and, at the same time, extend the ability of victims of intentional job discrimination to obtain monetary damages. But Bush had proposed his own bill, which limited monetary damages and retained part of the restrictions imposed by the Supreme Court.

While the primary intent of the legislation was to remedy the Court's rulings, the controversy and debates surrounding the bill made civil rights a looming issue in the presidential election. The Republicans steadily forced the Democrats into one compromise after another. The longer the Republicans could keep the debate going, the better it was for them: As recent evidence had shown, racially charged fears and resentments—especially as they bore on the issue of affirmative action—could readily be parlayed into white votes.

The Civil Rights Bill was but one example of legislation designed to mitigate the impact of the new Supreme Court, which was actively dismantling the long legacy of civil rights and liberal social policy. The Rehnquist Court had already handed down regressive decisions in the areas of minority rights, women's rights, capital punishment, and the rights of the accused. The retirement of Justice Thurgood Marshall, announced in June, further strengthened the conservatives' political hold on the Court. Marshall himself, in his last words from the bench, warned that "power, not reason, is the new currency of this Court's decision making." In his stinging dissent to a precedent-reversing 6-3 decision that removed restrictions on allowable evidence in death penalty cases, Marshall wrote, "Cast aside today are those condemned to face society's ultimate penalty. Tomorrow's victims may be minorities, women, or the indigent." The justices' new attitude toward the rights of society's most vulnerable members would, he added, "squander the authority and legitimacy of this Court as a protector of the powerless."

MIKE ROYKO
What about the Home Front?

With the Persian Gulf war over, a myriad of long-ignored domestic problems reclaimed public attention. Despite the war's purported revival of national unity and pride, Chicago Tribune *columnist Mike Royko saw little evidence that Americans were willing to join forces and take responsibility for the challenges on the home front.*

Col. David Hackworth is probably right about the nation's spinal cord. As he wrote in *Newsweek,* "Americans are standing tall for the first time in years."

The retired Army officer, one of the most decorated in history, says he has not seen such national pride since World War II ended.

That's what I'm hearing, too. It's pouring out of radio talk shows, newspaper and magazine editorials, and from the mouths of politicians everywhere. We've shaken off the doldrums: We're on the move as a great nation again: Pride has been restored, and we're No. 1.

Those who opposed the war are either slinking in dark corners or pleading 'Forgive me for having been a wrong-headed weenie.'

But I'm afraid that Col. Hackworth has allowed his euphoria to blur his vision. Or maybe it's because since retiring from the Army, he's lived in other parts of the world.

He goes on to write: "So, let's use our newfound confidence to turn America around. Yes, we need a new world order, but let it begin at home and not just with soaring polls and White House speeches.

". . . The key is to get American priorities right. We need to start with our education system, so our kids can read and write again. We need to take care of the homeless and poor, and attack drugs and crime. We must clean up our environment, rebuild our highways, railroads and merchant fleet. We must revitalize our industries to the point that Made in America will once again stand for quality. . . . Our vital national interests depend on a stable and secure America. Let's roll up our sleeves and make it that way."

Dream on, colonel, dream on.

In two or three years, Kuwait will be close to looking as it did before Iraq looted and plundered it. But I guarantee that the West Side of Chicago, much of the Bronx, and the slums of Newark, New Orleans and other American cities will be the same mess they are now.

That's because Kuwait sits atop an ocean of liquid gold. It can hire the giant Bechtel Corporation and other globehopping companies to perform a miraculous rehab job. Unfortunately, nobody is drilling gushers on the West Side of Chicago, in Detroit or the Bronx. And Bechtel doesn't take our IOUs.

It's not a matter of rolling up our sleeves. Dedicated teachers in poverty-plagued neighborhoods have been rolling up their sleeves for years. But baring their arm hair doesn't do much when most of their students come from broken families, with illiterate, jobless relatives.

But don't worry, colonel. Most American kids can read and write—those who live in suburbs and prosperous smaller cities. And many will go on to college and better jobs.

Then they'll reflect their parent's attitudes—resentment that they have to pay taxes to support that huge, lazy, welfare-sucking, crime-ridden underclass in the cities.

See, colonel, one of our biggest problems is that Americans don't really like or trust each other that much. They dislike each other for racial, class, regional, economic and political differences.

Does the good colonel really believe that Richard Nixon and Ronald Reagan were concerned about better education? If so, what did they do? Besides dubbing himself the "education president" what has George Bush done?

It's not going to get better, it's going to get worse. I know that because it's worse today than it was 20 years ago and 10 years ago, and there's nothing new in the works.

Take care of the homeless and the poor? (And you might throw in the poverty-level elderly.) Smack down crack, lock up criminals? That takes manpower, which means money, colonel. If you haven't noticed, we're running up a monster tab just rescuing the S&L industry, with the banks next. The time to have kind thoughts about the homeless, the poor, better schools, health care for the old, crumbling highways and collapsing bridges was before Ronald Reagan's crowd napped their way through the white-collar larceny of the bloated 1980's.

And even before then, when American industry became nearsighted while the Japanese and others developed long-range vision. We can roll up our sleeves, but only to dip into our pockets to see if we can cover the juice to all the countries that now act as our loan sharks.

No, all we've proved is that we can win a war. So maybe we should make that our national product. But at a better price. The Kuwaitis and Saudis, as trembly as they were, would have surely accepted a stiffer bill for our bodyguard and security service.

So the colonel will have to settle for those soaring polls and White House speeches. That's all we'll get.

And in a few years he should compare Kuwait City to Chicago's West Side—the schools, clinics, housing and job opportunities. To America's sick and elderly. To the wrecks in the V.A. hospitals.

And see how many yellow ribbons will be displayed for them.

The Chicago Tribune *May 3, 1991*

DOUG HENWOOD
The Uses of Crisis

High on the agenda of domestic problems were the crippling fiscal crises facing states and cities across the nation. Left Business Observer *editor Doug Henwood suggested that blame for the crisis was being placed everywhere except where it belonged: in the lap of conservative policymakers.*

Capital has pulled off a magnificent PR coup: it has convinced most of the world, including a few timorous lefties, that the market is the ultimate form of social organization, while managing to export, displace, or evade most of its problems. Apologists can point to the undeniable prosperity enjoyed by a privileged sliver within the world's rich countries, for example, while denying any responsibility for the Third World's endless depression. In the U.S., money's publicists can explain the fiscal crises now affecting every level of government by blaming the allegedly congenital inefficiencies of government—what else could you *expect* from the public sector, after all? Homelessness, crack, AIDS, and busted S&Ls, all of which are pushing public budgets deeper into the red, have nothing to do with *laissez-faire.*

Though federal deficits are hardly news, deficits among state and local governments (SLGs) are. SLG operating budgets started slipping into the red in 1987; only surpluses on social insurance funds (like pensions and workers' comp) have kept the overall accounts in the black. Previously, only full-blown recessions would shove operating budgets underwater; though the economy began slowing in early 1988, it didn't enter an official recession until July 1990. As with so many other things—bank failures and mass homelessness, just to pick two—even years of superficial prosperity were marred by slumpish features.

According to the latest *Fiscal Survey of the States,* published jointly by the National Governors' Association and the National Association of State Budget Officers, 30 states cut their fiscal year 1991 budgets and/or raised taxes in midstream. FY 1992—which ends in mid-1992 in most states—is the worst year for state finances since FY 1983, "when a severe and prolonged recession drained state resources. . . . While the current recession has been less severe, state budgets have been hit harder and spending growth has been reduced only months into the downturn." Given normal inflation and the recession's pressures on welfare budgets, modest spending increases actually "represent a reduction of services." Many cities are in similar shape.

The picture is getting worse by the day. A May survey by the Center for the Study of the States says revenues are in a "free fall."

California, the red-ink champion, is trying to close a $14 billion gap on a $56 billion budget—a deficit larger than the total budgets of 45 states. Republican governor Pete Wilson has ruled off limits the $220 billion in income hogged by the state's richest 10%. He'd rather close schools and cut welfare payments to single mothers by 9%—which is fine by him, since that will leave them less "for a six-pack of beer." Philadelphia is on the verge of bankruptcy, Massachusetts bonds are rated one notch above junk, and New York state and city plan deep cuts and regressive tax hikes. Only the midwest and Rocky Mountain states are unbloodied.

Part of the problem is recession, of course. As the economy sinks, tax receipts fall and welfare outlays rise. But recession isn't the only reason budgets are in trouble. The Feds have cut back on their aid to SLGs. In the 1970s, Washington's aid to local governments averaged 3.1% of GNP; now it's around 2.4%, even though the SLG share of GNP remained about the same. And Reagan's supply-side experiment —tax cuts for the rich and business in the name of promoting risk-taking and entrepreneurship—was duplicated by many jurisdictions. As a result, many SLG budgets are now structurally in deficit. . . .

Your average reactionary argues that public employment is out of control, public employees are paid too much, and welfare benefits are just too generous. Hack, deregulate, and privatize, and all will be well. Facts get in the way of all these arguments.

It's hard to claim that generosity towards the poor and sick gave us a fiscal crises. From 1980–88, old age and disability pensions in the U.S. fell by 4% relative to average national income; unemployment benefits, by 27%; and family assistance, 9%. Forty-six states will allow inflation to cut the real value of benefits under the Aid to Families with Dependent Children program.

According to OECD figures, the U.S. has had plenty of company in this official stinginess: during the 1980s, most of the rich countries reduced the value of unemployment and family benefits relative to average incomes. Though pensions rose in most major countries, they fell in the U.S. and Britain.

If you look at SLG expenditures as a percentage of total income, it's hard to make the case that spending is out of control, as conservatives would have you believe. General SLG spending was $203.25 per $1000 of personal income in 1976; in1988, the latest year for which the Tax Foundation has published numbers, the figure was $186.36. In 1977, SLG welfare spending peaked at $26.14 per $1000 of personal income; in 1988, it had declined to $22.95. Education expenditures by SLGs were $77.32/1000 in 1976; in 1988, $64.40. . . .

Nor has the pay of government workers gotten out of hand. In 1970, municipal workers' salaries were 2.06 times per capita personal income; in 1980, the figure was 1.62; in 1989, 1.60. In New York City, that hotbed of municipal socialism, the ratios were 1.95 in 1970, 1.72 in 1980, and 1.57 in 1989.

New York City, an old hand at fiscal crises, is one of the more prominent jurisdictions in the soup, with a FY 1992 gap of about $3.5 billion in a $28.7 billion budget. During New York's mid-70s fiscal crisis, democratic procedures, such as they were, were suspended, and the city taken over by a committee of bankers and bondholders, Felix Rohatyn foremost among them. . . .

And the social and political environment is a lot different [now]. The 1975 crisis came after a period of gains for minorities, the poor, and city workers—though nowhere near as extravagant as mainstream lore has it . . . New York became a national symbol for this failure of the lower orders to respect their betters, and the 1970s fiscal crisis was quite clearly a dress rehearsal for a national revolt of the haves.

In a 1976 op-ed piece in the *New York Times*, L.D. Solomon, publisher of *New York Affairs,* made this argument quite explicitly, "Whether or not the promises . . . of the 1960's can be rolled back . . . without violent social upheaval is being tested in New York City. . . . If New York is able to offer reduced social services without civil disorder, it will prove that it can be done in the most difficult environment in the nation." Thankfully, Solomon noted, "The poor have a great capacity to sustain hardship."

Solomon's experiment was a success. City welfare policies were redirected away from the poor and towards the rich. In the name of economic stimulus, financiers and developers were offered fat tax breaks, while inflation undermined the real value of welfare benefits and city worker pay.

David Dinkins, the city's first African-American mayor, who was elected by a coalition of blacks, Latinos, white progressives, and organized labor, has proposed a harsh austerity budget for FY 1992. Like that great liberal, Mario Cuomo, Dinkins rejects advice to tax the local rich, preferring a combination of nuisance taxes on those of modest means and deep service cuts. The $1 billion in annual tax breaks for real estate and "economic development," will go unchallenged. Class size in the public schools may reach 50, homeless shelters will be shut, children will go unimmunized, and thousands of workers will be fired—but the Mayor wants to spend almost $1 billion ($168 million from the expense budget, $800 million from the capital budget) on cops-and-jails.

It's quite consistent, actually: if you hack at social services with one hand, you better carry a big stick in the other to cope with the consequences. Dinkins' budget director, Philip Michael, told the *New*

York Times that "if it came down [to a choice] between the two, he'd cut day care before cops."

There's no better agent of austerity than a black Democrat with good liberal credentials: it disarms austerity's natural opponents. During the 1989 campaign, some Wall Street contributors worried that Dinkins was too close to the labor and welfare lobbies to be an effective budget-hacker. He dismissed these worries by saying, "They'll take it from me. . . ."

Fiscal crises are not forces of nature. The U.S. rich are undertaxed, and the public sector underinvests, even by the standards of the rest of the capitalist world. It comes down to a simple choice: fewer BMWs, or more shuttered libraries, malnourished kids, and collapsing bridges?

The Left Business Observer *June 3, 1991*

RUSSELL BAKER
Let 'Em Eat Photo Ops

New York Times *columnist Russell Baker noted that while America's cities groaned under the weight of insurmountable crises, the "Bush people" maintained a "magnificently cool indifference" through the age-old tactic of passing the buck.*

Washington's serenity is amazing. What do these Bush people take? They'd faint if offered pills or smoke, and you can't get Peruna anymore unless you know somebody with a great cellar. So how do they manage to stay way out in space treating the wrack and ruin with this magnificently cool indifference?

Whole states are going broke, cities bankrupt, booming unemployment—boy, there's a dull word—and Washington's response? Jim dandy, double-peachy photo ops: President at Mount Rushmore. President at good old-fashioned, salt-of-earth, Middle Western Fourth of July parade. President saluting heroes of gulf war. President setting up 10-second spots for next year's Monster Battle of TV Commercials, a.k.a. the 1992 Presidential campaign.

Should the Feds do something about the wrack and ruin? Sure, but you can bet this crowd won't. They hate domestic problems. Press them about people sleeping in the streets or 34 million Americans without medical care, and they talk public-relations cant about "points of light."

Besides, refusing to concede that domestic problems should concern them is justified by the wisdom of the philosopher Reagan. "Government is the problem," he declared. George ("Read My Lips") Bush hews faithfully to this Gipperesque principle, and with sound reason.

It was Federal government that led the states, cities and counties into the present pickle. They used to get back a lot of the money their voters sent to Washington. Then, obedient to Reagan philosophy ("Government is the problem"), Washington adopted a new policy. Basically, it said, "Your buck stops here."

The theory was that once you sent your buck to Washington, it became a government buck. And since government was the problem, terrible things would result if any fragment of this tainted money got back to its source. People would get hooked on good schools, fancy police work, clean water and such.

The government buck had to be disinfected, as it were, to prevent it from infesting the country. So it was sent to the Pentagon, which used it to buy goods for countries like Panama and Iraq, where its evil effects wouldn't matter much, since they needed to be taught a lesson anyhow.

Still the problem that government had caused long before Reagan made everyone see the light was gnawing at the national vitals. States, cities, towns, counties had become dangerously accustomed to getting their tainted bucks passed back.

So when Washington said, "The buck stops here, for your own good," the states, the cities, the towns and the counties were not altogether sincere when they said, "Mighty art thou, O Gipper and O Bush, and we thank thee for not burdening us with the terrible problem-causing buck which we have rendered unto thee."

(All right, governments don't speak such language, but wouldn't they be more lovable if they did?)

Why were they not altogether sincere? Because if the buck stopped in Washington, they couldn't replace it with the buck necessary to keep state, city, town and county voters contented unless they raised state, city, town or county taxes. Disaster! Because Reagan and Bush, preaching hellfire against evil government, had persuaded people that tax-raisers must be destroyed.

The states et al. had to avoid raising taxes without cutting services taxpayers demanded. In short, they had to pass a miracle once Washington, having decided that domestic governance was bad for people, got out of the business and turned it over to states, cities, towns and counties.

The end of all this is predictable: Hordes of governors, mayors and county supervisors will be voted out of business in 1992. At the same time the usual 95 to 98 percent of Congress and President Bush will enjoy re-election, on ground that by doing nothing about the wrack and ruin they are saving us from that awful government that is the problem.

All right, much of this is ham-handed irony. I don't apologize. Stating some of the truly silly arguments conservatives invoke to explain why "government is the problem," such as the theory that welfare breeds unemployment, would make me indictable for high-school sarcasm.

In Washington there are people who believe such stuff, those cool, cool, serenely re-electable Washington cats.

The New York Times *August 14, 1991*

WILLIAM GREIDER
The Next Bank Robbery

As Rolling Stone *national editor William Greider reported, by early 1991 it looked like some of the nation's larget banks were heading for an S&L–style crisis. But as in the S&L scandal, the government backed off from any action to limit the crisis early on. "When the big money gets in trouble," Greider advised, "Washington runs away from the facts."*

When the big money is in trouble, stillness falls over the nation's capital. The Bush Administration's proposed $70 billion bailout for commercial banks is quietly working its way through the system. If the Democrats and media cooperate, the veil of silence obscuring the banking crisis won't be lifted until 1993.

At that point, sometime after George Bush's re-election, the public will be given the full detail of another monstrous scandal. The media will belatedly begin searching for villains. Experts will explain that ordinary citizens have no choice but to cough up billions to clean up the mess.

Sound familiar? It's the same scenario that made the savings and loan debacle so devastating. In 1987, the Reagan Administration and Congress papered over that problem so they could get through the 1988 elections without bothering the folks back home. The Bush regime is following the same script, and so far the other players are playing along.

The facts of the banking crisis aren't a secret. Because of escalating bank failures, the federally guaranteed insurance fund that backs up deposits in commercial banks is effectively broke. The Federal Deposit Insurance Corporation still carries a positive balance of about $4 billion, but its funds are evaporating swiftly. Several conservative authorities testified before Congress in January that if the recession proved to be mild and short, F.D.I.C. losses would still be $32 billion. If the recession was deeper and longer, as now seems probable, losses would be $62 billion.

The Government is committed by law to fill that hole. After two years of smugly denying reality, Treasury Secretary Nicholas Brady and the F.D.I.C. chairman, William Seidman, rushed to Congress in late March and asked for a package of taxpayer-backed loans to the F.D.I.C. totalling $70 billion. There was lots of double talk about how this really wasn't a "taxpayer bailout," since the bankers promised to pay it all back once they get healthy again. That's what Reagan officials said in 1987, when they quietly arranged the initial bailout for the S&Ls. But, as everyone knows, the Government is now warehousing the carcasses of dead S&Ls.

The F.D.I.C. forecasts 440 bank failures this year and next, but the real losses are expected to come from the handful of gleaming money-center behemoths that are in deep trouble. No one can say which ones will fail, but the list of walking wounded is well known: Citibank, Chase Manhattan, Manufacturers Hanover, Chemical, First Chicago, Security Pacific and perhaps two or three others.

Henry Gonzalez, the astute chairman of the House Banking Committee, has a radical solution for the crisis, but it is not without pain, nor is it an approach the Administration is likely to adopt. Mr. Gonzalez argues that the Government should shut down Citibank right now and take the losses before they grow any larger.

To date, the Administration's strategy has been what bankers call forbearance: regulators are propping up the troubled banks with lenient accounting and hidden subsidies, and hoping for the best.

Citibank has received especially generous treatment. In December, the financial markets estimated the bank examiners would order Citibank to write off $2 billion to $2.5 billion more in bad loans. Why? Nearly one-fifth of its $13.3 billion in commercial real estate loans is "nonperforming"—the borrowers aren't making their payments. But instead of a big hit, Citibank got a kiss—a required write-down of only $400 million.

Wall Street relaxed, but Citibank executives are still scrambling to raise cash and cut losses. Though they've found a Saudi prince to invest $590 million, they're still searching for more to meet their goal of $4 billion in new capital. Meanwhile, the chairman, John Reed, has promised to cut operating costs by an additional $1.5 billion. "All big companies get sloppy," he said recently. "We're no exception."

In the forbearance strategy, however, the fate of Citibank and the other money-center banks rides largely on prospects for the economy: So long as the largest borrowers are failing, bad loans will mount and balance sheets will deteriorate. Everyone is hoping for an economic turnaround that would allow the banks to work their way out of their damaged loan portfolios. Maybe that will occur, but it's a gamble taxpayers already lost with S&Ls. "The savings and loan industry rotted away behind just such a regulatory smoke screen," says Mr. Gonzalez. "We know all too well that time and forbearance don't work."

While the S&L crisis was different in many respects, the banks are faced with the same essential dilemma: They've made bets on ventures unlikely to pay off unless the economy enjoys spectacular growth. For lots of reasons, including the mountains of domestic debt, many economists expect only slow growth for the next few years. Even if the recession ends soon, a weak recovery will not cure bankers' problems. Office buildings will remain empty and more developers will default. Inaction thus makes the F.D.I.C.'s hole, and the taxpayer's bill, grow much bigger. "If I had the power," says Mr. Gonzalez, "I would just go ahead and accept the fact that we've got insolvent institutions and shut them down—right away."

While Mr. Gonzalez is more forthright, other experts privately share his view, including some in the banking community. "In my judgment," says one banking expert, "you've got to close them down. Don't help the stockholders. Don't promise the large uninsured depositors that they will get away scot-free. Give them the bad news quickly and keep the banking system operating."

Facing the truth would be wrenching, but it wouldn't be the end of the world if handled correctly. A bank could be closed on Friday for example, then reopened on Monday with new management and new owners, either a Government-backed conservator or another bank. President Bush might have to speak up and offer assurances that the Government will protect the system's soundness.

The stockholders would lose their equity, of course, and the bondholders would lose their investment. But that's the way free enterprise is supposed to work. All deposits up to $100,000 would be made whole by the F.D.I.C., just as the law prescribes. Large-scale depositors would get most of their money, say 85 percent, with the rest held in escrow while authorities sort through the wreckage. If the Government ends up losing 10 cents on the dollar, then the largest depositors should take a hit, too.

The largest public benefit, aside from saving billions by stopping the bleeding now, would be to restore long-term market discipline to the banking system. Instead of riding free on Uncle Sam's protection, the big-money players—both large depositors and stockholders—would have to choose their banks more carefully and demand more responsible behavior from bank executives.

By keeping insolvent banks open, the Administration rewards not only depositors and investors but also executives. In private industry, when a company sinks into trouble and someone has to come to the rescue with new capital, the discredited C.E.O. is fired and a new team is brought in. If taxpayers are going to recapitalize the F.D.I.C., the least they might expect is a housecleaning. Regulators have the power to accomplish this, but don't hold your breath. It was executives like John Reed who proposed the bailout, and they did not have losing their jobs in mind.

The Republican solution to the crisis is more deregulation—Administration proposals that would let banks cross state lines and get into other lines of business. Democrats are more wary of loosening the rules, since this is how they got burned when they tried to help their S.&L. friends. Both sides are maneuvering for advantage and self-protection. Above all, they hope the public doesn't get interested. When the big money gets in trouble, Washington runs away from the facts.

Rolling Stone *May 28, 1991*

GARY SICK
The Election Story of the Decade

The serene facade of the Bush presidency was threatened by a potential scandal of major proportions, in the shape of the long-ignored "October Surprise." With revelations first published on the op-ed page of the New York Times, *former National Security Council staff member Gary Sick brought new credibility to the rumors of a secret deal between Ronald Reagan and the Ayatollah Khomeni.*

Suspicions about a deal between the Reagan campaign and Iran over the hostages have circulated since the day of President Reagan's inaugural, when Iran agreed to release 52 American hostages exactly five minutes after Mr. Reagan took the oath of office. Later, as it became known that arms started to flow to Iran via Israel only a few days after the inauguration, suspicions deepened that a secret arms-for-hostages deal had been concluded.

Five years later, when the Iran-contra affair revealed what seemed to be a similar swap of hostages for arms delivered through Israel, questions were revived about the 1980 election. In a nice, ironic twist, the phrase "October surprise," which Vice Presidential candidate George Bush had coined to warn of possible political manipulation of the hostages by Jimmy Carter, began to be applied to the suspected secret activities of the 1980 Reagan-Bush campaign.

I was a member of the Carter administration and on the staff of the National Security Council from August 1976 to April 1981 with responsibility for monitoring Iran policy. I first heard these rumors in 1981 and I dismissed them as fanciful. I again heard them during the 1988 election campaign, and I again refused to believe them. I had worked in and around the Middle East long enough to be skeptical of the conspiracy theories that abound in the region.

Then two years ago, I began collecting documentation for a book on the Reagan Administration's policies toward Iran. That effort grew into a massive computerized data base, the equivalent of many thousands of pages. As I sifted through this mass of material, I began to recognize a curious pattern in the events surrounding the 1980 election. Increasingly, I began to focus on that period, and interviewed a wide range of sources. I benefited greatly from the help of many interested, talented investigative journalists.

In the course of hundreds of interviews, in the U.S., Europe and the Middle East, I have been told repeatedly that individuals associated with the Reagan-Bush campaign of 1980 met secretly with Iranian officials to delay the release of the American hostages until after the

Presidential election. For this favor, Iran was rewarded with a substantial supply of arms from Israel.

Some of the sources interviewed by me or my colleagues are or were government officials who claimed to have knowledge of these events by virtue of their official duties or their access to intelligence reports. Most insisted on anonymity.

Other sources are low-level intelligence operatives and arms dealers who are no boy scouts. A number of them have been arrested or have served prison time for gun-running, fraud, counterfeiting or drugs. Some may be seeking publicity or revenge, but others have nothing to gain from talking about these events, and genuinely feared for their personal safety. Several sources said they were participants, personally involved in or present at the events they described.

Their accounts were not identical, but on the central facts they were remarkably consistent, surprisingly so in view of the range of nationalities, backgrounds and perspectives of the sources. Because of my past Government experience, I knew about certain events that could not possibly be known to most of the sources, yet their stories confirmed those facts. It was the absence of contradictions on the key elements of the story that encouraged me to continue probing. This weight of testimony has overcome my initial doubts.

The story is tangled and murky, and it may never be fully unraveled. At this point, however, the outlines of what I learned can be summarized as follows:

In December 1979 and January 1980, Cyrus and Jamshid Hashemi, two brothers who had good contacts in Iranian revolutionary circles, approached the Carter Administration seeking support for their candidate in the Iranian presidential elections. I met both of them briefly during that period. Although Washington was sympathetic, their appeal was over-taken by events. Their candidate lost, but they remained in contact with the U.S. Government, providing useful information about developments in the hostage crisis.

Cyrus died in 1986, only three months after his cooperation with the U.S. Customs Service in a dramatic sting operation that resulted in the arrest of several Americans, Israelis and Europeans on charges of plotting illegal arms sales. Jamshid Hashemi, who was also involved in international arms sales, was not implicated in that affair. I re-established contact with Mr. Hashemi in March 1990 and interviewed him a number of times.

According to Mr. Hashemi, William Casey, who had just become Ronald Reagan's campaign manager, met with him in late February or early March 1980 at the Mayflower Hotel in Washington. Mr. Casey quickly made it clear that he wanted to prevent Jimmy Carter from gaining any political advantage from the hostage crisis. The

Hashemis agreed to cooperate with Mr. Casey without the knowledge of the Carter Administration.

Mr. Hashemi told me that he and his brother helped to arrange two critical meetings. In a Madrid hotel in late July 1980, an important Iranian cleric, Mehdi Karrubi, who is now the speaker of the Iranian Parliament, allegedly met with Mr. Casey and a U.S. intelligence officer who was operating outside authority. The same group met again several weeks later. Mr. Hashemi told me that Mr. Karrubi agreed in the second Madrid meeting to cooperate with the Reagan campaign about the timing of any hostage release.

In return, he was promised that the Reagan Administration, once in office, would return Iran's frozen assets and help them acquire badly needed military equipment and spare parts. Two other sources subsequently described these meetings in very similar terms in interviews with me and my colleagues. The Carter Administration had no knowledge of these meetings.

At about the time of the second meeting in Madrid, according to two former Israeli intelligence officers I interviewed, individuals associated with the Reagan campaign made contact with senior Government officials in Israel, which agreed to act as the channel for the arms deliveries to Iran that Mr. Casey had promised. Israel had been eager to sell military equipment to Iran, but the Carter Administration, which was maintaining a total arms embargo on Iran, had refused to agree.

As the threat of war with Iraq began to mount in early September 1980, Iran opened direct hostage negotiations with the Carter Administration. In retrospect, it appears that Iran may have been playing both sides, seeking the highest bid for the release of the hostages. The Carter Administration, however, did not realize it was involved in a three-cornered bidding contest, and resisted Iran's apparent interest in military equipment.

The Iraqi invasion of Iran on Sept. 22, 1980, added both urgency and confusion to the various negotiating tracks. Two former Reagan campaign aides told me that this generated new fears with the Reagan-Bush campaign that war pressures would lead Iran to release the hostages before Election Day, thereby improving President Carter's chances.

Adding to the complexity, the Carter Administration secretly had been developing plans for a possible second hostage rescue mission, after the failure of its earlier mission, Desert I, in April. It became operational in September 1980. Richard V. Allen, Ronald Reagan's first national security adviser and a member of his campaign, told me that one member of the rescue team contacted him and gave him a description of the second rescue plan. Shortly thereafter, the Reagan-Bush campaign launched a major publicity effort warning that President Carter might be planning an "October surprise" to obtain the release of the hostages prior to the election.

From Oct. 15 to Oct. 20, events came to a head in a series of meetings in several hotels in Paris, involving members of the Reagan-Bush campaign and high-level Iranian and Israeli representatives. Accounts of these meetings and the exact number of participants vary considerably among the more than 15 sources who claim direct or indirect knowledge of some aspect of them. There is, however, widespread agreement on three points: William Casey was a key participant; the Iranian representatives agreed that the hostages would not be released prior to the Presidential election on Nov. 4; in return, Israel would serve as a conduit for arms and spare parts to Iran.

At least five of the sources who say they were in Paris in connection with these meetings insist that George Bush was present for at least one meeting. Three of the sources say that they saw him there. In the absence of further information, I have not made up my mind about this allegation.

Immediately after the Paris meetings, things began to happen. On Oct. 21, Iran publicly shifted its position in the negotiations with the Carter Administration, disclaiming any further interest in receiving military equipment. From my position at the N.S.C., I learned that Cyrus Hashemi and another Iranian arms dealer secretly had reported to State Department officials that Iran had decided to hold the hostages until after the elections.

Between Oct. 21 and Oct. 23, Israel sent a planeload of F-4 fighter aircraft tires to Iran in contravention of the U.S. boycott and without informing Washington. Cyrus Hashemi, using his own contacts, began privately organizing military shipments to Iran. On Oct. 22, the hostages were suddenly dispersed to different locations. And a series of delaying tactics in late October by the Iranian Parliament stymied all attempts by the Carter Administration to act on the hostage question until only hours before Election Day.

After the election, the lame-duck Carter Administration resumed hostage negotiations through Algerian intermediaries, but the talks stalled. On Jan. 15, Iran did an about-face, offering a series of startling concessions that reignited the talks and resulted in a final agreement in the last few hours of Jimmy Carter's Presidency. The hostages were released on Jan. 21, 1981, minutes after Ronald Reagan was sworn in as President.

Almost immediately thereafter, according to Israeli and American former officials, arms began to flow to Iran in substantial quantities. A former senior official in the Israeli Ministry of Defense told me that the shipments by air and sea involved hundreds and millions of dollars worth of equipment and that detailed lists of each shipment were provided to senior officials in the Reagan Administration. Moshe Arens, the Israeli Ambassador to Washington in 1982, told the Boston Globe in October 1982 that Israel's arms shipments to Iran at this time were coordinated with the U.S. Government "at almost the highest of levels."

Former officials and participants in the Reagan-Bush campaign team uniformly have denied any personal knowledge or involvement in such a deal, although none of them categorically denies that contracts with Iran before the 1980 election may have taken place. Richard V. Allen vehemently denies any agreement between the campaign and Iran over the timing of the hostages release. He told me and others, however, that there are "self-starters" in every campaign and that he cannot vouch for every "independent, free-lance, spontaneous, over-the-transom" volunteer.

Can this story be believed? There is no "smoking gun" and I cannot prove exactly what happened at each stage. In the absence of hard documentary evidence, the possibility of an elaborate disinformation campaign cannot be excluded.

But all of that must be balanced against the sheer numbers and diversity of the various sources, from eight countries on four continents. Some 20 individuals, including myself and some of the sources mentioned above, have been interviewed and can be seen tomorrow night on the Public Broadcasting Service's documentary series "Frontline."

The allegations of these individuals have many disturbing implications for the U.S. political system. One is the tampering with foreign policy for partisan benefit. That has, of course, happened before and it may well happen again, but it assumes special poignancy in this case since it would have involved tampering with the lives and freedom of 52 Americans.

Another implication is that leaders of the U.S. exposed themselves to the possibility of blackmail by Iran or Israel. Third, the events suggest that the arms-for-hostage deal that in the twilight of the Reagan Presidency became known as the Iran-contra affair, instead of being an aberration, was in fact the re-emergence of a policy that began even before the Reagan-Bush Administration took office.

But finally, it implies a willingness to pursue private, high-risk foreign policy adventures out of sight of the electorate. That may be real politik. Its practitioners may indeed win big. But it is profoundly antidemocratic.

During my research, I spoke to several of the former hostages. I was deeply moved by the response of one in particular. After listening to the evidence, he said simply: "I don't want to believe it. It's too painful to think about it." Painful it is. But the rest of us are obliged to think about it. Hard.

The New York Times *April 15, 1991.*

ROBERT KUTTNER
The Tyranny of the Economically Correct

While the nation faced a series of economic crises, columnist and economic analyst Robert Kuttner observed that the freemarketeers had come to dominate the field of economics, maintaining a tyrrany of ideas that dangerously "narrowed the scope of debate about our national economic well-being."

Ideological conformism on campus has come under wide attack as the last, pathetic gasp of the 1960s. Supposedly, students and teachers, especially in the humanities, are under pressure from leftover radicals to be "Politically Correct," both socially and in the classroom.

This is, of course, deplorable. But if you want to see truly rigid Political Correctness, take a good look at the field I cover—economics.

To be credentialed to practice economics today, one must accept a certain corpus of theology—a particular way of looking at human motivation and human society. Formal economics begins with the tautological premise that the process of buying and selling things—supply and demand—leads to optimal outcomes. It presumes that efforts to interfere with this natural order of things, notably by governments, are damaging to economic efficiency and, hence, bad.

The standard economic model of human behavior presumes that selfishness is normal, and hence desirable, while altruism is suspect. It tends to study economic phenomena by collecting statistics and building mathematical models rather than getting out of the office—as Adam Smith did—and seeing how things actually work.

By comparison, other academic disciplines are rich with healthy contention, in ideology, assumption and method. Nor did economists always view the world in this fashion.

There was a time when many economists were extremely curious about corporations, and unions, and communities and the development of technologies—as dynamic and necessary social phenomena. There was a time when economists understood that political power is inextricably linked to economic questions.

Once, most of the greatest economists studied history and society as well as mathematics, and recognized that the simple interplay of supply and demand through unregulated private transactions did not always lead to the best possible outcomes, either for citizens or nations.

There are, of course, still people who study the world in this manner. But they are unlikely to be tenured in the country's more prestigious departments of economics.

In fairness, there are a few exceptions to this conformism. The Massachusetts Institute of Technology's highly regarded economics department, for example, is more tolerant of diversity than most, as is Notre Dame's. A number of public universities still offer sanctuary to dissenters.

But for the most part, to be a tenured economist at an elite university one must be "Economically Correct." This also describes most economists at Washington's influential think tanks, whether nominally Democrat or Republican.

While conservative publications have had a field day attacking supposed liberals for their Politically Correct illiberalism, there has not been a peep from the belatedly civil libertarian right wing about Economic Correctness. And while pressure for Political Correctness, say, in literature classes may turn the heads of a few innocent sophomores, it is Economic Correctness that has the greater worldly influence and therefore does the real damage.

Unlike the national tempest over PC in Academe, the largely unreported scandal of EC narrows the scope of debate about our national economic well-being. It means that anyone who challenges the wisdom of, say, economic deregulation, or the systematic vilification of the public sector, or the U.S. government's backward priorities in its trade policy or the perversity of our income distribution, is likely to be someone other than a tenured economist from a famous university.

That, in turn, means that most of the prestigious "experts" who testify before Congress on these pressing public questions are likely to be on the orthodox side. What could be more stifling of genuine free inquiry?

For example, when Congress considers whether Japanese protectionism might be contributing to erosion of U.S. competitiveness, the overwhelming consensus of the economics fraternity is that the bigger problem is the U.S. budget deficit. To suggest that Japan's industrial policies might have helped that nation is, almost by definition, to be a non-economist.

To argue that the United States should target key technologies or industries for development is to be considered an economic illiterate—though this is standard policy in much of the world. For a practicing economist to hold such views is not only politically incorrect. More insidious, it is considered professionally incorrect.

The rare economist, like Northwestern's Robert Eisner, who contends that the perils of the U.S. budget deficit are exaggerated, or Harvard's John Kenneth Galbraith, who doesn't think planning is a dirty word, or Berkeley's Laura Tyson, who favors a degree of managed trade, have been all but ostracized from the economic fraternity. With a handful of younger exceptions like Tyson, most economists with heterodox views are graybeards who were tenured long ago, before EC took over.

The economics profession, mind you, doesn't censor heretics. It just makes sure those with incorrect views seldom get union cards. One awaits the appropriately indignant editorial in *The Wall Street Journal.*

Business Week *April 8, 1991*

BARRY COMMONER
Toward a Sustainable Energy Future

President Bush had employed the crisis in the Gulf to help him forge ahead with plans for a new National Energy Strategy, calling for more domestic oil drilling and nuclear power. But the real message of the Gulf war, argued veteran environmentalist and author Barry Commoner, was the need for clean and renewable energy sources.

For nearly 20 years, we have been on notice that America lacks a sensible energy policy and is bound to suffer for it. Now we have paid the price. The war in the Persian Gulf was the tragic outcome of our continued dependence on oil, for who can doubt that we would have quietly ignored the invasion of Kuwait—as we have numerous others—if, as one humorist put it, Kuwait produced broccoli instead of oil.

One of the lessons of the Gulf War is that it is long past time for an energy policy that will end our hazardous and costly reliance on non-renewable energy sources, especially oil. The basis for such an energy policy is well known, and most of the means of implementing it are at hand. What is lacking is the political will to affirm the policy, and to legislate it into effect.

One of the striking if melancholy features of American political life is that, despite repeated energy crises, there has been almost no debate on energy policy. Several weeks into the Gulf War, when President Bush already knew its potential human, economic and environmental costs, he proposed an "energy policy" that gave up the long held goal of energy independence—and no one challenged him. The energy debate is long overdue.

At present we rely on non-renewable resources—oil, natural gas, coal and uranium—for over 90 percent of our energy. What is wrong with that? First, these fuels generate serious environmental problems such as smog, acid rain, global warming and radioactive wastes. Second, because they are non-renewable, they become progressively more expensive to produce as they are depleted. Every barrel of oil taken out of the ground automatically makes the next barrel more expensive. Consequently, the cost of producing a non-renewable energy source is governed by inescapable mathematics: production costs rise exponentially as the source depletes. Third, energy's main-function is to power our systems of production, thus generating economic wealth. But since some of that wealth must be used to produce the energy, a non-renewable energy system inevitably diverts an increasingly larger fraction of the economic system's output from other uses. Thus, our non-renewable energy system cannibalizes the very economic system that it is supposed to support.

The upshot is simple: we cannot continue to rely on non-renewable energy sources. If we do, global warming, and the impact of less dramatic problems, will sooner or later overtake us. In addition, the escalating price of energy will eventually create an absurdity: the huge cost of producing energy will leave little wealth left to build the machines that use it.

There is a time limit on our ability to survive these hazards. We have perhaps 20 to 30 years to materially reduce both the global warming trend and the economic threat. Based on the underlying rising trend in the cost of domestic oil production, we can expect that, within 20 years, even without any political supply disruptions, the price of oil will rise to the point, relative to prices generally, that it reached in the 1981-82 crisis. From then on, we would be in the grip of a permanent, worsening energy crisis.

We can now define the basic thrust of a sensible national energy policy: it should call for the replacement of non-renewable energy sources with renewable ones; the transition should begin now and be completed in the next 20 to 30 years. The sun, of course, is a vast source of renewable energy; the amount falling on the Earth's land surface is about 1,000 times greater than present world energy consumption. The means for usefully capturing this energy are at hand: for heat, solar collectors; for electricity, photovoltaic cells, windmills and hydroelectric plants; for gaseous fuel, methane from biomass; for liquid fuel, ethanol from crops and algae. Some of these sources are now competitive in a number of specific applications; sooner or later all of them will be, as the cost of producing non-renewable sources escalates. . . .

Indeed, the EPA had prepared an executive order to set up a federal program for ecologically sound and energy-conserving purchases that was to be announced by President Bush on Earth Day 1990. It was killed by White House Chief of Staff John Sununu. Yes, the country needs an energy policy, and we know what it ought to be. But we'll never get it from the present occupants of the White House.

E Magazine *May/June 1991*

JEFF FAUX
The Biggest Export Will Be U.S. Jobs

Included in the White House's vision of a new world order was a free trade zone extending throughout North America, allowing the U.S. uncurtailed access to the hemisphere's resources. By the spring of 1991, negotiations for a comprehensive free trade agreement between the United States and Mexico were on a "fast track"—but the administration's proposed pact, argued Economic Policy Institute president Jeff Faux, would threaten workers on both sides of the border.

The Bush Administration's proposed free trade agreement with Mexico would harm our long-term economic competitiveness and do severe damage to millions of Americans whose jobs would be shifted to Mexico as a result of the treaty. It would also prevent any meaningful effort to relieve Mexico of its major economic problem—debt.

But the public debate has been one-sided; the truth of this flawed proposal's downside is not getting out. . . .

Bush says a U.S.-Mexico Free Trade Agreement (FTA) would "provide more and better jobs for U.S. workers" because increased exports to Mexico will exceed U.S. job losses brought on by increased imports from Mexico.

But this overlooks the fact that Mexico's capacity as a consumer of U.S. goods is very small, while its capacity to produce with cheap labor goods now made in the United States is large. Mexico's economic output in 1989 was only 3.6 percent of U.S. output. Mexican wages average one-seventh of ours and are even lower in the Maquiladora free trade zone in northern Mexico.

There won't be much improvement, either. A February report by the U. S. International Trade Commission, arguing for the FTA, admits that even under optimum circumstances, Mexican wages will not rise enough to close the gap significantly. Indeed, potential investors in Mexico were told at a recent conference sponsored by the U.S. and Mexican secretaries of commerce, that the wage gap will widen in coming years.

Most of the U.S. export gains to Mexico that can come from trade liberalization have already occurred. Drastic reductions in Mexican import barriers in the mid-1980s released the pent-up demand for American goods from Mexico's small middle class. Eliminating the last import restrictions will yield little further gain, due to extremely low income levels elsewhere in the Mexican population.

On the other hand, an FTA would have a much greater negative impact on the U.S. labor force than the administration admits. Numbers imbedded in the February trade commission report show declines in income for 73 percent of *all* U.S. workers!

The commission now says its own report is in error. But if anything, the commission understated possible U.S. job loss by refusing to calculate the potential effect of U.S. firms shifting production to Mexico. Yet, the large corporations are lobbying for FTA chiefly because it will eliminate Mexico's remaining restrictions on foreign investment in a way that cannot be unilaterally changed by any future hostile Mexican government. More than any other factor, U.S. firms are attracted by Mexico's labor force of almost 30 million willing to work for subsistence pay in unhealthy workplaces lacking environmental regulations. The protection of an international treaty for investments would give U.S. corporations confidence to expand from the Maquiladora zone to all of Mexico, thus lowering production costs while keeping U.S. market access.

Most of the lost U.S. jobs will occur among non-college workers (a majority of the U.S. labor force) whose real incomes fell dramatically in the 1980s. Hardest hit will be the least mobile and poorest workers. The apparel industry, for example, employs many disadvantaged minorities, immigrants and rural Americans for whom there will be few work alternatives when their jobs are lost to even cheaper labor in Mexico. In addition, Labor Department surveys show that U.S. workers dislocated by foreign imports in the 1980s have mostly found less skilled jobs at lower pay—if they were reemployed at all.

The lure of low wages is not limited to so-called low-wage U.S. industries. When the Maquiladora free trade zone was set up 20 years ago, the major activity was sewing garments. Today, apparel accounts for less than 10 percent of Maquiladora workers; almost 40 percent work in electronics and 20 percent in transportation equipment. Major employers include IBM, Hewlett-Packard, Wang and Westinghouse. But the Mexican worker has benefited little: Maquiladora wages are lower than the Mexican average, industrial pollution degrades the environment and educational and health services and physical infrastructure are abysmal. The Maquiladora experience also undercuts proponents' claim that the FTA will reduce illegal immigration. The desperate conditions of the Maquiladora sector have sent many migrants from southern Mexico and Central America further north.

Proponents say the Mexican government is committed to strengthening environmental and worker protection, but the promises of a transient administration alone cannot achieve such difficult goals. In the United States, such laws are made effective by strong institutions independent of government such as labor unions and environmental groups, and a genuine competitive political system—all non-existent in Mexico today.

The Washington Post *April 14, 1991*

JOHN TAYLOR
"Are You Politically Correct?"

John Taylor, writing in New York *magazine, encapsulated one side of a cultural controversy that was destined to rage on throughout the year when he attacked the legions of the "politically correct."*

In the past few years, a new sort of demagogic and fanatical fundamentalism has arisen. The new fundamentalists are an eclectic group; they include multiculturalists, feminists, radical homosexuals, and Marxists. What unites them—as firmly as Christian fundamentalists are united in the belief that the Bible is the revealed word of God—is their conviction that Western culture and American society are thoroughly and hopelessly racist, sexist, oppressive.

Defenders of Western culture try to point out that other civilizations—from the Islamic and the Hindu to the Confucian and the Buddhist—are rife with racism and sexism. They find it odd that while Eastern Europeans are rushing to embrace Western democracy, while the pro-democracy movement in China actually erected a replica of the Statue of Liberty in Tiananmen Square, this peculiar intellectual cult back in the States continues to insist that Western values are the source of much of the world's evil.

The new fundamentalists attack not just the opinions of their critics but the right of their critics to disagree. Alternate viewpoints are simply not allowed. Though there was little visible protest when Louis Farrakhan was invited to speak at the University of Wisconsin, students at the University of Northern Colorado practically rioted when Linda Chavez, a Hispanic member of the Reagan administration who opposes affirmative action and believes immigrants should be encouraged to learn English, was asked to talk. The invitation was withdrawn.

It is this sort of demand for intellectual conformity, enforced with harassment and intimidation, that has led some people to compare the atmosphere in universities today to that of Germany in the '30s. "It's fascism of the left," says Camille Paglia, a professor at the University of the Arts in Philadelphia and the author of *Sexual Personae.* "These people behave like the Hitler Youth."

Utne Reader — *July/August 1991*

SCOTT HENSON
On the Question of "Political Correctness"

As the "p.c." battle raged on college campuses around the country, the Texas Observer's *Scott Henson exposed the flaws in the terms of debate, and the real forces behind the curriculum wars.*

The controversy surrounding curriculum reform and efforts to diversify college faculty reached a climax May 4, when President George Bush attacked "the notion of political correctness" at a University of Michigan commencement address. Bush complained that "we find free speech under assault throughout the United States" by "political extremists [who] roam the land, abusing the privilege of free speech, setting citizens against one another on the basis of their class and race." While the notion that free speech is a "privilege" might surprise some civil libertarians, the President's specious dichotomy—free speech versus political correctness—mirrors the debates portrayed in a flurry of press accounts dating to just before the Persian Gulf war.

The President's attack on "political correctness" contributes to the already growing backlash by the right-wing and the liberal intellectual establishment against a growing student movement aimed at expanding universities' curricula and diversifying their lily-white and male-dominated faculties. Several national right-wing organizations, funded by a handful of northeastern foundations, currently spearhead this backlash. But after articles in *Newsweek, The New Republic, The Atlantic Monthly, The Wall Street Journal, The New York Times, Time, Fortune,* and others, the critique of curriculum reformers as advocates of "the new McCarthyism" has become embedded in the public psyche, with many a dissenting voice to counter the absurdities and misrepresentations of these arguments.

In fact, student reformers' demands not only aren't antithetical to free speech, but indeed are a precursor to real free speech and thought.

Concerns about abrogation of free speech rights stem primarily from universities that implement racial harassment or "hate speech" codes, which often include bans on racist, sexist,or homophobic speech. Invariably such regulations grow out of universities' responses to egregious incidents involving violence or the threat of violence. But these restrictions typically represent university administrators' responses, not the desires of student and faculty reformers.

For example, at the week-long UT-Austin fraternity function called "Roundup" in spring 1990, members of Delta Tau Delta fraternity exercised their free-speech rights by taking turns swinging a sledgehammer at a beat-up car painted with slogans like "Fuck You Nigs Die" and "Fuck Coons." In response, the UT Black Students Alliance (BSA) presented a comprehensive curriculum reform proposal—"Proposed Reforms to Institute Diversity in Education" (PRIDE)—that included the expansion of the number of black faculty and the number and types of courses dealing with black history and culture, as well as the creation of one required ethnic-studies class. The BSA argued, understandably, that Delta Tau Delta members' actions exemplified ignorance among supposedly educated people, and that education, not retribution, was the correct way to approach the Sisyphean task of confronting racism. In support of these demands, the BSA held the largest demonstrations at UT since the Vietnam War.

The university, however, refused to implement any of these well-thought-out proposals. Instead, UT President Bill Cunningham banned Roundup, an action for which neither the BSA nor the Black Faculty Caucus had petitioned. The result: Greeks' resentment of blacks, whom they saw as causing the loss of their party week. But to this day, UT has not brought forward a single substantive improvement in its achingly whitewashed curriculum.

Certainly UT restricted the expression of white, racist fraternity men, to the extent that it discontinued sponsorship of their event. But compared to the university's refusal to implement courses teaching black history, literature and culture, these restrictions are minor. The more destructive of UT's restrictions on speech and thought stem from its failure to supply students with opportunities to study thinkers and writers such as Frederick Douglass, W.E.B. DuBois, Ida B. Wells, Ralph Ellison, Toni Morrison, Malcolm X, Audrey Lorde and Bessie Head. Unlike relatively common sentiments like "Fuck Coons," these writers' speech and thought are structurally excluded from consideration within the university. . . .

But how *are* curriculum decisions made at the modern "multiversity?" As a case study, let's look at the University of Texas at Austin, the flagship institution in Hans Mark's UT System. When UT-Austin expands its curriculum, it does so in deference to programs that subsidize industry and create potential for corporate and individual profit from patented research. It takes into account neither the demands of students nor even the intellectual requirements of its faculty. Because industry is no longer willing to pay for its own capital-intensive R&D or job training, universities have increasingly assumed this work using public funds set aside for the education of the next generation of Texans.

Take, for example, the UT planning document, *The Strategic Plan, 1990–1995,* which outlines UT's intention to create four new degree programs—molecular biology, marine science, nutritional sciences and Slavic languages—as well as off-campus and evening programs that "respond to present and future needs of industry."

The University's decision to implement its molecular biology program, which *The Strategic Plan* says is designed "to meet the acute demand for professionals to develop Texas's embryonic biotechnology industry," illustrates UT's priorities in funding for curriculum expansion. The molecular biology building itself will cost $25 million, the same amount as, say, a new financial aid building.

Financial aid has been a continuing problem at UT for at least a decade. During peak periods of demand, students must often relate their families' financial status to aid counselors with other students present, since space constraints force counselors to share offices. Students wait in long lines every semester, and spend hours hoping to get through on the phone, trying to confirm their aid status. At the beginning of each semester, students typically attempt about 22,000 calls per day to the building—only about 700 of which get through.

This summer UT will move the financial aid office into a temporary space. A UT representative said the school has no concrete plans right now to build new facilities.

UT President Cunningham defends the molecular biology program as a "one-time expenditure," but a financial aid building would also be a one-time expense. The total expense for a new molecular biology program is estimated at $70 million over the next seven years, and of this $51.4 million goes to purchase research capital.

UT's spending priorities are clear: Expensive research capital takes precedence over student demands or societal needs. Financial aid is a class issue, and in America—especially Texas—class issues are race issues. The ethnic breakdown of students receiving financial aid demonstrates that point. . . .

But rather than spend $25 million to facilitate expedient financing for 24,000 students each semester, UT prefers to pay $70 million on a molecular biology program, which the administration intends to serve at most 100 students.

According to *The Strategic Plan,* one objective of the new graduate degree program in marine science will be to "furnish a modest flow of students uniquely trained to address practical environmental and natural resource problems common in the coastal zone, with an emphasis on Texas bays, estuaries, and the adjacent continental shelf." *The Strategic Plan* doesn't mention that "environmental . . . problems common in the coastal zone" often result from the very industries UT sees as its mission to subsidize.

These arguments should not be construed as opposing all scientific or technical training at universities—quite the opposite. To truly implement diversity, engineering and science programs must be opened up through increased financial aid and other mechanisms to facilitate the entry by people of color into those fields. But investments in science that benefit students must focus on *human* development, while most universities, certainly the University of Texas, focus their resources on developing *capital.* Capital-intensive R&D like that at Sematech—the semiconductor manufacturing consortium for which UT spent more than $12 million—is the real obstacle to bettering the college education in a time of shrinking state budgets.

The only non-technical curriculum expansion cited by UT's *Strategic Plan* illustrates similarly skewed priorities. UT will shape its new Slavic languages doctoral program to meet the needs of U.S. industries wanting to compete in newly opened Eastern European markets. According to *The Strategic Plan,* "recent studies indicate that the field is entering a period of sustained growth in terms of both employment possibilities and financial resources made available by governmental and private sources."

By contrast, the UT Oriental and African language department currently teaches not a single African language. This example embodies what multiculturalism advocates declare "institutional racism"—while students demanding diversity are denied access to African cultural and language studies, UT trains students, it hopes, to exploit newly opening economies in Eastern Europe. . . .

The times are not just a changin', they have changed. But campus reformers today battle, for the most part, the same canon Thorstein Veblen blasted in 1917. The new ideas and expressions of these segments of the population deserve their place in the academy—simple respect for others demands no less. The attack on "political correctness" amounts to a backlash targetting the handful of spaces created in the academy over the last 20 years for women and minorities to pursue their own scholarship. To this end, rightest scholars and pundits have defined disagreement with these newcomers as "repression" of their own ideas.

But, in the final analysis, losing an argument does not qualify as losing one's freedom of speech. The more odious repression comes when disputants refuse to allow an argument to begin, by fighting to exclude large fields of scholarship from the academic curriculum.

The Texas Observer *May 31, 1991*

HENRY LOUIS GATES, JR.
Whose Culture is It, Anyway?

Harvard professor Henry Louis Gates, Jr., observed that in the American past, "what has passed as 'common culture'" has been less than universal. The multiculturalism debate could only find fruitful resolution, Gates wrote, when both sides recognized that "culture is always a conversation among different voices."

I recently asked the dean of a prestigious liberal arts college if his school would ever have, as Berkeley has, a 70 percent nonwhite enrollment. "Never," he replied. "That would completely alter our identity as a center of the liberal arts."

The assumption that there is a deep connection between the shape of a college's curriculum and the ethnic composition of its students reflects a disquieting trend in education. Political representation has been confused with the "representation" of various ethnic identities in the curriculum.

The cultural right wing, threatened by demographic changes and the ensuing demands for curricular change, has retreated to intellectual protectionism, arguing for a great and inviolable "Western tradition," which contains the seeds, fruit and flowers of the very best thought or uttered in history. (Typically, Mortimer Adler has ventured that blacks "wrote no good books.") Meanwhile, the cultural left demands changes to accord with population shifts in gender and ethnicity. Both are wrong-headed.

I am just as concerned that so many of my colleagues feel that the rationale for a diverse curriculum depends on the latest Census Bureau report as I am that those opposed see pluralism as forestalling the possibility of a communal "American" identity. To them, the study of our diverse cultures must lead to "tribalism" and "fragmentation."

The cultural diversity movement arose partly because of the fragmentation of society by ethnicity, class and gender. To make it the culprit for this fragmentation is to mistake effect for cause. A curriculum that reflects the achievement of the world's great cultures not merely the West's, is not "politicized"; rather it situates the West as one of a community of civilizations. After all, culture is always a conversation among different voices.

To insist that we "master our own culture" before learning others—as Arthur Schlesinger Jr. has proposed—only defers the vexed question: What gets to count as "our" culture? What has passed as "common culture" has been an Anglo-American regional culture, masking itself as universal. Significantly different cultures sought refuge underground.

Writing in 1903, W.E.B. Du Bois expressed his dream of a high culture that would transcend the color line: "I sit with Shakespeare and he winces not." But the dream was not open to all. "Is this the life you grudge us," he concluded, "O knightly America?" For him, the humanities were a conduit into a republic of letters enabling escape from racism and ethnic chauvinism. Yet no one played a more crucial role than he in excavating the long buried heritage of Africans and African-Americans.

The fact of one's ethnicity, for any American of color, is never neutral: One's public treatment, and public behavior, are shaped in large part by one's perceived ethnic identity; just as by one's gender. To demand that Americans shuck their cultural heritages and homogenize themselves into a "universal" WASP culture is to dream of an America in cultural white face, and that just won't do.

So it's only when we're free to explore the complexities of our hyphenated culture that we can discover what a genuinely common-American culture might actually look like. Is multiculturalism un-American? Herman Melville didn't think so. As he wrote: "We are not a narrow tribe, no. . . . We are not a nation, so much as a world." We're all ethnics; the challenge of transcending ethnic chauvinism is one we all face.

We've entrusted our schools with the fashioning and refashioning of a democratic polity. That's why schooling has always been a matter of political judgment. But in a nation that has theorized itself as plural from its inception, schools have a very special task.

Our society won't survive without the values of tolerance, and cultural tolerance comes to nothing without cultural understanding. The challenge facing America will be the shaping of a truly common public culture, one responsive to the long-silenced cultures of color. If we relinquish the ideal of America as a plural nation, we've abandoned the very experiment that America represents. And that is too great a price to pay.

The New York Times *May 4, 1991*

IVY YOUNG
"Traditional" Family Disappearing

As the 1990 census had revealed, the structure of the American family was changing, too, but government family policy was still shaped by "a 40-year-old television rerun." Ivy Young of the National Gay and Lesbian Task Force called for domestic partnership legislation, and other measures that would respond to the new realities of family life.

The traditional family—father in the workplace, homemaker mother and the kids—is the model many of us grew up watching on television in the '50s. It was a black-and-white image of an Ozzie and Harriet kind of household.

For many of us it was not real life then, and, for most American families, it is not reality today.

According to the Census Bureau, only 11 percent of all families in the U.S. are so-called "traditional families."

American family life in the 1990s is extremely diverse. Look around at your neighbors, your co-workers, the kids you grew up with, yourself.

What you see is diversity: domestic partnerships, including unmarried heterosexual couples and gay and lesbian families; single parents; dual-income families; elder couples; adoptive and foster families; teenage, step-parent and extended families. Add to that quilt the role cultural and ethnic differences play in determining who is family.

Yet programs and policies designed to protect and nurture America's families were created long ago with the traditional model in mind, and do not meet the needs of 89 percent of U.S. families.

Many families fall outside of this model and are denied important benefits, ranging from health coverage and hospital visitation to survivor benefits and pensions.

That is why more than 17 jurisdictions around the country have enacted some form of domestic partner recognition. It is why some of the leading corporations in the nation now have family issues departments. And it is why a federal family and medical leave bill remains a high priority for our lawmakers.

Dire predictions of "skyrocketing taxpayer expense" are often used as reasons for not expanding programs to include non-traditional families. However, in several communities where domestic partner ordinances exist, city officials report no extraordinary costs.

The fundamental issue here is equality and respect for diversity. The quality of American family life should not be determined by the bottom line on a balance sheet, nor by a 40-year-old television rerun.

There is no one standard form for family life in America today. No one way to be a family. And just because my family looks different than yours doesn't mean it should be any less valued, respected or protected.

USA Today *April 5, 1991*

ANNA QUINDLEN
Banning the A-Word

The latest restriction on women's reproductive freedom to reach the Supreme Court was the regulation banning abortion counseling in federally funded clinics, whose clients include thousands of poor teenagers. As the Court heard argument in Rust vs. Sullivan, *columnist Anna Quindlen denounced the law that forced doctors to answer pleas for help with silence.*

There are three ways your average 16-year-old sexually active girl approaches gynecological care.

There are those who sit down with their mothers and discuss their sex lives. Then they visit the family doctor. This does happen, but not often.

The second group do nothing. They are believers in luck and the efficacy of standing up afterward. Not surprisingly, many of them get pregnant.

The third group go to Planned Parenthood. This was true when I was 16, and it is true today. Most of the girls I knew who carried the Pill in their purses got it at the local Planned Parenthood clinic. You might call Planned Parenthood the gynecologist to America's teen-agers, unless you believe that abortion should be illegal. Then you might call Planned Parenthood the evil empire.

In the South Bronx, Planned Parenthood has a center called The Hub, which serves 6,000 women a year. You can see some of them doing their homework in the reception area while they wait to be called for their appointments. Nearly all are poor, are black or Latino and live in a neighborhood that has the distinction of having one of the highest teen-age pregnancy rates in the nation.

Some of them come for birth control. Some come for prenatal care, which is meaningful in a community where prenatal care often consists of having a blood test at the hospital while you are in labor.

And some come for abortions. Although it has now become folk wisdom among middle-class white Americans that poor teen-agers of color—what they call "those people"—spend all their time having babies so they can live in luxury on public assistance, the Hub center gives the lie to that notion. About 80 percent of those who discover they are pregnant there decide to end the pregnancy.

Dr. Irving Rust has been The Hub's medical director for 12 years, and on Tuesday he watched from the gallery at the United States Supreme Court as he became part of history. The case is called *Rust vs. Sullivan,* and it challenges regulations barring family planning clinics that receive Federal funds from providing patients with any information—ANY information—about abortion.

If I say to Dr. Rust, whose clinic receives a quarter of its funding from the Federal Government, "Is my pregnancy too far advanced for a first-trimester abortion?" he is supposed to offer me prenatal care. If I say, "What abortion clinic could I go to?" he is supposed to offer me prenatal care. No matter what my situation, my state of health or my state of mind, this is what he is supposed to say about abortion:

Actually, that's not entirely true. The regulations do provide for this boilerplate response: "The project does not consider abortion an appropriate method of family planning." I think you're supposed to say it with your lips pursed.

Rust vs. Sullivan is a case about free speech sold out for political expediency. It has long been manifest that George Bush has no strong feelings about abortion; he does, however, have strong feelings about winning elections. His support of these regulations, proposed during the Reagan years, is meant to convince those opposed to abortion that the President is a true believer.

This is also a case about medical responsibility. Justice David Souter seemed dissatisfied when the Solicitor General said that a federally funded clinic could not even recommend abortion to a woman whose health would be threatened by pregnancy. "You are telling us that a physician can't perform his usual professional responsibility," the Justice said.

But ultimately this is a case about spitting in the face of the law. The Government demands that doctors like Irving Rust trade free speech and professional responsibility for scarce Federal funds. It has not yet managed to make abortion illegal, so it has decided merely to behave as if it were.

Dr. Rust remembers when it was. He was a resident in a hospital in the Bronx, and he remembers performing hysterectomies on women who had tried to abort themselves. He remembers the women who came in with septic shock and wound up in the morgue. He defies anyone to say these things did not happen. The Government says that when this man hears a woman, no matter how young, how poor or how desperate, say, "Doctor, I really need an abortion," that what he is supposed to say is:

"I couldn't do that," says Dr. Rust. "It would be wrong."

Finally, a sincere answer.

The New York Times *November 1, 1990*

HERMAN SCHWARTZ
Second Opinion

The May Supreme Court ruling in Rust vs. Sullivan, *observed American University law professor Herman Schwartz, revealed the true colors of the new conservative Court. It dealt a serious blow to abortion rights, the rights of the poor, and the First Amendment, and set ominous precedents for the future.*

With one 5-to-4 decision on May 23, the Supreme Court struck at abortion, the poor, doctors, the First Amendment and the welfare state—the "grand slam home run" that John Sununu promised a right-wing extremist who complained about the nomination of the unknown David Souter. Continuing his pattern since coming onto the Court, Souter joined the four hard-shell conservatives to uphold a 1988 regulation barring doctors in federally funded family-planning programs from counseling, or even mentioning, abortion except in medical emergencies; there are no exceptions for the sick, the young, or rape or incest victims.

Worse hit, of course, are the 4.3 million women who depend on the federally funded programs for family-planning advice. Many who have become pregnant—perhaps frightened, without money, non-English-speaking and bewildered—will now be getting this misleading advice. They may accept the distorted message as the final word and have the unwanted child regardless of physical and mental risks, a possibility airily dismissed by Chief Justice William Rehnquist and four of his male colleagues, each of whom is paid more than ten times the poverty level and gets excellent medical care at public expense.

Implicitly overruling prior decisions, the Court's ruling also prevents doctors from offering patients their best professional judgment, which in some states could expose them to charges of unethical conduct, to malpractice suits or other liability. Antiabortion activists claim that the defense in such actions would be the federal regulation, but the doctor's voluntary participation in the program and submission to the regulation, knowing the limitations it imposes, may preclude that defense.

The Court's simplistic premise is that since government is paying the piper, it may also call the tune. Does this mean that the government's support for medical and nursing education allows it to tell those schools that they may not teach how to perform an abortion and may not even tell their students that it is an option? that government financing of legal services not only allows the government to prevent legal services lawyers from taking cases to reform the law but also allows it to prohibit them from referring people to other lawyers? that criminal defense lawyers paid by the government can be barred from raising certain defenses? And doesn't the same logic apply to financial support given by state and local governments, which are often dominated by reactionary special interests?

The federal government has become a major source of funds for the poor, the arts and other public needs. The Court's decision gives the government enormous power over what Americans may be able to say and do in these areas. Obviously, a government subsidy may have some strings attached; but until now, certain strings seemed clearly forbidden. It seemed indisputable, for example, that a federal school aid program may not proscribe the teaching of evolution. That is probably still true. But beyond that extreme example, what restrictions *can't* the government impose if it can prohibit doctors from even mentioning how women can exercise their constitutional right to an abortion?

The Court's ruling and its probable aftermath will also tighten the squeeze play on the Constitution that the Reagan-Bush court packing has made possible. Although the Constitution makes Congress the primary if not the sole law-making body, the combination of the Court and the President can easily subvert the constitutional design, as we have seen in the efforts to undo the Court's misapplication of the civil rights laws. Adopting Justice Antonin Scalia's theory that administrative interpretations are to be given deference over legislative intent, which he actually considers irrelevant, the Reagan-Bush Supreme Court has consistently ignored Congressional intent and read statutes so as to deny the claims of minorities, women and the poor. When Congress has tried to overturn the Court's interpretation and reinstate its original intent, Bush has vetoed or threatened to veto, thereby governing by a combination of five activist justices and one-third-plus-one of either the House or Senate.

The result of such onerous and unfair federal regulations will be an increasing reluctance on the part of family-planning groups and others to take federal support. The ultimate result will be the shrinking of several programs—one of the long term goals of the Reagan-Bush administrations.

Efforts are under way in Congress to overturn the Court's ruling, but the bill may get bogged down with controversial amendments by right-wing opponents. Even if it is passed, the bill will face a presidential veto that will be almost impossible to override. Reagan's legacy continues to haunt us.

The Nation *June 17, 1991*

JONATHAN SHERMAN
Pictures at an Execution

The Rehnquist Court had also diminished the habeas corpus *rights of death row inmates, and capital punishment had gained the favor of an exceptionally large majority of Americans. Opponents of the death penalty were resorting to new tactics, but Stanford Law School student Jonathan Sherman warned that their "shock strategy" could backfire.*

Today, public television station KQED in San Francisco will return to Federal court to argue for the right to videotape and later broadcast the gas chamber execution of Robert Alton Harris, who murdered two teen-agers in 1978. Because the death sentence constitutes the most severe criminal penalty a state can mete out, KQED claims the public has a profound right to watch.

KQED neither opposes nor supports capital punishment. It has stated that it only wants to vindicate television journalists' First Amendment rights. For years, however, opponents of capital punishment have trumpeted televising executions for a different reason: They hope to shock Americans into outlawing capital punishment.

In 1985, for example, Senator Mark Hatfield of Oregon suggested that the public would turn against the death penalty once it peered into the execution chamber. Earlier this year, Pat Clark, director of Death Penalty Focus, a California anti-death penalty group, insisted that if executions are televised, "People will ultimately realize it's a human being murdered in a premeditated, calculated way by the state in our names."

This shock strategy is superficially appealing. It assumes that death penalty supporters—80 percent of all Californians—will vote with their stomachs after watching the show, and elect anti-death lawmakers.

But the strategy is also naive. It paints supporters of the death penalty as bumpkins who haven't thought carefully about their choice of punishment. Do the shock strategists believe that supporters of the death penalty don't visualize what goes on in the gas chamber? Do they actually think that by showing Robert Alton Harris' eyes explode, his chest shake, and his body squirm in agony people will be surprised?

Capital convicts commit acts of horrible violence. The whole point of the death penalty is to exact terrible retribution. I strongly oppose capital punishment, but its steadfast supporters know that violence is the price of vengeance—and they accept that price.

No, supporters of capital punishment won't be surprised. But they will react viscerally. And precisely because they accept the violence inflicted by the executions, the shock strategy will backfire.

Until the mid-19th century executions were public events in the U.S.; families picnicked at local hangings. States eventually outlawed the celebrations because the ritualistic violence precipitated raucousness, drunkenness and general disorder.

How would 21st century viewers react to death screenings? If televised executions are presented responsibly, coverage would no doubt begin with a "background piece" that would air as many gruesome details of the crime as time would allow. For moderate supporters of capital punishment, the sight of state-inflicted gore may be a turn-off, but its juxtaposition with criminal gore would produce only an irreconcilable conflict of emotions. And for ardent death penalty advocates, the turn of the switch will induce catharsis—and calls for more.

Disquieting images can have a salutary effect on public discussion. Pictures of Southern policemen firehosing black protesters galvanized support for the civil rights movement. But those horrible sights were news as well as powerful images. The marginal informational benefit of televised executions, on the other hand, would be small.

There is something fundamentally wrong with discussing closely contested moral issues in purely visceral terms. The death penalty is already one of the most heated of these issues. By reducing debate about it to a contest of shocking images, we diminish our capacity to resolve it—and we diminish our civic culture.

The New York Times *May 3, 1991*

TERENCE MORAN
Plain Truths from the People's Lawyer

Death row inmates, along with society's downtrodden and forgotten members, had cause to mourn the retirement of Supreme Court Justice Thurgood Marshall. Legal Times *columnist Terence Moran recalled one episode in the professional life of "the Court's great common man."*

Justice Thurgood Marshall has a knack for saying the wrong thing.

When decorum was called for—as at the end of Ronald Reagan's presidential term—he was abrupt. He called Reagan "the bottom."

When reassuring platitudes filled the air—as in the celebrations of the Constitution's bicentennial—he was brutally frank. "'We the people' no longer enslave, but the credit does not belong to the Framers," Marshall reminded the country in a 1987 speech.

When reticence might be expected—as in answering a reporter's rather rude inquiry about his medical condition last week—Marshall was forthright. "I'm old," he explained. "I'm coming apart."

Marshall's penchant for speaking the disquieting truth, for cutting through the crap that passes for much political and legal discourse in the country today, constitutes a substantive contribution to Supreme Court history that ought not to be underestimated. He was the Court's great common man—and he knew precisely what he was doing in that role. . . .

Marshall's tenure on the Court represents a triumph for democracy, and not simply because he was the grandson of a slave who made it to a position of such immense power. For most of this century, Marshall has worked as an advocate for the downtrodden and forgotten in America, from the back roads of Dixie to the chambers of the Supreme Court. By bringing that egalitarian experience to bear on the cases that came before him—in oral arguments, in conference, in memos circulated to his colleagues, and in his opinions, especially in dissent—Marshall brought the Court a bit closer to the country it judges. He wasn't a "lawyers' lawyer" on the Court, it's true. He was the people's lawyer. . . .

You could sense the comfort level on the Court, and among the lawyers who came before it, plummet during many oral arguments when Marshall would break into elevated discourse with an earthy reminder that the lives of real people were at stake in the case. . . .

One such moment comes to mind. On an October morning last fall, the Court convened to hear arguments in a death-penalty case,

Perry v. Louisiana. Entering the Court in single file with the other justices, Marshall labored to his seat on the bench, hauling his bear-like frame down the dais with pronounced difficulty. He settled heavily into his chair, breathing hard and peering over his glasses into the well.

At issue in the case was whether a state can forcibly medicate insane people for the sole purpose of making them mentally competent to be executed. Four years earlier, in 1986, Marshall had written a landmark opinion in the 5-4 case of *Ford v. Wainwright,* which held that the Constitution prohibits the execution of insane people. Now Louisiana was clearly trying to evade that mandate. The state was seeking to restrain convicted murderer Michael Perry and inject him with a psychotropic drug that would calm his disordered mind so that he would know what was happening to him when he was electrocuted.

An ancient principle of common law holds that the mentally debilitated are not to be punished for their crimes, but protected from themselves and from others, and cared for. Marshall has fought furiously to preserve such precepts because, alone among the justices, he knows from personal experience that the poor, the crazed, and the despised are the natural prey of the executioner. Perry's case, which came out of one of the poorest parts of the Cajun Country, dramatized that sad truth fully.

But when the Court took up the case for argument that morning, Perry's socioeconomic status was irrelevant. The justices long ago considered most broad-based challenges to capital punishment and dismissed them. Marshall, of course, knew all that, but he plowed ahead anyway, on what he sees as the path of justice.

Justice Antonin Scalia, as is his wont, dominated the questioning from the bench. He challenged Perry's lawyer to explain to him what right Perry had to refuse the medicine that would make him well enough to be killed. Scalia heaped scorn on the notion that such a right against forcible medication existed at all, calling it "a luxury" that condemned people might not have. Louisiana's scheme "seems a perfectly reasonable" course of action, Scalia mused.

Then the state's lawyer rose to make his case. He constructed an elegant analogy from the Court's precedents concerning the forcible medication of people deemed dangerous to themselves and others. "If you can medicate a person who's mentally ill to protect property," he reasoned, "you certainly should be able to do it to enforce the Court's interest in its laws and in obtaining its punishment."

As the lawyer concluded this neat syllogism, Marshall leaned forward and barked out a question. "Mr. Attorney General," he asked, "is this medicine given by injection or by the mouth?'"

"Both," the lawyer responded. "In this particular case, Mr. Perry. . . "

"Well, if all you say is true," interjected Marshall, "in the interest of Louisiana, while you're giving him the injection, why don't you just give him enough to kill him then? It would be cheaper for the state."

There was a pause, the lawyer smiled slightly, and explained that, of course, Louisiana was seeking to do no such thing. It would be "cruel and unusual," he said. He was about to continue, thinking perhaps the old fella was quite a character, but Marshall wasn't about to let him go.

"The state's sole interest is to kill him, right?" he demanded.

Taken aback somewhat by this raw expression of the case, the lawyer conceded the point, and Marshall continued. "If he had been sentenced to life, the state wouldn't be interested in his condition, would they?"

"Well," the lawyer stuttered, "the state would still be interested to the extent of providing beneficial medical treatment to a person that's ill."

Marshall was furious. "They would?" he thundered. "They would insist on it, in this Court? Do you really think they would?" The lawyer had no answer. After an uncomfortable silence, Rehnquist broke in to change the subject. But Marshall had exposed, for all to see, the rank hypocrisy and bloodlust at work in Louisiana's thirst for retribution.

A few weeks later, the Court sent the case back to Louisiana on procedural grounds. The judge who originally approved Perry's execution reaffirmed his ruling, Perry's lawyer appealed, and the case is back on the slow track to the Supreme Court.

When it gets there, Marshall will be long gone. And Michael Perry, a backwoods lunatic who spun through the mental-health-care system's revolving door; who could not afford the high-priced psychiatrists that John Hinckley Jr.'s parents bought for him; whose mother was a manic-depressive and whose sister lives in an insane asylum; and who, but for the grace of God, could be any one of us—Michael Perry will have lost his best friend on the Court.

Legal Times *July 1, 1991*

JAMES ALBRECHT AND JOSSELYN SIMPSON
Notes and Comment (The Supreme Court)

President Bush's nomination of Judge Clarence Thomas to replace Thurgood Marshall on the Supreme Court seemed to many a baldly political move, and promised the Court one fewer obstacle in its deconstruction of legal precedent. On the day he resigned Justice Marshall wrote that "power, not reason, [was] the new currency of this Court's decision-making."

The decision of Justice Thurgood Marshall to step down from the Supreme Court left President Bush with an unusually significant vacancy to fill. Justice Marshall, eighty-three years old and in failing health, isn't merely the first and only black Supreme Court Justice. A great-grandson of slaves, he has been a tireless defender of civil rights and individual liberties. But of late he has made no secret of his frustration with the changing climate of the Court. "We're not gaining ground, my friends," he said recently at a meeting of black civil rights leaders. "We might be losing."

An examination of the federal judiciary suggests some of the reasons for Marshall's frustration. More than half of that judiciary has now been appointed by either Ronald Reagan or by George Bush, and when the vacancy left by Justice Marshall's resignation is filled a majority of the Supreme Court justices will have been appointed by these two Presidents. The Court, which has greatly increased its influence on domestic policies in the last thirty years, has begun to "gouge precedent" to quote Marshall, and is sending "a clear signal that scores of established Constitutional liberties are now ripe for reconsideration." In the process, the Court has been constructing new legal precedents, which will last much longer than the policies of the Presidents who have created it. For President Bush, this is the perfect moment to make a special place for himself in the history books: with the nomination of Clarence Thomas, a black United States Circuit Court of Appeals judge in Washington, D.C., he is poised to establish a solidly conservative majority on the bench and to put his stamp on a Court that will affect our lives for decades.

However, this nomination has also put Mr. Bush on the spot. Because of who Justice Marshall is, and because of the positions he has taken in his quarter century on the Court, the selection of his replacement was necessarily a public-relations hurdle for the President. He has often spoken, however vaguely, of his commitment to advancing civil rights, but his actions have often seemed regressive. His has been an Administration unable or unwilling to compromise with a divided Congress, and his characteristic method of dealing with domestic issues has been to criticize others for his own inaction.

With the nomination of Judge Thomas, though, this "spin control" method of government has only exposed the faults in leadership it was designed to conceal. For one thing, Judge Thomas's brief judicial career is, like the career of Justice David Souter, notable chiefly for its lack of a "paper trail" and for stands not taken: stands on abortion, obscenity, the division of church and state, and the like. The President's choice seems to have been made partly to avoid a candidate who would provide any grounds for specific criticism. The nomination is also an attempt by the President to have things both ways when it comes to the "quota" issue. On the one hand, he has evidently sought—by selecting a black—to ward off complaints about the loss of a minority member on the Court, while, on the other hand, he has chosen someone whose stand against quotas and affirmative action is even stronger than his own. (In a letter to the *Wall Street Journal* in 1987 Judge Thomas deplored "race-conscious devices" that "only further and deepen the original problem.") It's likely that none of the groups the President is trying to please will be satisfied, since fulfilling the expectations raised by this vacancy on the Court requires more than public relations. That Judge Thomas is black is surely no guarantee that he will follow in the footsteps of Justice Marshall; that he is conservative may be no consolation to people who think that the President has created a "black seat" on the Court by nominating him.

Regardless of Judge Thomas's race, the goals achieved by his nomination are very different from those attained by Lyndon Johnson when he nominated Thurgood Marshall, then the Solicitor General, in 1967. Many people have questioned whether Johnson was truly committed to civil rights, but his choice of Marshall unambiguously furthered those rights. As counsel for the National Association for the Advancement of Colored People, Marshall had argued successfully before the Supreme Court twenty-nine times—most notably in Brown v. Board of Education, the landmark 1954 school-desegregation case. He was equipped with a keen sense of the practical consequences of civil law, and, as a lawyer and a "colored person," he understood the particular power that the Court has in the matter of preserving and extending civil rights. Though overt acts of racial discrimination have diminished in this country, Marshall's practical sense has remained keen. In January, he was once again forced to point out in a dissenting opinion "the unique harm associated with a system of racially identifiable schools"—words that he could have written half a century ago. "People say we're better off," Marshall said this spring, "but better off than what?"

Justice Marshall's influence on the Court extends well beyond desegregation and affirmative action—into the area of civil liberties. Here, too, he and his fellow-liberals have been losing ground; one example is the Court's ruling this term that the use of a coerced confession as evidence does not automatically invalidate a conviction. Justice Marshall has been a strong voice for the rights of criminals and prisoners, for a right to privacy, and against the death penalty. In its recent terms, the Court has broadened the authority of law officers to search people and their possessions without first obtaining a warrant, and has made it harder for victims of job discrimination to seek legal remedy; it has also ruled that certain appeals for death-row inmates and other state prisoners can be limited. In all these cases, Marshall dissented, and on the day he resigned he showed his discouragement at seeing the erosion of his legacy when he wrote, "Power, not reason, is the new currency of this Court's decision-making."

It may be fitting that Justice Marshall, the champion of the powerless, is stepping down now. When he wrote, in 1971, that "convenience and political considerations of the moment do not justify a basic departure from the principles of our system of government," he was writing about an attempt by the executive branch to arrogate power not granted by the Constitution. A different sort of departure is taking place today, as both the legislative and executive branches are unable to pay attention to anything other than the political aspects of the word "quota" in attempting to safeguard civil rights, and as the increasingly powerful judicial branch appears to be—as Justice Stevens put it, in a dissent joined by Marshall—caving in to "the hydraulic pressure of public opinion." With Justice Marshall's resignation, an important symbol of this country's achievements in civil rights has been lost and an influential voice in their favor stilled. When the Justice was asked what the Court should do after his resignation, he said, "Try to get along without me." The Court may fare better than the rest of us.

The New Yorker *July 15, 1991*

Epilogue

IN AUGUST OF 1991, THE ATTENTION OF THE WORLD again focused on events in the Soviet Union. The aborted coup, and the subsequent collapse of long-standing Soviet institutions, marked another turning point in the direction the Soviet Union had taken since Gorbachev came to power in 1985 and initiated the reforms of *glasnost* and *perestroika.* During the Gorbachev era, the world had witnessed sweeping change: the collapse of Soviet hegemony across Eastern Europe, unprecedented advances toward East/West accord, and a consequent shift in the balance of global power relations. Within the Soviet Union itself, however, Gorbachev had attempted to straddle the demand for reform and the calls for moderation within the still-ruling Communist apparatus. But the failure of the coup, which had been engineered by old-line party officials, heralded the demise of the centralized Communist power structure, and accelerated the momentum for change. Russian Republic president Boris Yeltsin's fortunes rose, and Gorbachev slipped, at least in the early tumultuous days after the coup, into the background. By early September, many were celebrating the dissolution of the Soviet Union, and trumpeting the emergence of a loose confederacy of member states, conceivably along the lines of the Canadian system (not an especially auspicious model, since it has long been suffering from internal discord that at times seems to strain its union). When Gorbachev regained a foothold on power, his first task was to begin negotiations toward this new and tenuous future.

Any new confederation of republics would, by all accounts, be dominated by Russia, the largest entity in the Soviet Union, which accounts for half its population and three quarters of its foreign trade and stretches from Europe across Asia to the Pacific. The prospect of an economic and political union dominated by Russia raised new questions regarding the disposition of the Soviet Union's vast natural resources and the revival of widespread ethnic animosities. Even in the recent period of reform, there had been a strong racialist undercurrent within Russia toward other peoples in the Soviet Union, as well as sporadic, bloody warfare between ethnic populations in the smaller republics. The dissolution of central control would, it appeared, make way for more violent ethnic struggles, as well as for struggles over the redistribution of the Soviet Union's wealth—not only its redistribution among the various republics, but also its redistribution out of the hands of the Communist party control and into the hands of the people. Would the emerging leaders sponsor land reform, for example? And what of the free market? How would it be introduced in the Soviet Union? Lacking the internal machinery needed to bring about privatization, the Soviets seemed destined to face, with even greater intensity, the problems that had plagued the Eastern European nations for the last year: corruption, foreign takeovers, and a reduction of the social welfare programs that even the most market-minded Soviet citizens hold dear. Finally, was it reasonable to expect the rapid emergence of Western-style parliamentary democracy in a nation with a lengthy and nearly unbroken history of totalitarian rule? And if this Western-style democracy and capitalism failed in the Soviet Union, what, then, would take the place of Communism?

Such questions were seldom adequately addressed in the United States, as the government and the press celebrated the new "Russian revolution." But the changes in the Soviet Union brought up new questions for the immediate political future in America, including the coming presidential campaign. With the threat of Communism declining, would either conservatives or liberals turn their attention to the problems of their own country? Would they show new willingess to reduce the defense budget and redirect billions of dollars to domestic infrastructure, education, and economic development? Or would the administration whose triumphs lay in the area of foreign policy press ahead with economic aid to the republics of the Soviet Union, and pursue its agenda for the United States—already made manifest in the Persian Gulf—of defining the new world order in its role as the world's only remaining superpower?

STEPHEN F. COHEN
Cold Dawn in Moscow

In the week following the failed coup, Princeton University Sovietologist Stephen F. Cohen outlined the sober realities facing the Soviet Union in the wake of the second "Russian revolution."

Carried away by the failed coup against President Mikhail S. Gorbachev and its turbulent aftermath, many commentators are issuing sweeping and highly dubious conclusions about the "former Soviet system." Though some of these conclusions may one day turn out to be valid, they are based more on today's euphoria than on Soviet realities. . . .

The argument that popular resistance demonstrated an ascendant democratic society is, alas, based less on evidence than wishful supposition. At most, a few hundred thousand people actively resisted the coup, mainly in the most liberal cities. Russia's other 180 million citizens seem to have been passive or calculating.

A democratic Russian journalist has cautioned against expecting rapid democratization: "People cannot jump out of their skins, or nations out of their history." Polls before the coup suggest he is right. At best, a barricade now runs through the nation's political soul. Nor is a transition to democracy abetted by the country's traumatic economic problems and ethnic strife or its lack of a system of constitutional government and political parties.

Democratic forces do now have their best chance in Russian history. But as a path-finding minority, those forces must be both scrupulously democratic and united. Here, too, the first signs were not encouraging.

After defying the tanks, Mr. Yeltsin and his pro-democracy associates began issuing decrees that exceeded their legal prerogatives, confiscating property, invading the homes of parliamentary deputies and suppressing a literary association of right-wing writers. Their hectoring of Mr. Gorbachev after his return from captivity also demonstrated an inability to distinguish between the friends and foes of democracy.

Without Mr. Gorbachev's leadership since 1985, there would have been no popularly elected President Yeltsin to symbolize resistance, no Russian Parliament to give him refuge and support, few if any anti-coup protesters in the streets, and little military or K.G.B. hesitation about using their overwhelming firepower. And had Gorbachev, isolated and worried about his family's safety, relented and signed documents endorsing the coup, the plotters' resolve would have been stiffened.

Perhaps all these pro-democracy violations of democratic behavior were merely first impulses. But first impulses often reveal a lot in politics.

Can we at least accept a third prevailing conclusion: Soviet Communism is dead? The party is discredited and suspended, but Communism has taken various forms and meanings during its almost 74 years in power. The party's institutionalized role in the state machine of economic administration is over, but millions of its longtime members remain functionaries in the nation-wide ministries, which still control more than 90 percent of the economy.

Indeed, many former party officials and large segments of the 15 million members will form the backbones of new parties. Like Mr. Gorbachev and Mr. Yeltsin, almost all of the prominent figures on the political scene today are Communists or very recent ex-Communists. They are diverse politicians, but they, too, cannot jump out of their skins.

Even more important, for most Soviet citizens, Communism really meant a cradle-to-grave welfare state. Opinion polls tell us that popular demands for those social guarantees remain widespread. Some effective movement, probably dominated by Communist fundamentalists, will emerge in response to them.

Finally, should we really assume that the coup's aftermath has swept away the obstacles to a market economy? The main obstacle was not a lack of pro-market intentions in high political circles. The real problem was how to carry out such reforms. State bureaucracies could not be trusted or forced to do so. And decentralization of economic control after the coup will not eliminate the problem; it will only shift it from Moscow ministries to their republic branches.

The only solution was empowering citizens to create a market economy from below, which Mr. Gorbachev tried to do. But in a country where many opposed such policies, change could only be slow and agonized. Here, the coup changed nothing.

Three days in August, however dramatic, did not produce "another country," as is being wistfully claimed from Moscow to Washington. The long, uphill struggle for democracy and markets, begun by Mr. Gorbachev, will go on. But if many Soviet citizens are wounded economically along the way, the old order will again strike back, next time in ways that will make the bungled coup look like a rained-out softball game. And if the U.S. really cares, we will suspend judgment and rush instead with the essential food and medical supplies to ease the pain.

The New York Times *September 4, 1991*

Notes

Chapter 1:

1. William Robinson and David MacMichael, "Intervention in the Nicaraguan Election," *Covert Action Information Bulletin* (Winter 1991).

2. Anthony Lewis, "Grasping Reality," *The New York Times* (February 6, 1990).

3. "Freedom Man," *The Economist* (February 7, 1990).

4. Jesse Jackson, "Racism's Comeback Is Destructive to All," *The Los Angeles Times* (January 18, 1990).

5. "Black Americans, Still Trailing Behind," *The Economist* (March 3, 1990).

6. Salim Muwakkil, "Living Fast, Dying Young in America's Inner Cities," *In These Times* (December 26, 1990).

7. Theresa Funicello, "The Poverty Industry," *Ms.* (November/December 1990). Statistics cited in this paragraph and the subsequent paragraph are also taken from this article.

Chapter 2:

1. James Ridgeway and Dan Bischoff, "The Leveraged Buyout of Earth Day," *The Village Voice* (April 24, 1990).

2. Eve Pell, "Corporate Environmentalism," *Mother Jones* (April/May 1990).

3. Kathleen Sullivan, "A Free Society Doesn't Dictate to Artists," *The New York Times* (May 18, 1990).

4. Martin Garbus, "Thornburgh's Morality Brigade," *The New York Times* (April 28, 1990).

5. Richard Bolton, "The Cultural Contradictions of Conservatism," *The New Art Examiner* (June 1990).

6. Henry J. Hyde, "The Culture War," *The National Review* (April 30, 1990).

7. Pat Buchanan, "Mission to Destruct?," *The Washington Times* (March 26, 1990).

Chapter 3:

1. Nan Aron, "No Vision, No Justice," *The Village Voice* (August 7, 1990).

Chapter 4:

1. Carl Rowan, "George Bush: Protector of the Rich . . . and Bigoted," *Chicago Sun-Times* (October 21, 1990).

2. "The Uruguay Round: Gunboat Diplomacy by Another Name," *The Ecologist* (November/December 1990).

Chapter 5:

1. William Arkin, Damian Durrant, and Marianne Cherni, *On Impact: Modern Warfare and the Environment—A Case Study of the Gulf War,* (Washington D.C.: Greenpeace, May 1991). All subsequent citations of Greenpeace refer to this report.

2. Nicole Volpe and James Ridgeway, "How to Win," *The Village Voice* (March 26, 1991).

3. Robert Fisk, "Free to Report What We're Told," *The Independent* of London (February 6, 1991).

Chapter 6:

1. George Miller, "White House Sleaze Factor," *The New York Times* (June 8, 1991).

Acknowledgements

Adams, Ike, "Ike's a Hillbilly and Proud to Be One," from the *Mountain Eagle*. Copyright © 1990 by the Author. Reprinted by permission.

Albrecht, James, and Josselyn Simpson, "Notes and Comment" (The Supreme Court). Copyright © 1991 by *The New Yorker* Magazine, Inc. Reprinted by permission.

Albright, David, and Mark Hibbs, "Hyping the Iraqi Bomb," from the *Bulletin of the Atomic Scientists*. Copyright © 1991 by the Educational Foundation for Nuclear Science, 6042 South Kimbark, Chicago, IL 60637. Reprinted by permission.

Anderson, Bruce, "A Plague on All Your Houses," Copyright © 1990 by *The Anderson Valley Advertiser*. Reprinted by permission.

Angell, Roger, "Notes and Comment" (A Country at War). Copyright © 1991 by The New Yorker Magazine, Inc. Reprinted by permission.

Arkin, William M., "The Gulf 'Hyperwar'—An Interim Tally." Copyright © 1991 by The New York Times Company. Reprinted by permission.

Bahouth, Peter, "World is on Brink of War to Protect Our 'Way of Life,'" from the *Birmingham News*. Copyright © 1990 by the Author. Reprinted by permission.

Baker, Russell, "Let 'Em Eat Photo Ops." Copyright © 1991 by The New York Times Company. Reprinted by permission.

Bari, Judi, "The COINTELPRO Plot that Failed." Copyright © 1990 by *The Anderson Valley Advertiser.* Reprinted by permission.

Berry, Wendell, "Unfair Trade for Farmers." Copyright © by the Author. Reprinted by permission.

Bork, Robert H., "At Last, an End to Supreme Court Activism." Copyright © 1990 by The New York Times Company. Reprinted by permission.

Bright, Stephen B., "Death Sentence Lottery." Copyright © 1990 by *The Washington Post.* Reprinted by permission.

Broad, Robin, John Cavanagh, and Walden Bello, "U.S. Plan for Latin Debt Relief is a Non-Starter." Copyright © by the Authors. Reprinted by permission.

Buchanan, Patrick, "Mission to Destruct?" Copyright © 1990 by Tribune Media Services. Reprinted by permission.

Butler, Stuart, "A Conservative Agenda for a War Against Poverty." Copyright © 1990 by the Author. Reprinted by permission.

Campbell, Brett, "The Feel-Good War," from the *Texas Observer.* Copyright © 1991 by the Author. Reprinted by permission.

Carothers, André, "The New Pitch of Battle." Copyright © 1990 by *Greenpeace* Magazine. Reprinted by permission.

Caudill, Harry M., "Corporations Should Provide for Adequate Public Library," from the *Mountain Eagle.* Copyright © 1990 by the Author. Reprinted by permission.

Cockburn, Alexander, "U.S.–Backed Terrorism Won in Nicaragua, Not Democracy." Copyright © 1990 by *The Wall Street Journal.* Reprinted by permission.

Cohen, Stephen F., "Cold Dawn in Moscow." Copyright © 1991 by The New York Times Company. Reprinted by permission.

Commoner, Barry, "Toward a Sustainable Energy Future." Copyright © 1991 by *E* Magazine. Reprinted by permission.

Crowther, Hal, "The Mystery of Jesse Helms." Copyright © 1990 by the Author. Reprinted by permission.

Ehrenreich, Barbara, "Tale of a Whale." Copyright © 1991 by *The Nation* Magazine/The Nation Co., Inc. Reprinted by permission.

Faux, Jeff, "The Biggest Export Will Be U.S. Jobs." Copyright © 1991 by the Author. Reprinted by permission.

Ferguson, Sarah, "Us Against Them." Copyright © 1990 by Pacific News Service. Reprinted by permission.

Francke, Rend, "How to Help Iraq's Innocents." Copyright © 1991 by *The Washington Post.* Reprinted by permission.

Galbraith, John Kenneth, "What Sort of Capitalism is Best for Former Communist Nations?" Copyright © 1990 by *Harper's* Magazine. All rights reserved. Reprinted from the April 1990 issue by special permission.

Galeano, Eduardo, "Language, Lies, and Latin Democracy."

Gates, Henry Louis, Jr., "Whose Culture is It Anyway?" Copyright © 1991 by *The New York Times.* Distributed by Special Features/Syndication Sales. Reprinted by permission.

Geiger, H. Jack, "Generations of Poison and Lies." Copyright © 1990 by The New York Times Company. Reprinted by permission.

Gonzalez, Juan, "The Best Heroes are Distant Ones." Copyright © 1990 by The New York News Inc. Reprinted by permission.

Goodman, Ellen, "The Long Death of Nancy Cruzan." Copyright © 1990 by The Boston Globe Newspaper Company/Washington Post Writers Group. Reprinted by permission.

Greenberg, Paul, "Decline and Fall of Civil Rights." Copyright © 1990 by The Los Angeles Times Syndicate. Reprinted by permission.

Greider, William, "The Next Bank Robbery," from *Rolling Stone* #606, June 13, 1991. Copyright © 1991 by Straight Arrow Publishers, Inc. Reprinted by permission.

Hamill, Pete, "Who Cares About Eastern Europe?" Copyright © 1990 by the Author. Reprinted by permission.

Harjo, Susan Shown, "October 12: A Day of Mourning for Native Americans." Copyright © 1990 by the Author. Reprinted by permission.

Havel, Vaclav, "The Great Moral Stake of the Moment." Copyright © 1990 by the Author. Reprinted by permission.

Hedges, Chris, "The Unilaterals," from the *Columbia Journalism Review,* May/June 1991. Copyright © 1991 by the Author. Reprinted by permission.

Henderson, Col. William Darryl, "How Army is Marketing the Gulf War to 'Soft' Public." Copyright © 1991 by the Author. Reprinted by permission.

Henson, Scott, "On the Question of 'Political Correctness,'" from the *Texas Observer.* Copyright © 1991 by the Author. Reprinted by permission.

Hentoff, Nat, "A Prosecutor's Judge—From the 19th Century." Copyright © 1990 by the Author. Reprinted by permission.

Henwood, Doug, "The Uses of Crisis." Copyright © 1991 by *The Left Business Observer,* 250 West 85th Street, New York, NY 10024. Reprinted by permission.

Jackson, Jesse, "Racism's Comeback is Destructive to All Men." Copyright © 1990 by the Los Angeles Times Syndicate. Reprinted by permission.

Kempton, Murray, "Keeping Up with the News." Copyright © 1991 by *New York Newsday.* Reprinted by permission.

Kuttner, Robert, "The Tyranny of the Economically Correct." Copyright © 1991 by *The Washington Post.* Reprinted by permission.

Lam, Andrew, "Why We Eat Dogs," from *Mother Jones.* Copyright © 1991. Reprinted by permission of The Foundation for National Progress.

Lasch, Christopher, "The Costs of Our Cold War Victory." Copyright © 1990 by *The New York Times.* Distibuted by Special Features/Syndication Sales. Reprinted by permission.

Lewis, Anthony, "When You Believe in Lies." Copyright © 1990 by The New York Times Company. Reprinted by permission.

McGowan, Judith, "In the Bronx, A Dubious Victory." Copyright © 1990 by *The New York Times.* Distibuted by Special Features/Syndication Sales. Reprinted by permission.

McIntyre, Robert S., "A Soaking (in Gravy) for the Rich." Copyright © 1990 by The New York Times Company. Reprinted by permission.

Mann, Judy, "The Justices vs. the Pregnant Girls." Copyright © 1990 by *The Washington Post.* Reprinted by permission.

Martin, Dannie M., "A Mount Everest of Time." Copyright © 1990 by *The San Francisco Chronicle*. Reprinted by permission.

Molnar, Alex, "If My Marine Son is Killed . . . " Copyright © 1990 by *The New York Times*. Distributed by Special Features/Syndication Sales. Reprinted by permission.

Moran, Terence, "Plain Truths from the People's Lawyer." Copyright © 1991 by the Author. Reprinted by permission.

Nader, Ralph, "Corporate Welfare State is on a Roll." Copyright © 1990 by *The Los Angeles Times*. Reprinted by permission.

Nairn, Alan, "Notes and Comment" (The Panama Invasion). Copyright © 1990 by The New Yorker Magazine, Inc. Reprinted by permission.

Nixon, Richard, "Why U.S. Policy is Right in the Gulf." Copyright © 1990 by *The New York Times*. Distributed by Special Features/Syndication Sales. Reprinted by permission.

Pines, Burton Yale, "The Eighties: Ten Years of Triumph." Copyright © 1990 by the Author. Reprinted by permission.

Pizzo, Stephen P., "S&L Scam: Deeper and Deeper." Copyright © 1990 by the Author. Reprinted by permission.

Postrel, Virginia I., "Greens Want to Make Peasants Out of Us All." Copyright © 1990 by the Reason Foundation, 2716 Ocean Park Blvd., Suite 1602, Santa Monica, CA 90405. Excerpted, with permission, from the April 1990 issue of *Reason* Magazine.

Quindlen, Anna, "Banning the A-Word." Copyright © 1990 by The New York Times Company. Reprinted by permission.

Rafsky, Robert, "AIDS Research: It's Killing Us." Copyright © 1990 by the Author. Reprinted by permission.

Reding, Andrew A., "A Brezhnev South of Our Border?" Copyright © 1990 by the Author. Reprinted by permission.

Renner, Michael G., "Military Victory, Ecological Defeat." Copyright © 1991 by World Watch. Reprinted by permission.

Rosen, Ruth, "It's Not Just a Tragic Part of Life." Copyright © 1990 by the Author. Reprinted by permission.

Roth, Kenneth, "Mass Graves in Kuwait." Copyright © 1990 by *The New York Times*. Distibuted by Special Features/Syndication Sales. Reprinted by permission.

Rowan, Carl, "George Bush: Protector of the Rich . . . and the Bigoted." Copyright © 1990 by North America Syndicate, Inc. Reprinted by permission.

Royko, Mike, "What about the Home Front?" Copyright © 1991 by Tribune Media Services. Reprinted by permission.

Ryan, Randolph, "U.S. Role in a Civilian Massacre." Copyright © 1990 by *The Boston Globe*. Reprinted by permission.

Sadowski, Yahya, "Power, Poverty, and Petrodollars." Copyright © 1991 by *MERIP Middle East Report*, 1500 Massachusetts Ave., NW, #119, Washington, DC 20005. Reprinted from issue #170, vol. 21, no. 3, May/June 1991, pages 4–7, 10 by permission.

Sale, Kirkpatrick, "The Environmental Crisis is Not Our Fault." Copyright © 1990 by *The Nation* Magazine/The Nation Co., Inc. Reprinted by permission.

Savan, Leslie, "The Face of the People." Copyright © 1991 by the Author. Reprinted by permission of the Author and *The Village Voice.*

Schanberg, Sydney H., "Censoring for Political Security." Copyright © 1991 by the Author. Reprinted by permission.

Schell, Jonathan, "Modern Might, Ancient Arrogance." Copyright © 1991 by The Los Angeles Syndicate. Reprinted by permission.

Schulman, Sarah, "Is the NEA Good for Gay Art?" Copyright © 1990 by the Author. Reprinted by permission.

Schwartz, Herman, "Second Opinion." Copyright © 1991 by *The Nation* Magazine/The Nation Company, Inc.

Sherman, Jonathan, "Pictures at an Execution." Copyright © 1991 by *The New York Times.* Distributed by Special Features/Syndication Sales. Reprinted by permission.

Shields, Mark, "The Neil Bush Case: Talk About Teflon!" Copyright © 1990 by *The Washington Post.* Reprinted by permission.

Sick, Gary, "The Election Story of the Decade." Copyright © 1991 by *The New York Times.* Distibuted by Special Features/Syndication Sales. Reprinted by permission.

Smith, Amanda, "Failure to Ensure Child-Care Leave Harms Employees, Employers." Copyright © 1990 by the Author. Reprinted by permission.

Taylor, John, "Down with PC." Copyright © 1991 by K-III Magazine Corporation. All rights reserved. Reprinted by the permission of *New York Magazine.*

Turnipseed, Tom, "Deserving David Duke." Copyright © 1990 by the Author. Reprinted by permission.

Weissman, Robert, "Prelude to a New Colonialism." Copyright © 1991 by *The Nation* Magazine/The Nation Company, Inc. Reprinted by permission.

Whitehead, Ralph, Jr., "Class Acts: America's Changing Middle Class Faces Polarization and Problems." Copyright © 1990 by the Author. Reprinted by permission.

Wicker, Tom, "Home of the Brave?" Copyright © 1990 by The New York Times Company. Reprinted by permission.

Wilkins, Roger, "With Mandela," from *Mother Jones.* Copyright © 1990 by The Foundation for National Progress. Reprinted by permission.

Will, George, "Thatcher, de Gaulle and Nationalism." Copyright © 1990 by The Washington Post Writers Group. Reprinted by permission.

Wright, Jim, "Seek Solutions, Not Scapegoats, in S&L Industry Collapse." Copyright © 1990 by the Author. Reprinted by permission.

Young, Ivy, "'Traditional' Family Disappearing." Copyright © 1991 by the Author. Reprinted by permission.

Zakheim, Dov S., "The Vietnam Syndrome is Buried in the Gulf." Copyright © 1991 by *The New York Times.* Distibuted by Special Features/Syndication Sales. Reprinted by permission.